# MASTERING
# WINE

*Also by Tom Maresca*

The Right Wine

La Tavola Italiana
(*with Diane Darrow*)

# MASTERING WINE

REVISED AND UPDATED

## Tom Maresca

GROVE PRESS
New York

Published by Grove Press
A division of Grove Press, Inc.
841 Broadway
New York, NY 10003–4793

Published in Canada by General Publishing Company, Ltd.

An earlier edition of *Mastering Wine* was published in 1985 by
Bantam Books, New York.

Library of Congress Cataloging-in-Publication Data

Maresca, Tom.
    Mastering wine / Tom Maresca.—Rev. and
  updated.
        p.        cm.
    Includes index.
    ISBN 0–8021–3298–7 (alk. paper)
    1. Wine and wine making. I. Title.
TP548.M3335      1992
641.2′2—dc20                                                    92-8288
                                                                  CIP

Manufactured in the United States of America
Printed on acid-free paper
Designed by Jules Perlmutter / Off-Broadway Graphics

This book is gratefully dedicated
to
the daring palates
and unflinching taste buds
of
The Kamikaze Tasting Squad

# *Acknowledgments*

THIS BOOK could not have been started or finished without the help of many friends and associates. Cathy Cashion helped lay the groundwork for it, and Susan and Tim Benthall led me to refine the idea. The goodwill and good palates of my volunteer tasters were indispensable, and hearty thanks go to Barbara, Bruce, Carey, Charlotte, Donna S., Donna W., Frank, Gene, Joan, Joe, Mary, Mary Lou, Nancy, Nick, Nino, Roger, Shirley, Steven, Susan, and Tim. Every stage of this project, from conception to consumption to completion, was aided and abetted by my wife, Diane Darrow.

Thanks are also due to many generous and efficient people in all branches of the wine trade, without whose cooperation this book could not have been completed. There are more of them than I can decipher from my scribbled notes, but among those whose aid showed clearest are Shirley Alport, Laura Baddish, Pio Boffa, Louis Bonaccolta, Kimberly Charles, Mike Citarella, the Colombini-Cinelli family, Claudia Conlon, Fiona Conover, Bill Deutsch, Philip Di Belardino, Paul Draper, Barbara Edelman, Robert Fairchild, Angelo Gaja, Mark Gould, Mireille Guiliano, Susan Henley, Nora Horan, Michelle Jones, Julie Ann Kodmur, Ed Lauber, Nancy Light, Giorgio Lulli, Mary Lyons, the Martini family, the Mastroberardino family, David Milligan, Mary Mulligan, Dominic Nocerino, Marsha Palanci, Kai Rosenthal, Patrick Séré, Niki Singer, Jodi Stern, Margaret Stern, Jan Stuebing, Christine Sullivan, Carm Tintle, Mara Todorovich, Bob Wiener, Anne Willets, and Bettye Yates.

Last but far from least, a large set of thank-yous to my tireless agent, Felicia Eth, and my patient editor, Walt Bode, who between them oversaw the start and the finish of this project.

# Contents

*x*                               Contents

# *Preface to the Revised Edition*

THIS NEW EDITION OF *MASTERING WINE* preserves the user-friendly format and unpretentious practicality that readers and reviewers enjoyed in the original publication. Many individual wines have been changed to reflect changes in the marketplace, but the bases of the original pairings are still intact—just updated with more recent vintages and, where necessary, more current data. One of the pleasures in working through these tastings once more was to discover all over again just how well the original comparisons and contrasts worked, and how validly the lessons and the enjoyment of each pairing were expressed. That was what the Kamikaze Tasting Squad and I had striven for, and it was—and is—gratifying to realize how well our program succeeded.

We hope this new edition will strengthen that evergreen quality. I've chosen wines for each tasting that maintain a reasonably consistent style and flavor from year to year, so that vintage variation won't dramatically alter the effectiveness of any particular pairing. And I've tried to suggest reasonable alternatives for the primary wines in each pairing, other wines that approximate the same qualities as the primary wines and which can be substituted for them in case of problems of availability or local supply. You'll find those possible substitutes prominently listed with each flight.

More than anything else, however, I've tried not to tamper with a good thing: I've kept hands off to let *Mastering Wine* do its work its own way, and to let readers and users meet the book and the wines on their own terms. Wine should be fun: not intimidation, not a test of sophistication, not a rigid set of "drink-thises" and "don't-drink-thats," but *fun*. That was the basic idea behind the original *Mastering Wine*, and it remains the soul of this new edition. I hope you enjoy it.

# READ
# THIS
# FIRST

THIS IS A DO-IT-YOURSELF WINE BOOK—a teach-yourself
project.

Its first premise is that wine is fun.

Its second is that most people would rather drink wine than read
about it or take classes about it.

Its third premise is that drinking wine is the only effective way to
learn about wine, anyway.

And its fourth premise, to let you in on everything all at once, is
that most people don't plan to become connoisseurs—at least not at
the start. They want to learn enough about wine to be able to enjoy
it—to stay calm when the wine list winds up in their hands, to avoid
sweaty palms when someone asks them what they think of the
wine, to be able to relax and enjoy a sip when the wine finally gets
into the glass.

Enjoyment is the premise of this book, and your own preferences,
your own likes and dislikes, are all the tools you need to learn as
much as you want about wine. Our procedure is going to be very
simple. You taste wines in pairs, and the wine you like better in each
pair will point the way to your next pair. Like leads you on to like,
and you increase your wine knowledge and your wine pleasure at
the same time. No terror, no anxiety, no questions you can't answer.
The questions don't even have wrong answers. Whatever you say in
response to "Which wine did you like better?" is bound to be right.

I've set up for you a whole gamut of wines, all arranged in pairs.
There are thirty-nine pairs in all—red wine, white wine, rosé, and
sparkling wine—thirty-nine steps to solving the mystery of wine.
They start from relatively simple and popular wines and gradually
move up a scale of complexity and distinctiveness.

3

You don't have to taste them all at once. You don't even have to taste them all. You'll follow the path of your own preferences through the book, and at your own pace. If you want, you could conceivably work through all the wines in this book in a month or less—even a few days if you could go at it full-time. But if you prefer, you can also stop at any point you like and resume tasting in a week, a month, a year. It's entirely up to you. You can taste alone or with your spouse or steady, with family or with friends. You can be solemn if that's your style or flip if you like—that's entirely up to you, too.

All you have to do is taste the specific wines (or their alternates) named in each pair and, after you and I have talked them over, decide which of the two wines pleased you more. That choice will lead you on to a pair of related wines so that you can sharpen your sense of the qualities you liked. I've deliberately chosen the first handful of wine pairs in both the red wine and white wine segments to display fairly sharp contrasts so that you should have no trouble at all tasting real differences between them. Later on, when you're narrowing down your range and really trying to focus on very specific elements you enjoy, the wines within the pairs will be more similar to each other and the differences between them subtler—but by that time you'll be subtler, too, and a lot more experienced at tasting and enjoying.

Yes, you'll need to practice enjoying. For many people, wine is an ordeal rather than a pleasure. It's so fraught with anxiety that they approach it not merely seriously but also tensely.

That's where I come in: what I'm going to do is write this book as if it were a conversation between us. I'll do and say everything I can—bad jokes and all—to put you at ease, to keep you interested, to keep you focused. I'm going to talk you through these wines exactly as I would if we were sitting across the table from each other. As far as I am concerned, there is one subject on which you are an indisputable authority: your own taste. Why drink a wine someone else thinks you should like rather than one you actually do like? Your own taste is going to be the key that unlocks the whole world of wine for you, because you're going to learn from what you like, with me on the sidelines cheering you on.

If you are already started with wine, or are not interested in the entry-level wines, or prefer particular kinds of wine, you can use this book to suit yourself. The book is organized so that each tasting concludes with directions for following three separate paths. You can simply follow your own preference: if, after the third tasting, you prefer the Jadot Beaujolais 1990 to the Sutter Home California Zinfandel 1989, you can skip to the tasting on page 74. Or you can choose to follow a special class of wines—those made from a noble grape variety such as Cabernet, for instance. Or you can explore the wines of a particular country.

Even more simply, you can just proceed through this book in sequence, page by page, pair by pair, ignoring the choices entirely. Because the overall sequence of the wine pairs in this book graduates from simple to complex just as the preferential sequences and varietal sequences and national sequences do, anyone, beginner or not, can simply taste the wines in the order of their presentation, work straight through the book, and come out the other end with a good amount of wine lore assimilated.

At any point in the book you can freely switch from one of these methods to another. Say, for example, that you are going along the trail of your own preferences and come upon a wine that really excites you—a German Riesling, for instance. You can at that point either continue on the path of your preferences, or explore the other wines made from Riesling, or explore German wines. You could either resume your original trail later on or just continue along your new track to its end. The book is designed to be helpful in any of these ways.

Whichever of these routes you choose, here's what you can get out of this book:

- a survey of and firsthand acquaintance with the major classes and classifications of dry dinner wines
- a painless introduction to wine terms, each presented in a situation in which it is immediately understandable because you are at that moment experiencing what it means
- practice, right from the start, with all of the seemingly mysterious and sophisticated techniques of wine tasting and wine analysis
- direct knowledge and experience—not descriptions, but the actual tastes—of most of the major kinds of dinner wines available in the United States
- a chance to explore your own taste in wine and find out what you really like, free from any pressures or constraints

If you are shy or embarrass easily, you can work through this book entirely by yourself. But if you'd rather, there is no reason you couldn't make the whole process into a festive social occasion. By gathering a few like-minded friends, you can turn your tasting sessions into predinner cocktails and finish the wines (and an important part of your lesson) at dinner. That even has the advantage of letting you divide the cost of the wines so no individual is very much out of pocket. (Just for the record, most of the wines included here are quite reasonably priced.) Even if you really feel that you know absolutely nothing about wine, this book is designed to let you teach yourself to enjoy it, or—to put it more accurately—to let you find out how very easy wine is to enjoy and how very well equipped you already are to understand and enjoy it.

Despite all the myths, Americans have no need to feel any inferiority about their knowledge of wine. Perhaps about their consumption of it and their capacity for it, but not their knowledge. The simple fact of the American marketplace forces a certain amount of knowledge on us: we can—and every day are solicited to—buy wine not only from all over the United States but from Canada, Argentina, Chile, France, Italy, Spain, Greece, Yugoslavia, Hungary, Germany, Austria, Portugal, Romania, Israel, Cyprus, Algeria, South Africa, and Australia, not to mention nongrape wines from China and Japan. Just to hold on to our dollars we have to learn to say no in several languages.

If you had grown up in a small city in France or Italy or Spain or any other of a number of winegrowing, wine-drinking countries, you would never have had an anxious thought about wine in the entire course of your life. As a matter of routine you would have drunk with your meals whatever wine was made in your locality, without ever wondering whether it was a good vintage or not. For your wedding or graduation or the birth of your child, you would have provided champagne if you could afford it, and if not, whatever sparkling substitute your region offered.

Maybe, if you went to the big city or to a fancy restaurant or were trying to impress someone, you would choose a special wine—but when you did, your ignorance about wine would probably be so abysmal that you would either put yourself blindly in the hands of the restaurateur or stubbornly insist on the one or two prestigious wines whose names you knew, whether or not they were appropriate to the occasion. As for wines made in another country: the odds would be very strong against your ever having heard of or tasted more than one or two, perhaps not even that.

The average European is as uninformed about vintages and vineyards as the average American. In this respect, the only difference between an American and a European is that we are intimidated by wine—maybe justifiably so, considering all the choices we're confronted with—and a European usually isn't. A European assumes wine as his or her birthright, so to speak, because the European has grown up with it. Most of us haven't. Wine on the table at every lunch and dinner is not yet an American tradition, though we can hope it will become so soon. Neither do we have the kind of communal or collective dining facilities, like British clubs, that allow the less-than-wealthy access to a well-stocked cellar.

By and large, American restaurants don't help, either: though things are slowly improving, the vast majority still have pathetically inadequate wine lists. Worse yet, even good restaurants with decent lists often charge a criminal markup on wine, so high in some cases that you'd think the restaurateur was being paid off by the temperance lobby to discourage wine drinking. More troublesome still, even the most conscientious restaurants find it very hard to maintain a cellar of properly aged wines—the overhead and cash tie-up are simply prohibitive—so most Americans never have the opportunity to taste a mature wine at its peak of perfection.

Because of that, a lot of the wine instruction starts at the wrong place for the beginning American wine drinker. Many, perhaps most, books and courses assume that the reader or student already enjoys wine, already knows something about it, and is working on developing a degree of connoisseurship or refining an expertise. They never say so explicitly, but that implicit bias shows clearly in the speed with which they pass over the mass of popular wines from which most Americans begin their acquaintance with wine.

That in itself might not be too serious a flaw if it were not usually compounded with two others, the failures to differentiate clearly, first, between what a trained palate discerns and what a beginner tastes, and second, between the ideal taste of a wine and the reality of its average market-specimen's flavor. Too often those very real distinctions are completely blurred. The student tastes nothing remotely like what the instructor describes, assumes that the fault lies in his or her own insensitivity, then either gives up on wine entirely or sticks with wine coolers. In either case, there is a real loss both to the apprentice wine drinker and to the world of wine.

The unspoken assumption of traditional wine lore is that the taster already knows or will instantly recognize the flavor of greatness in wine. The unfortunate truth is that most Americans have never tasted a mature claret, or a great Barolo, or an old Hermitage, and would probably not be able to recognize its greatness or understand what made it great if they had. Only a few very fortunate individuals who are blessed with the wealth that allows them to buy a—let us say—1959 Chateau Latour have ever tasted such wine. And fewer still are blessed with the extraordinary palates and palatal memories to learn from one bottle alone the standard that such a wine may teach. For most Americans, that bottle of Latour would be a dead waste. To learn wine tasting from great examples like that, you need to have a palate already active, a memory already stored with tastes and flavors and ideas. You have to be ready, so to speak, for that wine to hit you dead center and rearrange all your previous taste experiences around itself.

People who learned wine and wine tasting that way started at the opposite pole from where most Americans begin. There is a whole new crop of potential wine drinkers in the United States who are right now poised on the edge of wine, hesitant either to immerse themselves or to stay dry. Most of them have to learn wine from the ground up, working with what they can afford, moving tentatively from soft drinks and hard liquor and watery beer to the simpler domestic wines and inexpensive imports. And the wine courses and the wine books skim over in the first two pages or two minutes as unworthy of serious attention a whole class of wines that these wine drinkers haven't even tried yet! Even the drinker who has made the plunge finds precious little help in his or her first faltering attempts to figure out what makes a Rhine wine different from a Mosel, or a New York sparkling wine different from a Spanish *cava* from a French champagne.

## What You Need to Know

What do you need to know about wine to read this book?
Nothing. Zero. Zip. Zilch.

What is the one essential rule for learning about wine?
Don't be buffaloed.

NO MATTER WHAT YOU MAY HAVE HEARD, nobody knows "all about wine." No matter what great feats of recognition a few extraordinary palates are capable of, there isn't an expert in the world who can't be fooled in a blind tasting at least some of the time. Besides, that kind of expertise is totally irrelevant to most people's lives. It's the vinous equivalent of running the four-minute mile: most of us are content to admire it without seriously aspiring to do it. Most people who want to learn about wine wish to do so not to turn their lives into a constant process of testing, nor even for social points or one-upmanship: they simply want to enrich their lives by bringing something enjoyable into it. That is the best reason for learning about wine.

To become as much a connoisseur as most people ever aspire to, all you need do is discover what your personal tastes in wine are and develop confidence in your judgment. That's why nowhere in this book are you going to see any wine described as "better" than any other wine. The best wine is the wine you like best. That is one of the bedrock, working assumptions of this book.

If at the end of this book you've decided that you really prefer the simpler, less expensive wines with which the book begins, terrific!

9

Think of the money you'll save over the rest of your life! More to the point, you'll have the knowledge and the confidence of having tried other wines and knowing why you like the ones you do, and you'll have the language to explain those preferences to anyone who really wants to know.

There is nothing to embarrass anyone in a preference for simple pleasures. The embarrassment that people feel about wine comes

- from not knowing what they like
- from fearing that they don't know what they ought to like
- from fearing that they don't like what they should like
- from fearing that there is something wrong with what they do like because it is too inexpensive or too popular or too unsophisticated or too whatever.

That is nonsense. The greatest enemy of wine is the wine snob. I drink all sorts of wine, of every conceivable level of quality, character, and cost, and I find that there are few wines I cannot enjoy if they are presented in their proper setting.

Naturally, I have my own preferences, wines I think of as "better" than other wines. You will, too, as soon as you have enough tasting experience. But what I mean by "better" is, simply, more pleasing to my personal taste and more conformable to the standards applied by wine professionals—which, in fact, are not very standard at all. My taste and those unstandards are completely irrelevant to most of the rest of the world's.

It may be that such professional measurements will eventually become important to you. Ninety-nine percent of the wine professionals in the world and 100 percent of the gifted amateur connoisseurs did not become so by a cold-blooded, logical decision, but because at some point in their lives they drank a wine that just stripped their taste buds bare and made them stand up and cheer. After that, they became knowledgeable about wine simply by pursuing what they loved. Anyone can do the same thing the same way.

After all, the upper limit of what you can learn and enjoy about wine is simply the limit of what you can taste, what your palate and nose can perceive. If you've got the palatal equivalent of perfect pitch, or of the perfect 99-mile-an-hour pitcher's arm, you are going to taste and enjoy more and more acutely than the rest of us mere mortals. Your analysis and description of the taste of wines will be more complete and more precise than ours—but your preferences will still be every bit as subjective.

# Rules of the Game

WINE IN AMERICA IS 50 PERCENT ROMANCE and 50 percent pseudoscientific jargon—a bundle of unrealistic attitudes in a glossy high-tech package.

People think of wine in itself as complicated and of wine expertise as a sign of sophistication. Few people label themselves connoisseurs, but everyone loves being thought one. We shy away from the word, but we love the idea it conveys—the glamour, the discreet, worldly wisdom, the easy, offhand mastery of arcane lore. "Oh, yes," you say, smiling at your obviously wealthy, fashionable, admiring dinner companion and simultaneously nodding approval to the reverently attentive wine steward, "the Pichon-Lalande 1967. A pretty little claret, isn't it?"

So the romantic fantasy runs. The other side of wine in America is all Brix and pH, measures of residual sugar and acidity and alcohol. Experts earnestly argue the precise differentiations between the effects of new or old wood on Cabernets and Zinfandels and Chardonnays from one current superstar winemaker or another—California's updated version of Abbott and Costello's "Who's on first?" routine. We learnedly discuss the significance of climatic variations in zones I, II, III, IV, or V in Napa and Sonoma and Carneros and the Alexander Valley. We have university courses to teach us everything from winemaking to wine smelling, vinification to appreciation. Kits are available to help us analyze odors, charts to help us pin down colors, a whole lexicon of special terms from "ascescence" to "vinosity" to help us speak correctly of wine.

We do everything with wine, it seems, except drink it and enjoy it. That's too simple for our complicated world. In an environment like this, it's too easy to forget that all you really need to enjoy wine is a mouth.

The only secret of wine expertise, at least as far as tasting is concerned, is to pay attention. So this book is set up to prod you to think seriously about what you are tasting.

For most people, it's easier to distinguish and identify flavors and aromas when comparing two wines than when dealing with one in isolation. For that reason, you will taste a pair of wines at a time. The wines in each pair have been chosen both because they should be available just about anywhere in the United States and, even more important, because they clearly reveal important wine characteristics and components.

Since these pairs have been chosen for particular reasons, I urge you to try to obtain the wines specified. Wherever possible, I have listed alternate wines that will give approximately the same results as the primary wines in each flight. The biggest problem will be vintages, which—of course—change every year. If a particular wine is not available in the vintage I specify, a younger vintage of the same wine will always make the best possible substitute. This is especially true of white wines. But remember, no two wines taste exactly alike, so when you are using substitutes you will have to allow a bit more latitude to the descriptions and distinctions: the comparisons will still work, but they may not always be as sharp as with the primary pairing (on the up side, there is also always the chance that they will be better).

The paired wines should all be available throughout the United States. This doesn't mean that you can walk into a neighborhood mom-and-pop liquor store and expect to find them all. The odds on your finding every one of them even in a large wineshop are fairly long, given the vast number of wines on the American market. You may have to make a few phone calls or even have your dealer order one or two of them for you. That is rarely a problem. By far the most common difficulty you are likely to encounter in gathering these wines is the lazy shopowner who tells you there is no such wine and tries to sell you instead whatever is on hand. Be polite but firm. Give your dealer all the relevant data—you'll find everything you need in the pair entries—and tell him or her to consult the latest edition of *Beverage Media* to find out what company to call for any particular wine in your area.

One last preliminary assurance. I'm not going to bombard you with jargon. The necessary wine terms—you'll have to take it on faith for a little while that some are necessary—will be introduced only in a context where they are immediately relevant and where you will have (I hope in your glass or on your tongue at that very moment) a vivid example of what the term really means. Only by tasting wine can you learn anything about wine, and only by experiencing the precise sensation the wine terms are intended to denote will you understand that some pretentious-sounding words are really very exact. Should you come across a term whose meaning you're unsure about, the index will show where its principal explanation can be found.

## What You Need to Have

A T ITS MOST BASIC, all you absolutely need to use this book are wine, two glasses, and a corkscrew. That is bare bones, but it will still let you perform the basic task, tasting the wines. If you want to get the most out of this undertaking, however, here's a list of suggested paraphernalia.

- A good corkscrew (Screwpull is the best on the market)
- Clear, clean glasses, preferably tulip- or bowl-shaped, and preferably one for each wine to be tasted
- Paper cups or a bucket for spitting and pouring out waste
- A white tablecloth (to let you better see the wine's color)
- A pitcher of water and water glasses (for rinsing mouths and, if necessary, glasses)
- Note pad or tasting sheets and pencil for each taster
- Some good, fresh, crusty bread
- *Un po' di formaggio*: a little bit of an honest cheese—nothing too strongly flavored, and especially nothing sweet
- Some paper napkins
- The wines

That's not so bad, is it?

# What You Have to Do

AT FIRST, deliberate tasting is a very strange activity, and most people feel self-conscious about it. After all, your mother spent all those years teaching you to eat quietly and to close your mouth while you're chewing, and here all of a sudden you're expected to slurp and burble air into your mouth and slosh wine around in your cheeks and spit and God knows how many other things Mom would most definitely not have approved of. For a sophisticated activity, wine tasting sure seems to get off to a low start. It's no wonder so many apprentice tasters feel awkward.

Tasting all alone is a good way of avoiding the self-consciousness, but it deprives you of the benefits of other people's reactions—and it is almost certain that no two people are going to respond exactly the same way to a pair of wines (more about this and how it affects this book's descriptions of wine flavors later).

The optimum tasting situation would involve two, three, or four—rarely more—individuals who are at roughly the same stage of knowledge or ignorance, appreciation or curiosity. More important, they should be comfortable enough with each other so that embarrassment or shyness won't be a factor: better to taste alone than in a group where you can't say honestly what you think, because the whole point is to come to know your own taste.

Tasting with a small, congenial group not only lets you see how widely reactions to the same wine can vary but it also helps you discern elements in the wine you might otherwise overlook. Each taster can help teach the others and be taught in turn. And group tasting also has the practical advantage of spreading the cost of the wines so that nobody is out of pocket for any large sum.

In group tasting, you will be using everybody else (and they will

15

be using you) as a foil/comparison/contrast to your own experience. For this reason, no one should say anything about any wine until everybody has finished jotting down his or her remarks about it. Sorry if that sounds antisocial, but it's too easy to be persuaded— and to convince yourself—that you taste or smell something you actually don't, so it's important to get your own impressions firm before you hear anybody else's.

On page 17 is a sample tasting sheet. You can make as many copies of it as you think you'll need, or simply have your tasters copy out its categories onto blank sheets of paper. Its format is deliberately simple to focus your attention on the factors that matter most about a wine: its appearance, its aroma, and its flavor. You'll notice there's space for overall comments: this is because, surprisingly often, tasters find themselves saying quite glowing things about the components of a wine that on the whole they don't really care for, or making disparaging comments about aspects of a wine that they like a lot *in toto.*

You'll also notice there are no numbers, no points to be assigned, no mathematical games to be played. Just words, and your job is to find the right ones. This is in part to generate sympathy for my job, but mostly to force you really to think about what you're smelling and tasting. Numbers seem to be exact, but in fact they allow you to slide over a lot of important details.

The actual process of tasting involves what you will come to think of as the "infamous s's": see, swirl, smell, sip/slurp, savor/slosh, and spit. Not a prepossessing bunch, but a lot of fun when you get to know them.

### See:

Look closely at the color of the wine. How would you describe its shade? Is it clear? Is it brilliant? Is it attractive? Tilt your glass slightly and look closely at a thin edge of the wine. Is the color true to the end? Or does it fade off? Or does it show other tints there?

Different wines have different color patterns, and as you come to know wine better, this will be a useful clue to you about how well a particular wine has been made or how well a particular bottle is holding up. Initially it won't tell you too much beyond whether you find the appearance of the wine attractive, but prettiness is also one of the pleasures of wine, so don't ignore it.

---

**Tasting Notes: Pair Number____          Taster_____**

Wine 1: _____          Wine 2: _____



Appearance:                    Appearance:



Aroma:                         Aroma:



Taste and Texture:             Taste and Texture:



Overall Impression:            Overall Impression:



In spite of
          my remarks above, I prefer wine number _____.

Because of

---

## Swirl:

With a gentle wrist motion or even gentler forearm motion, slowly start the wine circulating around the glass. You do this to release the aroma of the wine by bringing more oxygen in contact with it. Remember, gentleness is the key: too much exuberance leads to wine stains on the walls, the guests, and the precious self.

The much-revered ancient Greeks, when they weren't being wise and venerable, used to unwind after dinner with a wine-swirling game. The rules were simple: a large bowl was placed in the middle of the floor, and seated guests tried to swirl their remaining wine out of their cups and into the bowl. This only goes to show that even the ancient Greeks weren't impressive all the time, and anyone is entitled to look a little silly where wine is involved.

## Smell:

After you have swirled the wine, put your nose right down in the glass and draw in a long, deep breath. Don't worry about what it looks like: if anybody is there with you, they ought to be doing the same thing at this point. The crucial thing is that as you are breathing in, you are concentrating as hard as you can on what you are smelling. Use your nose as you've never used it before. Think about the traces of things you recognize in the wine's aroma. Nuts? If so, what kind? Fruit? Vanilla? Violets? Earth? Grass? This is where you really have to work, because smell is a major factor in our enjoyment of wines. Even what we call flavor is mostly made up of smell. And literally hundreds of different aromatic elements have been identified in wine, while most of us nasally impoverished humans recognize only a few of them.

Many wine aromas change in the glass, developing and/or fading as the minutes pass. This is why so much fuss is often made about exactly when to uncork and whether to decant a very old or very fine wine. Contact with oxygen releases the aroma, but too much contact with oxygen will also kill a wine—everything it has will literally vanish in air. So go back to a wine every now and again to smell it anew. Any young wine that disappears like that after, say, twenty minutes in the glass is a badly made wine.

## Sip/Slurp:

Take in a small amount of wine—not a whole mouthful—with as much air as you comfortably can. That's where the slurp may come in. The point of the air is, once again, to get maximum flavor out of a small amount of wine so you can taste everything that's in it. A small amount of wine keeps alcoholic intake to a minimum, because alcohol will eventually tire and numb the palate, and you want to be fresh for the next wine or wines.

## Savor/Slosh:

Let the wine run slowly over the entire surface of your tongue. Move it about both sides of the mouth. Expose it to every surface you've got that's capable of sensation.

This need not look silly, and it can be done very quietly. People who sit in posh restaurants and ostentatiously *chew* their wine (usually with wine steward or captain in patient attendance) are doing so not because they must but because they want you and everyone else in the restaurant to know what they are doing. The difference between true wine connoisseurs and such performers is the difference between people who do what they do out of sheer love and people who haven't the slightest idea of the worth of their activity unless it's noticed by an audience.

The action of tasting shouldn't look or sound like a mouthwash commercial, but don't rush it, either. Again, concentrate on what is actually going on in your mouth. Are you tasting one flavor, or many? All over the mouth, or in different parts? Are several flavors present at the same time, or do they succeed each other? What kind of flavors are they? Related to the aroma, or very different? What do they taste like? Fruit? Nuts? Tobacco? Minerals? Grass? Be as specific as you can—and remember to taste both with and without a bit of food (this is where our little bit of cheese comes in) and note carefully how the wine changes. If you've never done anything like this before, you're going to be amazed by how many different things you become aware of.

If you're tasting with a group, you're also going to be surprised by how very different each individual's description of the same wine's flavor can be. Don't let this bother you, not even if everybody in the group says the wine tastes like plums and you're all alone in insisting it tastes like asparagus. If it tasted like asparagus to you, it tasted like asparagus. That's all there is to it. The important questions are, Did you like it? Or did that asparagus flavor put you off? Once you know that, you can also know, for example, that there are other wines made from this same grape, or vinified the same way, and the odds are you're going to find them tasting something like this wine, and you'll like or dislike them accordingly.

All this holds true for my own comments about the wines, when you come to them. Just because I describe something I found in a wine doesn't mean you have to experience exactly the same thing. There's a fifty-fifty chance you will or you won't. That's not important. The important thing is to develop and sharpen your own taste.

To help you do that, I will provide you with some reactions to the same wine you are tasting, comments and descriptions made by varying groups of nonprofessional wine tasters—people at more or less the same level of wine knowledge as yourself. You may be surprised by some of these comments. I know some of them surprised me. But they should help you to get over any lingering doubts or self-consciousness about your own reactions and also provide you with a makeshift frame within which you can locate your own response to an individual wine. And every now and again I'll tell you what connoisseurs look for or hope for in the very best examples of a particular kind of wine.

I've deliberately avoided anything like a statistically significant sampling or a rigorous, scientific gathering of reactions, in order not to risk intimidating you into feeling that you had to taste exactly what other people had described. All the comments I have included are intended simply to help you come to know your own palate better, by letting you know what other tasters of skills similar to yours have tasted and what professionals look for as standards for the breed. But I cannot say this too often: all that matters are what you taste and how you react to it.

## Spit:

It means what it says. Spit, no matter how much you like the wine. Why? So you won't get sloshed, that's why. Obviously, the more wines you plan to taste at one sitting, the more important this becomes. Remember, too, that even though you spit every mouthful, you still absorb some alcohol directly through the mucous membranes that line the mouth, so it is possible to get a bit tiddly—and considerably more, if your tolerance for alcohol is low—without actually drinking a drop.

After you spit out the wine, once again concentrate. Does its flavor persist in your mouth? Does a component of its flavor, or a new flavor element, persist in your mouth? This is what is called a wine's finish (congratulations! you've just learned your first piece of wine jargon), and it, too, is an important part of a wine's overall effect and pleasure. Most beginners with wine have a bit of trouble discerning the finish without actually swallowing, so for that purpose it may be a good idea at first to let a little of the wine slide down your throat. But after you get used to paying attention to the sensations in your mouth, you won't find that necessary.

Professional tasters always spit out their wine, so no matter how distasteful this may seem to you, it's actually got quite a lot of professional prestige attached to it. Your mom may think you unmannerly, but your fellow wine drinkers will recognize real sophistication when they see it. If you plan to taste only one or two pairs of wines at a sitting, you can certainly skip the spitting if you wish to—it's not crucial where the number of wines remains small. So suit yourself. Either way, you win: swallow and enjoy the wine, or spit and look impeccably professional.

Don't worry about memorizing this sequence of steps. I'll go through them with you in detail in the first tasting, and after that I'll remind you of them at appropriate places. After you've done them a few times, they will come naturally to you. The watchwords are relax and enjoy.

Let me stress that each time you taste a wine, try to taste it with a little bit of food. This runs counter to almost every other wine-tasting method, but I strongly recommend it. Have something along with your wine, even if it's only a nibble of a mild cheese, because—unless you are very unusual—that is the way you are going to consume most of the wines you'll have in your lifetime. And food changes wine—in some cases, very dramatically.

That fact is what lies behind the ancient piece of wine-business lore that says "Buy on apples, sell on cheese." Acidic foods like apples strip bare every flaw and blemish in a wine. Fat foods like cheese bring out all that is best in them. Similarly, all sorts of food affect differently the way wine behaves. Some wines that do not seem impressive when tasted only against other wines simply blossom alongside food. And many wines that do very well in formal judgings fail miserably with food. Many a huge, high-alcohol wine has won a gold medal because it has the effect on the judges' palates of a double martini: you simply can't taste anything else after it.

There is a not-so-apocryphal story of a California winemaker who was proudly displaying his medal-bedecked, 18-degrees-of-alcohol (that's 36 proof for you whiskey drinkers), 6-degrees-of-residual-sugar, late-harvest Zinfandel: a monster Zin, as they call it in California, for which he was also charging a monster price. When asked what kind of food one would drink such a wine with, he answered—with a straight face, mind you—"It's terrific with peanut butter."

After you have finished all of the infamous s's, and after you have finished jotting down your comments, proceed as follows: if you are tasting alone, turn at that point to this book's comments on the wines you just tasted and use them to refine your own perceptions. Retaste step by step with the book if you find that that helps you. If you are tasting in a group, thoroughly discuss the wines among yourselves before turning to the book's comments. Go through each wine category by category as they appear on your tasting sheets—appearance, aroma, taste, etc. Then and only then look at the book's comments. As I have said before and will remind you many times again, you laid out your hard-earned money for this book to sharpen *your* taste in wine, not to defer to mine or anybody else's.

With the exception of the first flight, where I will conduct a guided tour, these basic tasting procedures remain the same throughout the book. The initial few sets of wine have been chosen to present fairly sharp contrasts and to introduce the basic terms and concepts you will use through the rest of this book. For that reason, I urge beginning tasters especially to taste the first four pairs in sequence. Your preferences there will lead you to subsequent groups of wines, different groups according to your preferences in each pair, and so on through the book. What you like will be leading you on to more complex examples of related wines or related kinds of wines. If at any point you can't make up your mind—if you either like or dislike both wines of a pair—go on to either or both of the next sets: strong preferences are almost bound to make themselves felt pretty quickly.

Leftover wine shouldn't be a very great problem. If you're tasting at the cocktail hour, I urge you to complete the tasting process by drinking the remaining wine with dinner. Otherwise, if you tightly recork the bottles, most wines should hold pretty much unchanged for a day or two; whites should be refrigerated. If the wines do change, it will usually be for the worse, unfortunately—but that, too, is part of the learning process.

# *What You Need Not Do*

To TASTE THE WINES AS FULLY AS POSSIBLE, it would be wise to approach them with your mouth and nose and eyes as fresh as possible. For this reason, many professionals taste only in the morning. There is also a mystique that claims that everyone can taste more accurately in the morning; all of us who awaken slowly and ineptly know just how much hogwash that is. In any event, for most people, morning tastings are going to be difficult at best, impossible at worst. Don't worry about that, but do pay attention to your own metabolism and your bodily clock. Try to block out for tasting a time of day when you are normally alert and energetic, whenever it may fall, and try to schedule all your tastings for that same time. Many people find early evening convenient.

Try to keep your palate fresh for tasting. I'm obviously not urging you to fast all day if you're tasting in the evening (your palate would still get stale anyhow), but at least don't try to proceed directly to wine tasting from wolfing down a deli-special pastrami, salami, and Swiss-cheese hero with peppers and onions and coleslaw and Russian dressing: it won't work.

This is also true if you are a smoker: sure, your palate has made the adjustment and you can taste wine just as well as a nonsmoker; nevertheless, your judgment will be skewed if you've been smoking heavily immediately before tasting. As for smoking during tasting: if everyone in your group also smokes, it might be okay in moderation, but it can very easily get tricky. If there are nonsmokers present, anyone smoking during the tasting will make it impossible for them to smell anything other than the smoke and will seriously impair their tasting ability.

Other things that will also skew the functioning of your taste

23

buds and interfere with your perceptions: alcohol and sugar, alone or in combination. A cocktail before the tasting (people do stranger things) will diminish your ability to discern flavors, as will heavily sweetened foods. In fact, if you are a sweets eater of more than average dimensions (take that how you will), you will have trouble coming to appreciate many very fine wines: you will find them too dry, perhaps even sour. You can make things easier for yourself by gradually drying out your palate: reduce the amount of sugar you consciously add to things, and start avoiding the kinds of food that have already been laced with sugar before they come to you. Sugar is a palate-killer: it masks the flavors of other elements in a wine or a dish, and it seems to have almost addictive effects on some people, so they find anything without sugar insipid.

# Setting the Table

NOW IS THE TIME, for convenience's sake, to provide yourself with all the wines you're going to need for your first tasting or two.

Remember, these tastings can be conducted at your own pace. You may choose to do one pair of wines at a sitting, or two, three, or four. You can do even more than that at one time if you choose, but you'll find that your ability to concentrate gets increasingly impaired as you go along. Even if you are conscientiously spitting out every mouthful of wine, you're bound to lose both mental and physical sharpness. You won't quite be able to pick up the aroma, flavors will be more blurred and vague than at first, and the words to describe them won't come as readily.

If you're doing this sort of thing for the first time, you might want to start very gently—say, two pairs of wines at most, and if that goes well, you could consider trying three or four pairs the next time. But don't push beyond your physical limits—which is good advice for most situations, but especially where alcohol is concerned. I'm not even being moralistic here so much as pragmatic. Go beyond your capacity, and you're just wasting your time and money.

My policy in working with you through this book is going to come pretty close to total disclosure, so let me start off on the right foot by telling you that you are here, on the verge of your first tasting, about to commit an oenological heresy. (Do you like that word, "oenological"? All it means is "having to do with wine," but do you notice how I let you get this far along before I sprung one of those on you? A man can smile and smile and be a villain.)

Your crime—maybe it's mine—consists in tasting red wines before whites as all of you were innocently just about to do.

Conventional tasting and teaching procedures always put white wines before reds, for the usually very sound reasons that white wines are for the most part lighter-bodied, less alcoholic, and less markedly flavored than red wines. That means that tasting red wines before whites in the same tasting session would all but make the white wines disappear.

We're starting off with red wines, however, because none of those reasons applies to our case. First and most obvious, we're not tasting reds and whites at the same sitting. Second, I like red wine better (total disclosure, see?). Third and most important, you can learn more about wine faster from red wines than from whites.

Because the flavors of red wines are both more distinct and more varied than those of whites, it's easier for any taster, beginner or experienced, to pick out individual tastes and characteristics, and it's easier to come to grips with concepts such as balance and maturity in wine. On the other hand, precisely because the flavors of white wines are more subtle than those of red wines, it makes sense to approach white wines after you've gained some tasting experience and have a better idea of how to taste and what to taste for.

One last piece of information. For reasons that are totally obscure to me, any number of wines grouped together for tasting are known as a flight—just like darts—so our pairs are really, in technical wine jargon, flights of two. Got that? If so, get ready to earn your wings. *Avanti!*

# RED WINES

# THE FIRST FLIGHT

❧

## Monterey Vineyard
## Classic Red 1989
## and
## Banfi Cuvée Placido
## Red Tuscan Table Wine

❧

I'M GOING TO WALK YOU THROUGH the tasting of this first pair of wines step by step so you get a good, clear sense of what your tasting procedure is going to be throughout the book. So for this one time only, read my golden words as you are actually performing your various tasting maneuvers. In all the flights that follow this one, I'll ask you to read only the preliminary remarks (if any), then to taste and take your notes, and only after that to look at what the book has to say.

Okay: you've provided yourself with glasses, water, a little nibble, pads, pencils, good lighting, and the two bottles of wine named above. Now, get your corkscrew and pull the corks or, in the case of Banfi's Cuvée Placido, unscrew the cap.

First lesson: Cork both is and isn't essential to wine. For wines designed to be drunk young, as both of these bottles are, modern bottling techniques can seal a bottle so efficiently that cork closure is not necessary. That screwcap on the Cuvée Placido is keeping its bottle just as airtight as is the cork on the Monterey Classic Red, perhaps even more so. The difference, however, lies in the public mind: people associate corks with quality wines, screwcaps with more plebeian drinks. But if you're going to explore the complicated world of wine, the first really serious lesson you should learn is not to be impressed by packaging. A badly made wine in a fancy bottle is just a badly made wine that costs a lot. A well-made wine in a no-frills presentation is often a bargain. Shop for good wine: don't buy glitzy packages and, above all, don't buy labels.

### That's a Corker

Cork became the standard stopper for wine somewhere in the late seventeenth or early eighteenth century, just about the same time that glassblowing techniques had progressed enough for bottles to become the standard wine containers. Now that technology has made many other materials available for the same purpose, we are starting to see wine in cans (so far unsuccessful: the wine tastes metallic) as well as wine in cartons, and various metal and plastic stoppers are also being tried on wine bottles. For the time being, cork has the upper hand. However, right now there is a big argument among wine professionals about whether the long corks that traditionally seal the finest wines are really the best material for that purpose. Some people swear by cork; because it is slightly porous it allows the wine to breathe and develop over a long period. Others argue that that is exactly what's wrong with cork: any oxygen at all is bad for wine and will eventually kill it. If you want to see what oxygen does for wine, leave a glass of one of these testers out overnight and then taste it: compare your reaction then to the notes you'll be taking in just a few minutes.

One final note: a wine is said to be "corked" or "corky" when it either smells of cork rather than wine or it smells stale, old, and sour. This is usually the result of oxidation, which in turn can result from a soft or crumbling cork. This is the reason wine stewards make so great a show of presenting you with the cork they have just extracted from your bottle of wine: so that you can see it is sound. In the case of most young wines, this is hardly necessary, since the cork will not have been in the bottle long enough to have deteriorated.

Back to business. Pour a little bit—no more than two ounces, and even one ounce is sufficient—of each wine into a glass. You can always pour more wine if your tasters need it, but most people find this quantity ample. Also, you will want to swirl the wine in your glass, and until you get the knack of that, a smaller amount of wine can spare you quite a few lurid stains.

If you're not sure how much an ounce or two of wine comes to in the glasses you're using, take a standard bar jigger—shot glass to most people—and fill it with water; then pour it into one of your wine glasses. That should be an ounce and a half of liquid precisely. If you have lived a life so temperate that you don't own a shot glass, two ounces equal a quarter of a cup equals four tablespoons equal twelve teaspoons—and bless you.

Always pour in the same direction, especially if you are tasting several wines or several pairs of wines. Most people find it easier to keep track of their wines if they arrange them like print on a page, moving progressively—or regressively, depending on the point of view—from the left to the right. This is wine advice, not political advice.

Now is the time to put the infamous s's to work: see, swirl, sniff, sip, savor, and spit. Celebrate and cerebrate. Those last two are constants.

## Appearance.

First, see. Look at the color of the wines carefully. It's a good idea if you can contrive a uniform white background to do this best. If you don't mind risking a tablecloth, that would obviously be ideal. Otherwise you can make do with the sheet of paper on which you will write your comments.

Any wine should look pleasing to the eye. Its color should be bright and clear, and it ought to look somehow lively. This may sound crazy, but a wine that looks dead usually tastes dead. The difference is hard to verbalize but is as apparent to the eye as the difference between a sleeping dog and a dead dog.

Wines that look cloudy or muddy are, if not dead, dying; they will almost certainly be marred by off-flavors. If one of the wines in front of you looks like that, go no further: return the wine to the dealer and try another bottle.

Of the two wines before you, the first, the Monterey Red, is a clear ruby, while the Cuvée Placido is somewhat lighter in color. This

difference in appearance will probably prompt you to expect the
Cuvée Placido to taste lighter than the Monterey Red, while the
Monterey Red by contrast looks as if it ought to be weightier or
fuller, somehow heftier to correspond to its deeper color. As it turns
out, although such correlations are by no means guaranteed, they
work out often enough so that color can often provide a usable clue
to the character of the wine in the glass.

The shade of the Monterey Classic Red, by the way, is pretty close
to a textbook example of what wine jargon means by describing a
wine as ruby. Remember the shade and the term: both will be
getting a lot of use.

A professional taster, in examining the color of a wine, will always
tilt the glass to about a 45-degree angle in order to make a thin lip of
wine for the light to pass through. What you look for in that lip is
whether the color of the wine is true all the way out to the edge,
whether it thins and fades, or whether bands of other colors appear.
In more complex wines, those bands of color can be important
indicators of the wine's maturity or youth, how fast or how slowly it
is developing. For relatively simple wines like these two, however,
this shading of color is neither apparent nor important. So, if you
like, you can practice looking professional—and professionally—by
tilting your glass slightly and regarding it judiciously. While you're
having fun, just don't forget to jot down your notes on the colors
you see.


## Aroma.

All right, now swirl and smell. Gently rotate the wine in the glass.
The idea is simply to get it moving and expose a bit more surface to
the air to liberate the aroma. Really concentrate now on what you are
doing. Bring the glass right up close to your nose and take a long,
deep whiff, just as if you were savoring the aroma of fresh-baked
bread. Put the glass down, think for a few seconds about what
you've just smelled, and jot down your impressions right away. Trust
your first impressions, even if they seem silly or irrelevant.

If the smell seems fruity, force yourself to be more precise: what
kind of fruit? or at least what color fruit—red like cherries or strawberries? or white like pears or bananas or apples? If it smells to you
like growing things, what sorts of growing things? Fresh grass?
Flowers? A woods after a rain? Herbs? If so, which? Spices? If

it smells of earth—is it like wet soil? or dry, dusty soil? or chalk?

Be as detailed as you can, and if you wish, take a few more sniffs—but remember that our noses overload very fast. You've probably noticed that phenomenon yourself when you first enter a new olfactory environment—a florist shop, say. The scent of flowers immediately demands your attention; then after a minute or so you aren't even aware that the flowers have any scent at all unless you bury your nose in them. That's why your first impressions are so important in analyzing the aroma of a wine.

Don't be embarrassed by anything that occurs to you about the scent of wine. Smelling is not a test—at least not of *you*—and even if it were there are no wrong answers. What you smell is what you smell, and that is all there is to it. So if one wine smells to you like horse manure and another like maple syrup, just jot those impressions down.

Smelling attentively and analytically does not come easy to us human beings. Because of the relative weakness of our smelling apparatus and our lack of experience in identifying and classifying smells, this is going to be the area where the greatest divergence of opinion—or at least of description—is going to take place.

I say "at least of description" because you may very well discover here that several of you are using different words to say the same thing about the wines, or are using the same words to denote different things. The latter case is by far the most confusing aspect of describing wines—or anything else, for that matter.

For instance, if there are four of you, the odds are very strong that at least two of you will use the word "musty" (it seems to be a popular word among beginning wine tasters) in describing one of these wines' aroma. The odds are also strong that one of you will mean the Monterey Red and the other the Cuvée Placido. There's an even greater chance that what at least one of you means by "musty" is not the conventional notion of stale or mildewy but something more akin to the smell of overripe fruit, fruit on the verge of fermenting, perhaps combined with a slight smell of earth.

In fact, neither of these wines has a pronounced scent nor a very complicated one, so you've been put very much upon the stretch here. Most people tend to find that both aromas seem to share, in slightly different proportions, elements of earth and of generalized fruit—an unspecific scent that at most leans toward sweet fruits such as berries rather than acid fruits such as apples.

Let me underline that you should not be distressed if what you smelled was nothing like what I just described. Everybody's sense of smell is different. Everybody's way of linking specific smells with specific objects is different. The crucial thing at this stage is smelling attentively, thinking about what you're smelling, and thinking about the language you're using to express your thoughts. "Earth" and "fruit" are two very important wine terms, and you are beginning to learn the concepts behind them and to see how what might before today have seemed totally vague to you can in fact have a quite concrete meaning. That's not bad, considering I haven't even let you taste a wine yet.

### Taste.

Now we're ready. Take a big sip or a small mouthful, with a lot of air. Don't worry about the noises you make. Let the wine flow all over your mouth and tongue, and pay attention to what sensations you are getting from it and where they occur in the mouth. Is there a prickle on the tip of your tongue? Is there astringency (a puckering, contracting sensation) at the sides of your tongue or on your cheeks? Are you getting flavor only at the front of your mouth, or at the back, or all over? Finally, what flavor? What does it actually taste like? Is the flavor similar to the aroma or different? Think of those categories we used before: fruit, growing things, earthy flavors. Do any of these fit here?

Don't forget to spit. And don't forget to write down your thoughts.

Now for the great wine instruction heresy: take bite of food. Do the whole thing once more, tasting all over your mouth again. Does food change the wine's flavor at all? If so, how? Once more, be as specific as you can, and make your notes as detailed as you can. Memory is untrustworthy, especially when alcohol is involved.

A few things about the action of these wines on the palate can be stated as fact—which means that about 90 to 95 percent of you ought to agree with them. First, the two wines have a different feel on the tongue. The Monterey Red feels heavier, bigger somehow, and definitely soft in comparison to the Cuvée Placido, which feels lighter and a tiny bit thinner; a very few individuals may even detect a slight spritziness, a sensation as if the wine were the slightest bit carbonated, in the Cuvée Placido. If this sensation were more pronounced and more universally discernible, it would approximate what the French call *pétillant* and Italians call *frizzante*—both words usually meant as terms of praise.

This entire package of weight-and-feel of the wine is what is meant by the texture of a wine. Notice especially that what we are talking about here are tactile sensations: lightness, heaviness, thinness, and softness, smoothness or prickliness are what the wines *feel* like on the tongue. They aren't tastes or flavors at all: they're pressures, textures, surface sensations. Taste again if you're not sure of any of this.

If you were really paying attention when you tasted, most of you will have noticed that the preponderance of the taste of the Monterey Red came on the back and sides of your mouth, while most of the taste of the Cuvée Placido came from the center of the tongue and felt as if it were higher in the mouth than the flavor of the Monterey Red. Go back and taste again, if you wish, to see if this isn't so.

The upper edges of the tongue are the primary receptors for sourness, the sides of the tongue for saltiness, the back the primary locus for perceiving bitterness, and the tip for sweetness. So the Monterey Classic Red is making the greatest impact on your sensors that read saltiness and bitterness. The Banfi Cuvée Placido, on the other hand, is striking those sensors that pick up sourness, normally in wine a product of acid.

Both wines are of course by any sane definition dry—that is, wines with no perceptible residual sugar. The sensation of sweetness that different tasters can receive from either wine is purely a function of their differing combinations of fruit and acid, not to mention the literally hundreds of other "trace elements" that are found in even the simplest wine. Depending on your sensitivity to these different factors, you are going to find the Cuvée Placido anything from bright, light, and lively to a bit thin and astringent, even vinegary, because what you are reacting to is the combination of fruit and acidity in that wine. The taster who finds the Cuvée Placido bright and lively is by the same token likely to find the Monterey Red flabby and over-fruity, even sweetish, with a different sort of astringency of its own (the result of tannin, which we will talk about in a little while). Conversely, tasters who prefer the Monterey Red will in all likelihood do so because they find it mouth-filling, smooth, and relatively fruity. For them, the Cuvée Placido may be too light and sour.

Monterey Classic Red Table Wine is produced by The Monterey Vineyard, a large vineyard and winery operation now owned

## Chemicals in Wine

Wine, like any other organic product, is a construct of naturally occurring chemical components. Moreover, fermentation is not only a natural process but also a chemical operation. Yeasts attack grape sugars, digest them, and convert them into alcohol and several different kinds of acid. A good many other by-products result from both this process and the other components of the grapes themselves. Because of this, there are as many different naturally occurring minerals and chemicals in wines as there are in, say, bread or pickles, and for much the same reasons.

In modern winemaking, science and technology play an increasingly important part at every stage, from protecting the vines from parasites to cultivating selected strains of yeasts, from manipulating the musts (grape liquids resulting from pressing) to bottling the wine in an oxygen-free environment. Most of this leaves little if any trace in the finished wine. The introduced trace element that the winedrinker is most likely to encounter is sulfur dioxide ($SO_2$), and that most often in white wines, where it is used to discourage wild yeasts and pave the way for the desired strain. Sulfur is also sometimes used to clean wine barrels. Any perceptible level of sulfur in the aroma or especially in the taste of a wine indicates flaws in the wine-making. This is far more likely to occur with white wines than with reds.

by The Seagram Corporation. It makes sound and often very interesting wines from all the classic California grape varieties. Most of its Classic series of varietal wines offer excellent value for the money.

Cuvée Placido is produced and marketed by Banfi Importers, an American importing firm that now has extensive grapegrowing and winemaking operations of its own in some of Italy's most prestigious wine zones. It imports just about every level of Italian wine from simple to complex, from blended table wines like this to fine single-vineyard bottlings.

## Substitutes:

The best alternative for the Monterey Vineyard Classic Red is a younger vintage; failing that, try Seghesio's Sonoma Red, Trefethen's Napa Valley Eschol Red, or Fetzer's California Premium Red as alternatives: depth of color may vary considerably, but in other respects these will serve very well. If Banfi's Cuvée Placido is unobtainable, try Folonari's Red Table Wine.

That ends the first wine-tasting session. There are several ways for you to proceed from here.

*Following the lead of your own preferences:*
   No matter which of these two wines you liked better, the
   Monterey Classic Red or the Banfi Cuvée Placido, you should at
   this point proceed straight on through the next three flights in
   order to equip yourself with some basic tasting categories,
   concepts, and terms.

*Following the kind of grapes:*
   At this point, there is no way to follow any particular grape
   variety, because both these wines are pretty miscellaneous
   blends. Later on in the book, however, a varietal approach will
   become possible and I will give you appropriate directions.

*Following the wines of the country:*
   Wine One: Go on to the Third Flight.
   Wine Two: Go on to the Second Flight.

Happy trails to you, as Gene Autry used to say.

# THE SECOND FLIGHT

◦◦◦

## *Bolla Bardolino 1990*
## *and*
## *Jaboulet "Parallèle 45"*
## *Côtes du Rhône 1989*

◦◦◦

YOU'RE GOING TO TASTE THESE TWO WINES, as you will all the others from this point on, exactly as you did the first pair: pour an ounce or two in each glass, look at it carefully to gauge the color and limpidity, swirl it to free the aroma, then smell and assess that, and finally take a good-sized sip, taste attentively, and spit. Take a nibble of food and taste again. Remember to take your notes promptly at each step, because each succeeding sensory stimulus can smudge the clarity of the one that preceded it. You're going to get sick of reading reminders like this before you've finished with this book, but what we are trying to instill here are new—and it is to be hoped permanent—patterns of attention.

The only change you'll make from Flight 1 will be that you'll complete the whole tasting procedure on your own first, before coming back to see what the book has to say about the wines. If you are tasting as a group, make sure to discuss among yourselves your responses to these wines before going on to read my comments on them. Try to sort out your terms and clarify as much as is humanly possible that you all mean the same things by the same words. For instance, if some of you are using terms like "tart" or "acidic," are you describing two different things or only one? A dictionary may come in handy to resolve amicable disputes.

38

Push each other for some details: if you like a wine, why? What is there about it that pleases you? If you describe an odor or a color as lovely or as displeasing, why? What about it appeals or offends? You don't all have to agree about your responses to the wines, but you should all have a good idea of why you are reacting as you do.

Okay; if you're ready now, go perform the ritual of the s's and make all your notes. Take your time: wine is a leisure activity (or so I'm told). After you've made all the comments you want to about these two wines, check back here to see what some other people like you have tasted in them.

### Appearance.

The Bardolino and the Côtes du Rhône present an even sharper color contrast than did the Monterey Classic Red and the Banfi Cuvée Placido Red (Flight 1). The Rhône wine shows a deep ruby, almost but not quite purplish, while the Bardolino is a much paler red, not pale enough to describe as a rosé, but nearing that; more-over, it has orange or amber highlights or glints. Both wines are limpid and attractively clear.

The differing colors suggest depth and lightness, respectively. Both are characteristic of their kinds of wine: that is, these are exactly the shades that good examples of these kinds of wine ought to show. Let me underline that for you, since people sometimes think that the Bardolino's paleness or (less often) the Rhône's depth of color indicates a poorly made wine, either watery on one hand or coarse on the other. Not so: a Bardolino is always lightly colored and a Rhône always deeply colored because of the vastly different grapes from which they are made. A Bardolino as dark as the Rhône or a Côtes du Rhône as light as the Bardolino would be wines to worry about, but these two are right as they are.

### Aroma.

The Bardolino's aroma will strike most people as very light and evanescent: little hints of fruit, perhaps of mint, but delicate and not persistent. The Rhône, on the other hand, has a markedly stronger aroma, with some depth to it. It will suggest to most tasters things in the spicy, peppery, sweet-fruit range—at the extremes, perhaps raisin or a more vegetable smell. Many tasters will be surprised that the aroma is not as big as the color of the wine led them to expect.

Once again, as with the colors, these aromas are perfectly typical of these kinds of wine. Different vintages might yield some variations in strength of aroma, but the general polarity of delicacy vs. strength that these two wines illustrate will persist.

Taste.

This pair of wines offers a case study in the deceptiveness of appearances. From looking at the wines, you would expect the Bardolino to be very light, perhaps watery, with little to it, and the Rhône by the same criterion to be a powerhouse. In fact, the Bardolino strikes most palates as more substantial, and the Rhône less blockbusterish, than appearances suggest.

The Bardolino *is* light, but it does show some tasty fruit and plenty of bright acid. How do I know that last quality? By its effects: it's the acid that makes it feel so lively on the tongue. Try to log that piece of information in your palatal record book. It's important, since that function of acidity goes a long way to determine the character and style of a wine, especially a not very complex one like this Bardolino.

Other elements in its flavor? Well, if you concentrate really hard, you may even discern hints of something like cherry in it, but not too much more than that. All in all, most tasters would describe it as a pleasant, very light wine, small-bodied and straightforward.

The Rhône, on the other hand, does not deliver the big-bodied wine its color and aroma lead many tasters to expect. What you do get is mouth-filling enough, but very soft in texture. There is some fully dry fruit and an astringency, most apparent in the almost bitter finish (the finish, remember, is the taste that persists in your mouth after you have spit or swallowed the wine).

That astringency is almost certainly due to tannin, a substance that enters wines both from the grape skins themselves and from wooden (especially oak) barrels, where it occurs naturally. Consequently, you'll come across tannin far more frequently in the flavor of barrel-aged red wines than in white wines, which are normally vinified in stainless steel without any skins in the musts (musts being the grape liquids resulting from pressing). We'll be talking a lot more about tannin, so take note of that astringent sensation in the finish and log it into your memory.

Tannin usually makes itself felt in the mouth by a drying, puckery sensation on the cheeks and/or a raspy sensation on the tongue and throat, neither of which feeling—despite what that description sounds like—is always unpleasant. Tannin's taste in the purest form is reminiscent of that of over-strong or over-steeped tea or the bitterness you get from biting into a raw acorn. You rarely find it that concentrated in any wine, but even lesser degrees of tannin can make themselves felt quite forcefully.

Tannin is crucial in wines of any pretensions to greatness because it is one of the key elements that promote long life in a wine. Consequently, balance and harmony are also quite crucial to the success of any such wines: otherwise we would have have undying tannin monsters roaming the shelves of our wine shops.

Tannin enters wine from the grapes themselves (particularly from their skins, where it occurs in widely varying concentrations according to grape variety) and from the barrels the wine is fermented and/or stored in, especially from new oak barrels. Thus, wine-makers can control, with some degree of precision, the amount of tannin presence they want to achieve in their wine by altering the containers in which that wine is fermented, stored, or aged.

For beginning tasters, the effects of tannin are sometimes difficult to distinguish from the effects of acid. Consequently, there is a possibility of confusing the two different sets of flavors of these wines. You feel acid as a prickly sensation, usually pleasant, and almost always most intense all over the tongue, as if thousands of little carbonation bubbles were gently scratching it. You feel tannin as a distinctly puckering or astringent sensation, definitely unpleasant when strong. It occurs mostly on the cheeks and, to a lesser extent, at the side of the tongue.

Despite the fact that they are very different sensations, some people may in fact experience the fruit-and-acid of the Bardolino and the fruit-and-tannin of the Côtes du Rhône as almost the same thing. Consequently, they may describe these two wines as only slightly different versions of each other, or they may describe the Rhône as being like the Bardolino, only more so. Don't worry if you've done this: it doesn't mean your wine career is already over. As you get more practice tasting wines, you'll start to make that distinction a lot more sharply. You'll very quickly be able to feel the difference between the drying effect of tannin and the enlivening effect of acid on your mouth. Then all you'll have to learn is how to differentiate more exactly between kinds of fruit.

Fruit is a difficult but absolutely crucial wine term. After all, all wine is made from fruit and inevitably, unless Better Living

Through Chemistry has intervened, all wine must taste of fruit. But different varieties of grapes have different flavors to start with: even humble table grapes like Concord and Thompson Seedless can show you that. The highly bred varieties that go into fine wines are even more distinctive, and the whole process of vinification and aging—especially barrel-aging—can accentuate or modify, blend or isolate those differences. Grape juice always tastes like a grape: wine can taste like the whole range of fruits and many other substances as well.

So what do wine people mean when they talk about fruit? Fair question.

First of all, they most commonly and most generally do not mean a specific fruit, and emphatically not grapes. To call a wine grapey is in fact often an insult: it implies a kind of excessive simplicity, even coarseness.

When wine professionals say of a young wine, as we have said of the Bardolino and the Rhône in this pair, that "it has fruit," they mean first to compliment the wine, second to denote a quality of freshness and refreshingness, often linked with the presence of a kind of sweetness without sugar, that almost immediately calls to mind for most people a loose and unspecific idea of fruitiness.

Probably the most graphic way to describe what they mean is to remind you of the way you think of a nice, juicy piece of fruit on a blistering hot summer day. You may not even have in mind a specific kind of fruit, just a broad idea of succulence, moisture, pleasing flavor, and refreshment. That's the ideal that wine professionals are mentally referring to when they describe wines as having a lot of or a little fruit. Above all, fruit is those elements in a wine that convey to our palates and our imaginations the sensations and ideas of freshness and vitality. That is the most important meaning of fruit in wine jargon, and I think you can see how it is possible for one wine to have more or less fruit than another, or more or less vivid fruit.

Beyond that basic notion, you enter on greater complexities, because as your taste buds get sharper and your experience broader, the wines you're going to taste in the course of this book are going to get more complicated, and you will begin to be able to discern in some of our examples not simply fruit but classes of fruit and even, perhaps, individual kinds of fruit.

In fact, the second most important use of the concept of fruit in talking about wines lies in the broad distinction between flavors that align themselves with the red fruits like berries and cherries, and those that align themselves with the white fruits like pears, apples, and, at an extreme, bananas.

Lest you think that all this is so much hokum, remind yourself about what you already know that is just like it. Macintoshes and Winesaps and Golden Delicious and Greenings can't be mistaken for one another, but you wouldn't take them for anything but apples either. A Greengage and an Eldorado taste very different from each other, but both taste of fruit and both taste like plums. You can already recognize sameness and differences within the general flavor of classes of fruits: all you have to do now is transfer that ability to wine flavors.

In the two wines of this second flight I think you can readily distinguish two very different "tonalities" of fruit (I put that word in quotation marks because I'm using it loosely at the moment: it's not a conventional wine term). By that I mean that the fruit present in the Bardolino is not simply more delicate or less pronounced than the fruit in the Côtes du Rhône, but that it strikes the palate as if it were in a higher register than that of the Rhône: tenor, or perhaps even soprano, to the latter's baritone.

I know, I know: this kind of language is going to drive you crazy. You think it's the worst thing about wine, and you're right. The sad truth is, however, that this kind of language is unavoidable: we are talking here about personal perceptions which have so far resisted scientific measurement. No one has yet found a way to quantify what goes on in our mouths or our minds when we taste something. The French—who else?—are working on the problem, but until they come up with a solution, we are stuck with the imprecision of language. We are essentially driven to metaphors and figures of speech to try to convey the varying shades of what we perceive. It needs goodwill and an effort at understanding on everybody's part to make it all work.

Besides, would it really help you any if I could tell you that Wine A was 5.4 on a salinity scale and 3.2 pH, while Wine B was only 4.7 and 3.1, respectively?

After all that palatal palaver, here are a few facts about these two wines to balance against all this subjectivity.

Bardolino is made from four localized varieties of grapes grown in the hills around Lake Garda in north-central Italy. It should be drunk as young as possible, and specimens over four years old can be dead if they have not been stored very well. Generally speaking, it's wise to drink Bardolino before its third birthday. In Italy it is often served lightly cooled: chilled, not iced. Bolla is one of the largest and most reliable shippers of Bardolino and other Veronese wines to the United States.

"Parallèle 45" is the Jaboulet firm's proprietary name for their Côtes du Rhône wine. The area in which the several varieties of grapes for this wine are grown lies along both banks of the river Rhône in southern France. Simple Rhône wines like this one are usually pleasant drinking, with a straightforward, robust style, and they often offer very good value for your money. Jaboulet is one of the largest and most important winemakers and wine dealers in the Rhône area.

Bardolino and Côtes du Rhône are both usually described as "fruity" wines, in case you needed any further proof how one wine term can cover a multitude of *vins*.

You're probably thinking that this has been an awfully long discussion of the flavor components of what you thought of as only two simple, enjoyable wines. Well, you're right. It was a very long discussion, but it's worth every word, because even though you may not have realized it at the moment, you have just acquired the essential key to understanding red wine. Congratulations.

What do you mean, what is it?

I told you. Tannin, acid, fruit. Fruit, acid, tannin. Acid, tannin, fruit.

That's it?

That's it. From the taster's point of view, tannin, acid, and fruit are the basic building blocks of dry red wine, just as you will find later on that acid, fruit, and sugar serve the same function for tasters of white wine. The nature and relative proportions of tannin and acid and fruit will account for most of the distinctive flavors of the whole world of red wine. At very least, that trio of elements will explain the large differences among the major kinds of red wine. They can describe, for example, the differences between wine made from the same kind of grapes in different parts of the world. So from here on out, every red wine tasting you do is going to force you to one degree or another to consider the relations of tannin, acid, and fruit in each wine.

As I said before, congratulations: you're well on your way to knowing wine.

**Substitutes:**

First choice should be a younger vintage of these two wines. After that, try a Bardolino from some of the other reliable makers in the region (for example, Anselmi, Bertani, Folonari, Masi, Pasqua, Sartori, Tommasi, Zenato) or, if Bardolino is completely unavailable, its near kin Valpolicella (from any of the same producers). Be aware, however, that Valpolicella is fuller-bodied and in all respects more forceful than Bardolino. If the Jaboulet "Parallèle 45" is not obtainable, try a Côtes du Rhône from either a regional maker (for example, Chapoutier, Guigal, Petite Ferme), or a good Burgundian shipper (Bouchard, Jadot), or, as a last resort, Petite Ferme's Côte du Ventoux.

This is the conclusion of the second tasting session. To increase your basic wine knowledge and armory of tools, it would be best to go right on to the next flight. However, should you choose otherwise, there are several ways for you to proceed from here.

*Following the lead of your own preferences:*
    If you liked the first wine better, Bolla Bardolino, go on to the
    Third Flight.
    If you liked the second wine better, Jaboulet "Parallèle 45" Côtes
    du Rhône, go on to the Fourth Flight.

*Following the kind of grapes:*
    Go on to the Nineteenth Flight.

*Following the wines of the country:*
    Wine One: Go on to the Fourth Flight.
    Wine Two: Go on to the Third Flight.

# THE THIRD FLIGHT

❧

*Jadot Beaujolais 1990*
*and*
*Sutter Home*
*California Zinfandel 1989*

❧

HERE AGAIN ARE TWO WINES which are frequently described as fruity, so be prepared to compare them in those terms. With all of these pairs of wines, it is a good strategy to seek those ways in which they are alike as well as the elements that distinguish them from each other. Since we don't have any sort of objective measurements to use, we've got to construct a makeshift set of yardsticks out of the ideas of sameness and difference. Every new wine you learn and every new wine element you recognize extends that ruler a fraction of an inch. By the time you finish this book, you should have built your own private yardstick for measuring what you like in a wine.

Are you ready? Perform the ritual: see, swirl, smell, sip, savor, and spit.

And take notes. And talk it over. And then read on.

Appearance.

Once more, we have sharp color contrasts between the two wines. Both wines, however, should be equally clear and bright, with no trace of muddiness. The Beaujolais shows a very pale ruby, really a light cherry red, almost soda-pop looking, though definitely not as pale as a rosé. In fact, although it can appear almost faded alongside the ruby of the Zinfandel, this bright, clean, lively looking wine has a fine, deep color for a Beaujolais: 1990 was a lovely vintage, and its wines are more marked in every respect than Beaujolais usually are. The dark shade of red with bluish tints, almost moving into purple, that you see in the Zinfandel is quite a characteristic color for that wine. The Zinfandel is a very robust grape that makes an exceptionally deeply dyed young wine.

### Aroma.

With these two wines, you should be able to start making some more elaborate distinctions between aromas. Both of their bouquets ought to suggest to you a pretty large assortment of components.

After you finished your visual survey, you were probably surprised that the Beaujolais had so big an aroma: it is no pantywaist wine, despite its lighter color. Most people perceive it as, in effect, tutti-frutti: a medium-strong, distinctly fruity aroma, all ripe cherries and berries (some tasters discern apples too). Many people pick up a pleasing earthy or stemmy undertone and a small scent of pepper as well. This is a classic Beaujolais aroma, and most tasters love it, though a few find it too soda-poppy for their pleasure.

Most people will describe the aroma of the Zinfandel as a combination of alcohol (perceived as a kind of headiness or warmth), fruit (perceived as intensely ripe grapes), spice (cinnamon, nutmeg, pepper), and earthy odors, with one or another of these predominating. Some will also discern a deeper earth scent, almost a slight smoky aroma. Usually, for the majority of tasters, the fruit takes charge, and what they smell, though they may use differing terms to describe it, is the brambly, berrylike scent that distinguishes this style of Zinfandel from almost every other wine. Overall, this particular Zinfandel has an aroma that can technically be called full, forthcoming, and absolutely characteristic of the grape variety—in other words, this too is a classic varietal aroma.

While most of you will probably agree about what's in the aroma, you'll no doubt disagree sharply over whether it is pleasant or not. In fact, it is not hard to get a consensus on the description of the aromas of these two wines, but in both cases the house divides on the question of whether they are attractive or not—which is a very nice illustration, if you needed one, of the limits of objective measurements of wine and the importance of plain old-fashioned personal taste.

### Varietal Is the Spice of Life

Varietal is a key word—and an overworked one—in wine jargon. Its usage derives, obviously, from a grape variety, but in wine circles it is used primarily in connection with the prestige grapes, the so-called noble varieties of *Vitis vinifera* (the European wine grape, as opposed to the native American *Vitis labrusca*).

Important red varieties include Cabernet Sauvignon, Merlot, Pinot Noir (all three cultivated in both France and California), Zinfandel (California), and Sangiovese and Nebbiolo (Italy). Major white varietal wines include Chardonnay (almost everywhere in the world, but especially France and California), Riesling (Germany, France, California), Sauvignon Blanc (France, California, Italy), and Gewürztraminer (France, Germany, California). The finest wines of California are usually varietal wines, meaning that they bear the name of the grape that (by law) makes up at least 75 percent of their contents.

Varietal character refers to the total package of sensations—aroma, taste, feel—produced by a noble grape variety. This remains to some degree the same in any wine made from the grape, but it can vary in intensity and it can be manipulated by growing practices and techniques of vinification. Consequently, varietal character, varietal intensity, and fidelity to varietal become important considerations in professional evaluations of, for example, California Chardonnay and white Burgundy (made with Chardonnay).

In case you're wondering: yes, it is certainly conceivable that someone might find a wine pleasing to drink but a terrible version of the varietal, and vice versa.

### Taste.

First of all, let's talk about fruit in these two wines. In the Beaujolais, you will probably taste a bit less fruit than the aroma led you to expect: most people react that way. The fruit is still ample, however, flavorful and round and definitely falling into that cherry/berry range (most tasters will probably call it strawberries).

The Zinfandel, on the other hand, has almost a super-abundance of fruit: it strikes most people as full, soft, deep and very fresh. And most tasters have no trouble pinning it down to a specific fruit: they taste a distinctly spicy blackberry flavor in the wine, accompanied by what you have to describe as a kind of pleasant scratching sensation on the tongue. Both these flavors are absolutely characteristic of these kinds of wine.

What you are perceiving here, in whatever terms you may be using to describe it, is both varietal flavor and varietal intensity. The basic difference in the tastes of these two wines is directly traceable to the grapes from which they are made, the Gamay and the Zinfandel. Varietal flavor is a constant in varietal wines: that Gamay flavor will persist in all well-made Beaujolais just as the basic Zinfandel flavor will persist in all decently produced Zinfandel wines.

On the other hand, the differences between the freshness of this Beaujolais and the force of this Zinfandel show what is meant by their degree of varietal intensity, and that is a variable that can be affected dramatically by the conditions of the harvest and of the wine's vinification. You'll have to take my word for it, but the degree of varietal intensity a wine possesses can make a great deal of difference to your appreciation of it: a more intense Beaujolais (though that is hard to imagine; this is a big one as Beaujolais goes) and a less intense Zinfandel (much easier to imagine) might be very difficult for you to distinguish at this stage of your wine apprenticeship.

In fact, this whole distinction may not be as simple for you to perceive as I have been assuming, since in these two wines you don't taste the fruit by itself. It doesn't come to you in isolation, but rather is surrounded by other components of the wines that modify the intensity of the fruit and the way it strikes you. To talk about this at all, we've got to artificially select out elements one at a time and look at them in sequence, but when you actually taste the wine you get them all together and all at once.

One of the major elements in a wine that alters the way you taste its fruit is acid. There are of course all sorts of acids in the world, many of them not so pleasant. The ones that occur naturally in wine—and they are numerous—mostly tend to contribute to the liveliness of the wine. It is acid that makes a wine taste fresh, gives it a little lift, lets the fruit sing.

In the case of the two wines we're dealing with here, the Beaujolais has a lot of acid: that's why it tastes so bright. Fortunately, there is enough fruit there to sustain all that acid, so the wine doesn't taste thin or insubstantial. The only sign that the acid may be a little excessive is a slight tingling sensation, as if the wine were nearly *pétillant*. In all fairness, I have to say that many Beaujolais fans find that quality very attractive and not a defect at all.

If the Zinfandel is at all unbalanced, it is in the opposite direction: too much fruit for its acid to carry, which makes for a certain limpness or flabbiness in the wine. Again, this is my palate speaking. For many tasters, a lot of softness in a wine like this can be as big an attraction as an acid tingle in the Beaujolais. The sensation it creates on the tongue for them is soft, but round and live.

"Round" in wine language means two similar things: the way a wine tastes and the way it feels on the tongue. In both cases, smoothness is the key: the wine doesn't feel sharp; no single flavor component sticks out. If other important qualities are also present, the overall impression a round wine makes is completeness and harmony—not necessarily richness or fullness, though those may be present also. If other key qualities are absent or insufficient, a round wine may taste merely bland or excessively soft.

Whether they like it or not, however, most tasters will agree that the Zinfandel's softness stands out, especially in comparison to the Beaujolais.

This is true despite the fact that the Zinfandel is what we call a heavy wine. Try it again; you'll see what I mean. The Zinfandel actually feels as if it weighs more on the tongue than does the Beaujolais. That is the effect of, among some other lesser elements, alcohol, and it is this sensation that is usually meant by the term "body." So if you were going to convey some of the characteristics of these two wines succinctly and technically, you would describe the Beaujolais as fruity and acidic, with a medium body, and the Zinfandel as relatively full-bodied, soft, and markedly fruity.

A final word about body: Even though the major component of body is alcohol, all of the other elements of the wine also contribute. A high-alcohol wine with little fruit and little acid would not strike you as a big, full-bodied wine: you would taste it as harsh and biting. It is for reasons like this that concepts like harmony and balance are so important in talking about fine wines—and they obviously become increasingly crucial as the wines you taste possess more and more elements that need to be harmonized.

You're coming along just fine, and you should take a minute here to think about what you've done so far. Already, in only our third pair of wines, you've gotten to the point where you've dealt at least once with fruit and acid and tannin, and body and texture and finish, and I've just taken it for granted that you can taste dryness or sweetness. Even in wines as relatively simple and straightforward as this Beaujolais and this Zinfandel—and these are regarded as very simple wines, wines a professional would not ordinarily subject to the kind of close analysis you've just done—even in wines this simple you've had to deal with the interplay of several of these components.

Your preference, in a pair of wines like this, is going to depend on things like whether the vivacity of the Beaujolais pleases your palate more than the bigger, more abundant fruit of the Zinfandel. That kind of information about yourself, as you gradually accumulate it through this series of tastings, is what is going to help you to define your own taste and select the kind of wines that are going to give you pleasure. It can also, if you let it, show you what the limits of your taste are at present so that you can expand them if you wish to. No one ever pitched at ninety-nine miles an hour the first time he threw a baseball: practice strengthens your palate just as surely as it does your arm.

If you found something lacking in both of the wines in this flight, that doesn't mean there's anything wrong with your taste: on the contrary. Taking a very hard-nosed view of them, both the Beaujolais and the Zinfandel, for all their pleasantness, are one-dimensional wines: fruit is really all there is to them. That's just about all you really should be looking for in wines of this class—but that doesn't mean that that is all wine has to offer, nor is it all you have to settle for. The world of wine offers a great variety of attractions, and the honest pleasures that these wines afford are a starting point, a base line from which you can move as far afield as you wish.

The important thing about these and all wines is not to criticize them for what they lack but to enjoy them for what they have to offer. These are simple, unpretentious wines to drink with simple, light foods: they are not wines to make a fuss about or use to show off your newfound expertise.

For your information and files, here are some data on these two kinds of wines.

Beaujolais is one of the most popular wines in the world. It is produced in south-central France, between the southern end of the Burgundy region of great wines and the city of Lyon. It is made from the Gamay grape, which is grown also in California.

Beaujolais is so widely enjoyed because it is a simple, straightforward wine, light, fresh, and modestly fruity. An even lighter version now enjoys great popularity, even though many red-wine drinkers (myself, alas, included) find it too soda-poppy for their taste: that is what is called Beaujolais nouveau or Beaujolais *primeur*, which is rushed to market with great fanfare every November. This is the first wine of that fall's harvest, and it is always very light and often distinctly *pétillant*—lightly fizzy. The house of Jadot is a major Burgundian *négociant* and one of the foremost shippers of quality Beaujolais.

Those latter two French terms are in wide use among wine people—*négociant* because there really isn't an English word that quite expresses the combination of wine-related activities a firm like Jadot is involved in (they are grapegrowers and buyers, winemakers and buyers and blenders and sellers), and *pétillant* because it sounds much more sophisticated than "fizzy." Fizz is what kids' drinks do.

Zinfandel comes close to being a native American wine grape. Certainly the wine it produces is unique to California, and the grape's origins are obscure enough (current theory holds the vine is related to the Italian Primativo from Puglia) so that it can be regarded as an American classic.

This is a hearty grape that makes all sorts of wine, from a simple, fruity, picnicky style up to the level of estate-bottled, complex wines for long aging. What we have here, as indicated by its simple California appellation, is a Zinfandel blended from grapes grown in several counties of California and showing hints of the provocative varietal flavor that specimens from the best growing areas can achieve.

Sutter Home is something of a Zinfandel specialist: most Americans will probably know of the firm from its popular, sweet, white Zinfandel. It makes Zins in every style: its Amador County Reserves are among the biggest-bodied you can find. Its simple Zinfandels, like this example, offer great value for their modest price.

**Substitutes:**

Once again, choose younger vintages of these same wines first. After that, look for Beaujolais from other reliable *négociants*

(Bouchard, Duboeuf, Ferraud, Fessy, Latour, Pasquier-Desvignes, Sarrau, Tete) and simple Zinfandels from other good California growers (e.g., Buena Vista, Martini, Montevina, Seghesio, etc.).

Here, at last, ends the third tasting session. Pour yourself a drink: you've worked hard. If you intend to follow the trail of your own preferences through this book, you'd be well advised at this point to go straight on to the Fourth Flight and begin your preferring there. Nevertheless, there are several other ways for you to proceed from here.

*Following the lead of your own preferences:*
   If you liked the first wine better, the Jadot Beaujolais, go on to the Seventh Flight.
   If you liked the second wine better, the Sutter Home Zinfandel, go on to the Fifth Flight.

*Following the kind of grapes:*
   Wine One: Go on to the Seventh Flight.
   Wine Two: Go on to the Seventeenth Flight.

*Following the wines of the country:*
   Wine One: Go on to the Fourth Flight.
   Wine Two: Go on to the Fifth Flight.

# THE FOURTH FLIGHT

~∞∞∞~

*Valbon Rouge
and
Ruffino Chianti 1990*

~∞∞∞~

**O**NE OF THE WINES in this pair is a nonvintage bottling, the second such you will have had so far. If you have not finished the wines from previous tastings, you might learn something further by tasting the two together—Valbon Rouge from this pair and Villa Banfi Cuvée Placido from the first.

Alternatively, you might try blind tasting them and two of your vintage bottles to see if you can actually taste any difference between them. To do that, simply wrap each bottle tightly in a brown paper bag right up to the lip—or better yet, have somebody else do that—number the bags, pour, and taste. Don't unveil until everybody has cast every ballot. It can be fun, instructive, and often surprising, especially if you have exaggerated notions about vintage. But we'll talk more about that after you taste this pair.

Ready? Proceed through all of the s's as before, trying to remember and utilize everything we've said so far. Bear in mind those categories we've touched on: fruit, acid, tannin, alcohol, body, texture, and balance. Don't feel you have to mention—or even experience—every one of them with every wine, but have them ready as usable categories if you need them. Above all, concentrate on what is in your eyes and nose and mouth.

After as many of you as are tasting together have all said your piece about these two wines, read on. (I hope by now you see the value of your talking out your own responses to these wines before you read what I have to say: it's too easy to be bullied by the printed word into thinking you tasted things you didn't. People need to develop greater skepticism about what they read. That *is* political advice.)

## Appearance.

In color the Valbon Rouge and the Ruffino Chianti are very similar. Both are essentially a medium ruby, the Valbon in the brown-red range and the Ruffino in the blue-red spectrum, and perhaps showing a few amber or tawny highlights.

Those amber highlights, by the way, are typical of many Italian wines, and in some of the best Chiantis and Barolos and similar wines the tawniness increases markedly with bottle-aging, so that it is often a good indication of maturity in those wines. In many French or California wines, on the other hand, a heavy amber tone often indicates that the wine is over the hill.

## Aroma.

As far as aroma is concerned, most tasters will get a definite scent of alcohol, almost a rush, from the Valbon. Some will say it smells warm, or hot: what they will in all probability be referring to is the alcohol. This doesn't mean that this is a particularly strong wine, simply that the other elements are sufficiently subdued for the alcohol to show strongly. The aroma is in any event a light one, with some slight "sweetish" (as most people describe them) elements and a subdued but definite scent of fruit. The Chianti too has a light aroma, but it is a bit more intense and drier-smelling than the Valbon—many people find the odor reminiscent of freshly cut stems and twigs. Some people may also detect slight suggestions of tobacco in it.

## Taste.

In flavor, the Valbon is what I would call a mannerly wine. It's not very assertive, and you taste it more as a blending of components than any single thing. There is some fruit, some tannin, some acid, and they all seem to get along quite nicely. The wine gives the impression that it was blended to fit unobtrusively into as many niches as possible, to accompany almost any kind of food.

Smoothness and roundness are its major characteristics, and in that respect it is a distant echo of the great Burgundies that are its inspiration.

The Ruffino too offers itself in a rather understated way. It is nicely balanced, and it shows both a bit more fresh fruit than the Valbon (many people may even pick up a suggestion of cherries) and a bit more acid to bring the fruit to the fore—discreetly. You may feel on your tongue a slight prickly sensation: this usually results from an abundance of acid or tannin. The Valbon feels fuller and strikes the taster as a single flavor. This Chianti seems smaller-bodied but more complicated: you taste a greater variety of elements in its flavor. To differentiate it firmly from the Valbon, I would describe it as drier and more acid and brisk, not as full, and a touch more austere and more complex. In these respects it too echoes its nobler relatives, the older Chianti Classico Riservas.

Valbon is made by Bouchard Père et Fils, a major Burgundian firm whose wines are distributed in the United States by Heublein. The Ruffino firm makes a complete range of fine Chiantis as well as other wines: Schieffelin is its distributor in the United States.

With this pair of wines, you have embarked on a whole new path in this book. (Rotten trick, isn't it, just when you thought you were finding your way around?)

Up to this point, the pairs of wines I've been presenting to you were chosen for contrast, so that differences would stand out with some clarity. With this pair, you've begun to taste wines that possess some affinities to each other and a subtler range of differences, differences that have to be talked about less in terms of stark contrasts ("This wine has guts and that one's a wimp") and more in terms of degree ("This wine has less fruit than that, but it is fuller and seems more balanced"). It's less dramatic, and it means you're going to have to work harder—but you're also, from this point on, going to have increasingly more to work with. This does not mean I'm demeaning the wines you've tasted thus far—no one should ever condescend to a well-made wine, no matter how simple—but I am saying that the real fun is just beginning.

Before we go too far down this new garden path, however, we ought to talk a bit about vintage and what it means. The labels you are looking at illustrate the basic dichotomy, vintage-dated bottlings and nonvintage (almost always abbreviated "nv"). The Valbon Rouge is not vintage-dated. That means that it is probably blended from more than one vintage in much the same way as it is blended from grapes from more than one growing area. At very least it means that the maker wanted to retain that option. Why? Lots of reasons.

Before the big wine boom in California, for instance, it was more the exception than the norm to vintage California wine, and old habits die hard. (In fact, sometimes they don't die, but we then call them traditions and honor them without question.) In Champagne, as another example, nonvintage bottlings are still the norm and vintage dating the exception—and no one regards Champagne as any the less prestigious for that.

There are sound economic reasons not to vintage: you are then free to use one year's big crop to eke out another year's small one. And crops vary from year to year not only in size but in quality in all of the world's fine wine areas—even in California, despite the popular delusion that the sun always shines there. For the winemaker, it's a decided advantage to be able to prop up an ailing vintage with a hearty one.

And then there are the intangibles: things like house style, the sense of the market, and the desire to make accessible wines or affordable wines. This is the area where economics and family pride, a sense of public spirit, and the long-range hope of developing a market go hand in hand.

California is the example closest to home. Many very reputable California wine firms adopted vintage dating reluctantly, and many continue to make nonvintage wine as well. Blending different vintages enables them to produce a wine—a house wine almost—that will be consistent in taste and style and quality, bottle after bottle, year after year. It enables them to make a wine that could be the equivalent of the table wine you would have drunk almost every day had you grown up in that small town in a winegrowing country that we spoke of at the start of this book. And it enables them to make wine at an affordable price so you can drink it every day if you wish. Valbon and Cuvée Placido are such wines, wines like those served in carafes in little restaurants all over France and Italy, wines about which you would never dream of asking the vintage. Even if you did, odds are the restaurateur, perhaps even the maker, wouldn't know for sure.

Obviously, the reason for making such a wine is not pure altruism: these firms are strongly hoping you *will* drink such wines every day, and that it will teach you the custom of taking wine with all your meals, and that you will in the long run turn into a regular customer not only of their simple wines but also of their more complex, more costly ones as well—in short, that you will become something between a fan and a connoisseur. (Heartless wretch that you are, you have probably never spared a single moment's thought for the hundreds of thousands of winemakers around the world who go to bed every night piously praying for your increased sophistication.)

So much for nonvintage: what then is the point of vintage dating? The answer to that one is simple: uniqueness, and the variety that comes with it. Every vintage is different: this means you have to take your chances on some disasters, but your highs can be very, very high indeed.

Vintage, in fact, increases in importance according to the potential of the grape varieties you are dealing with and according to the capacity of the soil you are growing them on. Vintage matters most when you have a combination of noble grapes and great vineyard, and from there on down the scale it matters less and less as grapes and vineyards decline in quality. Naturally, a great harvest can make even normally mediocre wine very pleasant indeed, just as a miserable harvest can make normally superior wine very mediocre—but under average circumstances, vintage becomes a serious consideration only when you are dealing with a very limited number of fine grape varieties growing in a very limited number of environments: Napa, Sonoma, the Carneros, and a few other choice locales in California; some spots in Washington and Oregon and New York; Bordeaux, Burgundy, Champagne, Alsace, and the Rhône in France; Piedmont and Tuscany and a few other areas in Italy; Rioja in Spain; and the Rhine and Mosel valleys in Germany. Those are close to all the truly noble winegrowing zones in the world. With Central Valley Zinfandel and Algerian Cabernet, vintage is not a serious consideration.

From here on you will be dealing with wines of a caliber where vintage becomes an increasingly important factor. I have specified vintages throughout this book: wherever possible, try to get the exact vintage I name. I have also tried to select wines from makers who have achieved a reasonably consistent style, so that even if the vintages I've used in this book are no longer available, a younger wine from the same maker should display the same elements (even if not in exactly the same proportions to each other) as the wines I describe. Where I can do so, I'll also indicate as reasonable substitutes other wines that approximate the primary wines in each flight.

The vintages I select will not always be the absolute top-ranked, twenty-out-of-twenty best: sometimes the typical is going to be more useful for us than the stratospheric. Sometimes I will have gotten cold feet about asking you to spend as much money as a really terrific vintage would cost. And sometimes we'll just have to work with what is available in the marketplace: there would be very little point in my talking about a wine none of you could find.

So you're going to be getting a very mixed bag of vintages in the wines that follow, and I wanted to let you know that so none of you thinks that the simple fact of a wine's appearance in this book means that it is automatically superb. 'tain't so: some of them are, some of them aren't. Besides, if I told you they all were, or all the odd-numbered ones were, you'd then feel obliged to admire them whether you really liked them or not. Be prepared to hate some wines that the rest of the world calls great and to love some wines everybody else thinks very ordinary. Remember, you drink only with your own mouth.

## Substitutes:

As always, seek first for younger vintages—in this case, of the Chianti. Failing that, try simple Chianti or Chianti Classico from Frescobaldi or Pagliarese, Capezzana or Cecchi, Fossi or Ricasoli, Santa Cristina or Villa Cusona, Villa Banfi or Villa Cafaggio. Young Chianti from Placido or the Conti Serristori would also work very well. If Valbon is unavailable, consider Bucheron's Cuvée Rouge or Moreau Rouge or Maufoux's Cuvée Rouge; Drouhin's Laforet Pinot Noir will also just work, though it is a vintage wine and possesses a more marked varietal character than any of the others.

This is the conclusion of the fourth tasting session. There are several ways for you to proceed from here.

*Following the lead of your own preferences:*
   If you liked the first wine better, Valbon Rouge, go on to the Sixth Flight.
   If you liked the second wine better, Ruffino Chianti, go on to the Fifth Flight.

*Following the kind of grapes:*
    Wine One: This is a very miscellaneous blend. Try either the
    Seventh Flight or the Twelfth Flight.
    Wine Two: Go on to the Fourteenth Flight.

*Following the wines of the country:*
    Wine One: Go on to the Sixth Flight.
    Wine Two: Go on to the Ninth Flight.

*Excelsior.*

# THE FIFTH FLIGHT

## *Federico Paternina "Banda Azul" Rioja 1986 and The Monterey Vineyard Classic Gamay Beaujolais 1989*

HERE IS YOUR CHANCE TO SEE what happens to a little French immigrant in California: the Gamay Beaujolais, whether or not it is the same grape from which the French Beaujolais is made, has at least been definitely identified as French in origin. Rioja is the name both of one of Spain's most important wine-producing regions and the wine made there.

Once more into the breach, my friends: see, swirl, smell, sip, savor, spit, take notes, and talk it over. Remember to concentrate particularly on the aroma, since that is the sense function we normally exercise least. With practice you can wind up with an Arnold Schwarzenegger–class smelling apparatus.

### Appearance.

The Rioja shows a typical distinct ruby, perhaps a little pale, but very clean and bright, with the slightest of orange edges. This is just about middle of the range for Rioja: you will see a few lighter or darker, and in this kind of wine at least those shadings of color will usually be a good indication of the wine's body—that is, lighter color usually comes with lighter body in Rioja reds.

The Gamay is much paler, almost a bright strawberry, but not quite moving into the rosé range. This is a bit lighter than normal for wines of its type. You will find many California Gamays of a more pronounced ruby than this.

### Aroma.

The Rioja offers a good, strong, but not overpowering aroma. It gives a pronounced suggestion of earth and oak, a tannic scent that some tasters may liken to the smell of cold tea, others may describe as a mix of earth and pepper. Fruit, dry and ripe, emerges for most people well underneath those heavier scents. There is a warm alcoholic strand in the aroma, too, and some tasters may actually feel a slight alcohol tingle in their noses. Overall, this is a very representative set of Rioja characteristics. Most tasters respond very favorably to it. Those who don't like it usually call it too strong or rubbery smelling.

A lot of the oaky, tannic odors derive from the wooden barrels the wine ages in. Barrel oak is most commonly perceived in a wine's bouquet as whiffs of caramel or vanilla: some tasters discern those scents in this wine, and some do not. Naturally, the longer the wine is aged in oak, and the smaller the barrels, the more effect the wood will have on both the aroma and the taste of the wine when it is finally bottled. We're going to have plenty of chance later on to talk about wood and what it does to wine.

In comparison to the Rioja, the Gamay has a smaller aroma but a much fruitier one. Most people immediately spot acidic red fruit in it, and alcohol, and then, far behind, a bunching of light floral or shrubby scents. This is not at all a big aroma, but it is distinctly fresh and clean. Some will describe it as sprightly and find it very attractive; others will call it cloying and describe it as smelling artificial, or smelling like soda pop.

However the aroma strikes you subjectively, it is objectively, even though a bit small, rather typical of the scent of California-grown Gamay. The degree of ripeness the grapes normally achieve there develops their sugars and their scents to what sometimes seems an exaggerated degree. For this reason, the aroma of this Gamay is simpler and more one-dimensional than that of the Rioja. Fruit really almost completely dominates it, and you either like that or you don't: there is little else to consider.

**Taste.**

In this pair of wines, the lines drawn by their aromas hold true in their flavors as well: the Rioja is fuller and more complex, the Gamay lighter, simpler, and more immediately appealing.

Let's take the Rioja first. Just about everybody tastes it as a medium-bodied wine, dry, with a good feel in the mouth. It is neither soft and flabby nor overacidic and biting, though it has a discernible touch of tannin, either from the grapes themselves or from the barrels. Most people can feel that along the insides of their cheeks or on the very top of their tongue—a drying, slightly puckering sensation.

In addition, most people also taste a generous burst of fresh, sprightly fruit, more than the Rioja's aroma might lead them to expect. A good number of them will specify the fruit as tasting of black cherry or raspberry (some may even find this particular wine vaguely reminiscent of Zinfandel). Finally, the wine finishes long and dry, with a slightly bitter aftertaste, in which some people will detect the barest suggestion of tar (in other vintages it may suggest almonds) and others will find woody/oaky traces, perhaps even an oversteeped-tea tang. With food all these elements plump up a little bit larger, but only a little. Those who don't take pleasure in this flavor range may taste all these things as sour, or astringent, or unpleasantly bitter.

In the flavor of the Gamay, as in its aroma, fruit overweighs almost everything else. The wine is soft and definitely lighter than the Rioja. Most tasters credit it with good bright acid, both because of the liveliness of its fruit and because of the slight spritzy sensation many of them feel on their tongues. Very few find any but the smallest trace of tannin here. The fruit flavors fall definitely into the red fruit group in most tasters' reports: the majority taste strawberries, a few taste black cherries, but neither flavor is strongly distinguished. Some detect sufficient ripeness in the fruit for them to experience it almost as a hint of sweetness, as if there were the merest trace of residual sugar left in the wine. Those who dislike it report that as a sort of soda-pop flavor.

This Gamay has a nice dry but short finish—that is, its flavor ends rather completely with the swallow. In a simple wine like this, one intended to be drunk young and without fanfare, that is not a serious flaw, but for a mature claret or Burgundy or estate-bottled

California Cabernet to finish so short would be a very grave defect indeed.

This pair of wines illustrates—or at least I mean them to illustrate—a fundamental and too often ignored wine distinction, the difference between a simple and a complex wine. This distinction is the Grand Canyon and the Continental Divide of the wine world. Between simple wines and complex wines there is a great gulf, and the gulf is not simply the prestige accorded one group and withheld from the other but a gulf of taste and temperament—and that can be the most unbridgeable depth of all.

In his play *Man and Superman*, George Bernard Shaw has Satan explain the abyss that separates Heaven and Hell as the incompatibility of the heavenly and hellish temperaments. Angels and demons would be bored to tears in each other's domain. In the world of wine, matters stand very much like that. People who really love complex wines can tolerate and on the right occasions even enjoy simple wines—but most of the time they are bored by them. Vice versa, lovers of simple wine aren't palatally tone-deaf: they appreciate what complex wines can offer, but it's just not what they want most of the time. Would you want always to dine on caviar and foie gras? Never eat any fruit but kiwis? Read only *War and Peace*? See only Antonioni movies? Ninety-nine percent of us would find that unbearable. So why should it be any different with wine?

Because, unfortunately, someone a long time ago impressed us all with the fact that some wines are *better* than others, and we, damn it, are not going to settle for anything less than the best. What's the point of being American if we do? Anything else we're willing to admit is a matter of taste—even of mood, of whim—and we'll fight to the death to maintain that our opinion is just as good as anyone else's. But with wine, somehow, an absolute ranking takes over and we become servile in the face of it. We all know—or think we know—that there are wines we *ought* to swoon over even if we don't know anything else about wine. So we feel embarrassed about liking simple wines. We apologize because we don't appreciate, or know about, or have any experience of the prestigious classified growths and noble wines. It's hard to think of any other area of life in which Americans allow themselves to be bullied as thoroughly as they are about wine.

Well, it's time to make your own personal declaration of independence and own up to what you like. As an apprentice wine taster, your opinion about the different elements you can discern in a mouthful of 1945 La Tache doesn't amount to a hill of beans compared to what an Alexis Lichine or a Michael Broadbent can tell you about that wine. Informed opinion, opinion based on knowledge and experience and skill, is what matters there. But on the subject of your preferences, on the matters of your own tastes and your pleasures, no one is better informed than you. On the subject of what you like, you are the final authority: your opinion is absolutely incontrovertible.

All this amounts to saying that there is nothing at all wrong or stupid or embarrassing about preferring simple wines—especially if you have tried complex wines and found that they just don't suit you. The relevant factor here is *informed* opinion. No one need ever feel embarrassed for not knowing what he could not know—and that simple fact lets most of us off the hook about wine knowledge. Wine lore is simply something that was not readily available to us. Wine was something we didn't grow up with, unlike chopped-and-channeled Chevvies for one generation and the Beatles for another.

What you should be embarrassed about is knowledge that is available to you that you ignore. For that, shame on you. This book is your opportunity for that kind of wine knowledge: even if you think you already know what you like, try a few more wines, explore a few more kinds, give some new sensations a chance. You might find something you like. If you do, you're that much ahead of the game. If you don't, you've lost nothing but a little time, and that is a good investment if the return makes you feel secure about your taste and free from qualms for the rest of your life. So sip on for a while.

All right then, what is this distinction between simple wines and complex wines that I'm making all this ridiculous fuss about? You've got a graphic example of it in the glasses in front of you now: two pleasing wines, but pleasing in different ways and for different reasons.

Simple and complex are the most honest and precise of all wine terms, because they mean exactly what they say. A simple wine is easy to deal with, easy to understand. It's not elaborate, not complicated. A complex wine on the other hand requires more attention: it has parts, components, facets. It rewards concentration by revealing more and more aspects of itself.

Our Gamay Beaujolais here is an example of a simple wine: its fruitiness of aroma and flavor—what amounts to a mild varietal flavor, the taste of the Gamay grape—is its main and almost its exclusive feature. Other sorts of simple wines can be more intense or more subtle, more lively or more restrained, with greater or lesser depth of flavor, but they will share the essentially single thrust of this Gamay. This is in no sense a dismissal of this wine. It is an excellently made example of exactly what it was intended to be, a light, enjoyable Beaujolais-style wine.

The Rioja, on the other hand, offers us a medley of sensations, and the longer we linger over it the greater the number of suggestions it makes to us. Many of them are muted, it is true, but the wine nevertheless presents differing facets and ideas to us, revealing different aspects of itself by its variety of parts—hints of vanilla and oak, scents of earth and wood and fruit. This is not because this Rioja is a great wine: objectively speaking, it is a well-made, sound, and typical young Rioja. But it is a wine whose vinification (the process by which its grapes were turned into wine) and whose grapes themselves (maybe) opened many possibilities of development. It is a wine that was made differently from the Gamay, in a manner that tamed the fullness of its fruit flavors somewhat to allow other elements present in the wine to express themselves.

The broadest goal of a vintner is always to make a drinkable wine: the more competent the winemaker, the more interesting and pleasing he will try to make it within the limits of the available material. Within this objective, these are two chief goals for which vintners can strive in handling grapes: to achieve the fullest possible expression of fruit, to the exclusion of other elements; or to create a harmony of fruit and other components.

Even so, the limits and the variables are myriad. First, the grape variety and its characteristics: some grapes achieve great sweetness. Some stay relatively tart. Some have a very pronounced and distinct flavor, readily identifiable. Others are much more subdued. Some naturally have a lot of tannin, which means that they have a greater potential for aging and development. Many of these characteristics are themselves not constant even within a grape variety but alter dramatically with the soil the vines are grown in, the sunlight or moisture they get, the stage of ripeness at which the grapes are picked.

Then there are the conditions of vinification, starting right with fermentation. Is it produced by naturally occurring yeasts or controlled introduction of selected yeasts? If the latter, which ones? Is the temperature controlled during fermentation? Is the fermentation long or short? In wood or steel or glass? How long are the skins of the grapes left in the liquid? How is the wine kept after fermentation?

There are even more variables. Just to give you a sense of the possibilities: If the wine is aged in wooden barrels, what capacity barrels? (because volume determines the actual degree of contact between wine and wood surface); what kind of wood? (it's usually oak, but there are variations from that); young or old? toasted (lightly charred) or raw?; and, finally, for how long?

All these things alter the taste and style and heft of the finished wine. But don't be fooled if making wine begins to sound like the return of Doctor Frankenstein or Better Living Through Chemistry. For all the technical apparatus and scientific expertise, winemaking still remains more an art than a science: that's why there are still only a handful of really transcendent complex wines in the world. The most all that technical know-how can guarantee is that basic wine is sound, that good, simple wines can be made reliably and consistently and inexpensively. Beyond that level in winemaking and in wine enjoyment, there can never be any guarantees.

The Monterey Vineyard has already been introduced (pp. 35–36). Paternina is a large and much respected Rioja firm producing both the red and the white wines of that region.

### Substitutes:

Younger vintages of both wines are the first substitutes to look for. If those are unavailable, try, for the Rioja, wines from makers such as Gran Condal, Marques de Caceres, Marques de Murrieta, Marques de Riscal, or Montecillo. For the Gamay Beaujolais, look to other California makers such as Almadén or Mirassou.

This is the conclusion of the fifth tasting session. There are several ways for you to proceed from here.

*Following the lead of your own preferences:*
If you liked the first wine better, the Paternina Rioja, go on to the Sixth Flight or the Fourteenth Flight.
If you liked the second wine better, the Monterey Classic Gamay, go on to the Seventh Flight.

*Following the kind of grapes:*
Wine One: There is really nothing else like this Rioja in our tastings.

Wine Two: Go on to the Seventh Flight.

*Following the wines of the country:*
Wine One: There are no other Spanish wines in the red-wine
tastings.
Those who are pleased by the style of the Rioja might want to
try other examples of young Rioja from different makers.
Marques de Murrieta, Muga, Privilegio, Gran Condal, Marques
de Caceres, and Marques de Riscal all offer sound and
interesting wines. Most of these firms also market older Riojas
with longer barrel- and bottle-age (Rioja Reserva). These are
frequently very fine wines of great complexity.
Wine Two: Go on to the Sixth Flight.

# THE SIXTH FLIGHT

~~~ ၄၉ ~~~

## Mouton Cadet 1988
## and
## Beaulieu Vineyard Beautour Napa
## Valley Cabernet Sauvignon 1989

~~~ ၄၉ ~~~

**H**ERE'S A PAIR OF WINES to give your budding skills a chance to cope with complexity. Mouton Cadet is a very popular wine from France's famous Bordeaux district. Cabernet Sauvignon is the grape variety that constitutes the major component of the finest red wines of that area, and it is now intensively and very successfully cultivated in California's best wine districts.

Once again perform the ritual, concentrating especially on smelling the wine and remembering during tasting to let the wine run over the entire surface of your mouth and tongue. Take your notes, discuss the wines with other tasters, and then push on to the next paragraph.

Appearance.

These two wines show some kinship in their coloration. Both are an attractive deep ruby, the Beautour slightly darker than the Mouton Cadet. Most Cabernet-based wines display this color range when young: it lightens to the traditional claret color (traditional because claret is the collective name by which the great red wines of Bordeaux are known) as they age, acquiring a distinct tawny (some call it mahogany) rim when you tilt the glass in the proper light.

Aroma.

In both wines, the aroma has developed several facets. Different tasters will emphasize different elements according to both their sensitivity to those elements and their ability to recognize and put names to them. In the Cadet, most people are likely to detect just a little fruit in the red range: they are likely to specify currants, if anything at all. Other vegetal aromas are more noticeable. Common descriptions might include peppery, herbaceous, grassy, mossy, and/or earthy. Some may pick up slight vanilla tones. Those tasters for whom this combination of aromas falls into an unpleasant range most often use words like "chemical" or "cooked" to describe the odor they perceive.

For most people, the scent of growing things is prominent in the Beautour as well: grass and fresh twigs or a medley of herbal smells. But in this Cabernet fruit is important too, and many tasters will remark on its aroma of ripeness. Again, those for whom that particular level of olfactory intensity is unpleasant will describe it as the smell of overripe or rotting fruit, or as artificial-smelling. Either group of tasters may detect alcohol in the aroma of this wine.

Taste.

The differences between these two related wines continue to multiply and intensify as we progress from color and aroma to taste.

In tasting the Cadet, many people will experience prickly sensations at the tips and sides of their tongues or a feeling of astringency all through their mouths. These are, respectively, the result of acid and of tannin, which is also often felt as a puckering sensation on the cheeks. For many (though by no means all) tasters they so dominate this wine that little else is discernible in its taste. Many people report that only a bare minimum of fruit comes through, and it has no special characteristics and no particular force. The wine finishes short and, for many people, somewhat bitter. While a few tasters wax enthusiastic about this wine—they particularly like its dry, balanced attack—most find it drinkable and forgettable, a bland, inoffensive wine.

After tasting the Beautour, many people will express a divided reaction—disappointment that the wine doesn't fully live up to the promise of its aroma, and pleasure that it gives more than the Cadet. Once again, the relationship between the two wines makes itself felt: tasters will almost invariably find in the Beautour the same elements they experienced in the Mouton Cadet. The difference here is the presence of a much larger amount of fruit to balance somewhat the still plentiful acids and tannin. That fruit unhappily lacks the distinctive ripeness the aroma possessed. The majority of tasters describe it as having at most a slight berrylike or black currant quality. Its finish is short but pleasing. The whole wine is usually described by tasters as like the Cadet but having more character: fuller, or rounder, or more interesting, or more assertive.

This pair of wines seems to me very instructive for what they can teach you about the importance of complexity and balance even at an unsophisticated level of wine. Both are well-made wines in the sense that there is nothing adulterated in either of them and no short cuts have been taken in their vinification: they are the products of sound ingredients treated respectfully. The Mouton Cadet is a blend of Cabernet Sauvignon and other grapes (Merlot and Cabernet Franc are traditional in Bordeaux). So too is the Beautour, though it seems a safe guess that there is a considerably higher percentage of Cabernet Sauvignon in it (California law mandates a minimal 75 percent if a wine is to be called Cabernet Sauvignon on its label).

By itself, that higher percentage of Cabernet Sauvignon would not necessarily make the Beautour the more balanced wine. Cabernet Sauvignon is a very tannic, very hard grape—hard in the sense that young wine from Cabernet grapes is often harsh and unpalatable. California sunshine has a lot to do with the balance of this wine: riper fruit has more sugar and more fully developed flavor, which in turn yields a bigger, more alcoholic wine with greater fruitiness surviving to balance the natural acids and tannins of the grape. California vintners normally achieve levels of ripeness that remain quite exceptional in other viticultural areas. The small advantage in balance that ripeness confers amounts to a great difference in enjoyment.

Let's make no mistake about it: by the criteria of connoisseurs, these are still simple wines we're dealing with. Mouton Cadet lives by its name (and Baron Philippe's at the bottom of the label), whose associations with Château Mouton Rothschild, one of the world's most esteemed wines, lead many people to believe they are getting something like an estate-bottled claret when all they are actually getting is a shipper's Bordeaux Rouge, exactly like Prats's Maître d'Estournel or Eschenauer's Olivier de France, or any other red wine, with or without brand name, that simply bears the appellation *vin rouge de Bordeaux*. The BV Beautour Cabernet Sauvignon we're here tasting is similarly a blend of grapes from all over Napa, which is a particularly prized but also large and variegated California viticultural region. My point, however, is not to belittle these wines: this kind of wine offers decent value for price and a degree of consistency from bottle to bottle that more ambitious wines find it difficult to match. It offers security and reliability—in a minor key, to be sure, but it also saves you a lot of thought and trouble.

My point is that the thinking-man's (and I emphatically mean thinking-woman's too) palate can make trouble in paradise, because this class of wines is not uniform across the board. You *can* taste differences among them. You just did, as a matter of fact. The simple fact of the matter is that at every level of production, you can get better or worse wine, more pleasing or less pleasing wine, for about the same amount of cash—so it makes sense both in terms of your enjoyment and in economic terms to explore your palate and the wines it likes and to learn to make these sorts of distinctions.

In the cases we have before us in our glasses, we have a distinction drawn by the element of balance. One wine has it; the other doesn't. In one wine, acid and tannin dominate the fruit, so the overall flavor, while not displeasing, is rather slight and quickly passing. In the other, more fruit and a bit more alcohol (take a look at the labels) turn the duet into a quartet, with the result that the total flavor is more interesting and more lasting. Ninety-nine percent of the time, in drinking this Cabernet you wouldn't even think twice about its balance: but the fact that it is there is what would enable you to enjoy this wine more than once.

Mouton Cadet is produced by Baron Philippe de Rothschild, the proprietor of Château Mouton Rothschild. Mouton Cadet is one of—probably *the*—largest-selling brand of red Bordeaux.

Beaulieu Vineyard—"BV" to wine lovers—has been one of the benchmark makers of Cabernet Sauvignon and the whole range of Californian varietal wines almost since the beginning of this century. It produces a ladder of Cabernets, from this first-step Beautour through its Rutherfords to its justly esteemed Georges de Latour Reserve. BV's prices are always very fair for the quality of its wines.

**Substitutes:**

Your first choice should be younger vintages of these same wines. If they are not available, try the following alternatives: for the Mouton Cadet, Prats's Maître d'Estournel rouge, B & G 1725 Bordeaux rouge, or B & G Bordeaux Cabernet Sauvignon; for the Beautour, Christian Brothers Napa Valley Cabernet Sauvignon or Monterey Vineyard Classic Cabernet Sauvignon.

So concludeth the first case of red wines. If you've made it this far, consider yourself a B.A., Bachelor of Alcohol. There are several ways for you to proceed from here.

*Following the lead of your own preferences:*
  If you enjoyed either the first wine, Mouton Cadet, or the second wine, Beaulieu Vineyard Cabernet, go on to the Tenth Flight.

*Following the kind of grapes:*
  Go on to the Fifteenth Flight.

*Following the wines of the country:*
  Go on to the Seventh Flight.

# THE SEVENTH FLIGHT

~~∞∞~~

## *Buena Vista Carneros Gamay Beaujolais 1990 and Sylvain Fessy Beaujolais Villages 1990*

~~∞∞~~

A FINE CALIFORNIA WINE FIRM and one of the most respected Beaujolais *négociants* provide the wines for this flight. Beaujolais is the name of the district in France where the Gamay grape makes its most enjoyable wine, a fruity, lively wine meant to be drunk quite young. Despite the California wine's name, it is not in fact made from the Gamay grape, though for many years this was thought to be the case. It is, however, intentionally cultivated and vinified to emulate the style of French Beaujolais, so in this tasting you will be making your first full-scale attempt to differentiate between the styles of similar wines.

Remember to perform the whole ritual of observations: note the color of the two wines; swirl them gently to release their aromas and then sniff; sip the wines and taste them all over your mouth before spitting them out. A little trick you may find helpful in tasting the wines is to put a little of it "in the hole." Let a little wine run down into the space below your tongue and behind your front teeth. Let it sit there for a few seconds, then taste with the tip of your tongue: you should get the full effect of whatever sweetness and fruit the wine has, plus a generous sense of its acid and tannin. The technique is unnatural, but the effect is frequently worth it.

After you have untwisted your tongues and talked over your notes (remember: only after all have finished tasting, not while anyone is still reacting), go on to the descriptions of the wines.

## Appearance.

Both are attractive wines of a clear, bright ruby color, very lively looking. Due to bottle variation—a normal occurrence in all wines—either one of these wines might look a touch lighter or darker than the other in any particular tasting.

You can also expect the color in wines of this sort to vary a great deal from harvest to harvest. They can be anything from a slightly dark rose shade to purple as mimeograph ink, and often the color is a good indicator of just how much body or guts they're actually going to have. The colors you have in the glasses before you are almost textbook examples of what these two wines ought to look like in their best vintages: a pretty translucent ruby, neither paling to pink nor darkening to purple.

Brick or orange tones in a Gamay wine this young would definitely not be good signs. They are usually manifestations of aging, and their premature appearance can be a warning sign about the condition of a particular vintage. Beaujolais and the whole class of red wines like it, wines whose claim to fame is youthful zest and fruit, should not be held for maturation, because the changes they undergo in bottle do not improve the wine but rather kill it. The rule with Beaujolais-type wines is to drink them as young as possible.

But don't be too literal-minded about this. I don't mean you can't buy a case or two of Beaujolais for drinking over the course of a year—or even two years if it's a very good vintage—but that's the outer limit. Beaujolais is not a wine to cellar for five or ten or more years. Even the best vintages should be drunk before they are three years old: they gain nothing from bottle-aging.

## Aroma.

Ideally, what you ought to smell in a Beaujolais is fresh fruit and not too much else. The aroma ought to be inviting in a kind of healthy, outdoorsy way: nothing subtle, just a direct sensuous appeal. The better the vintage, the bigger the aroma and the stronger the appeal should be.

### The Name of the Gamay

There are in fact two grapes called Gamay in California, and neither of them is the Gamay grape cultivated in Beaujolais. The one known in California as Gamay Beaujolais has in fact turned out to be a subvariety of Pinot Noir, which is, in its own right, the most important variety cultivated in Burgundy and just beginning to show what it can do in California. The other variety, the Napa Gamay, appears to be no relation to Burgundian grapes at all. Because of longstanding practice, however, both are legally permitted to bear the name Gamay Beaujolais on their labels.

The wines of Beaujolais are bottled with several different types of regional designation on the label. The simplest, Beaujolais, designates a wine made from grapes drawn from all over the zone. Beaujolais Superieur does not designate a better wine, but a wine with a slightly higher percentage of alcohol. The next regional class, Beaujolais Villages, indicates wine blended from grapes drawn only from a designated cluster of townships in the north of the zone.

The class above Beaujolais Villages is a single *cru* Beaujolais, one made exclusively from grapes from a single one of the ten named crus (classified growths) of the region—in other words, the ten villages with the best soils or climates for producing the wine. They are Brouilly, Chenas, Chiroubles, Côtes de Brouilly, Fleurie, Julienas, Morgon, Moulin-à-Vent, Regnie, and Saint-Amour. The final classification of Beaujolais is cru Beaujolais with an estate designation, indicating that the wine is the product of a single vineyard. Normally only the very best vineyards find it economically worthwhile to bottle and sell their own wine under its unique designation. All of these classifications are covered by the French *Appellation d'Origine Controllée* (AOC) laws, which legislate and police the accuracy of the regional designations.

Happily, most tasters find exactly that kind of aroma in these two wines. There are differences, of course, from wine to wine and from taster to taster, but the vast majority describe both wines as first, aromatic; second, fruity; and third, alcoholic (sensed as a kind of warm or hot component in the aroma, sometimes even as a tingle in the nose).

Do you want particulars? Here goes.

Most people describe the Buena Vista Gamay as strongly fruity and alcoholic, and they specifically sense very ripe fruit—usually they say strawberries, though a few may smell peaches in there. A very few find the scent too strong and call it overripe and off-putting. But most find the fruit aroma very pleasing. Some may also report a sort of mixed stemmy or woody or earthy undertone that builds up somewhat as the wine opens in the glass.

The Fessy Beaujolais Villages is similarly called very fruity, though usually its scent is said to be slightly more delicate, or in a higher register, than the aroma of the Gamay. People may describe this scent as spicy or slightly sweetish. It too is warm and alcoholic. Almost everybody agrees to strawberry as the fruit component that they smell in it, and almost everybody likes it.

Vintage and age do make a real difference, even in wines like Beaujolais, whose attractions are simplicity and directness. The fresh, lively fruit that you're smelling in both these wines isn't always there with the clarity and vitality it has in this vintage. Sometimes acids will be more prominent, making the wine very bright and lively, but also thinning it a little, making it sharper and less easy on the nose, sometimes even acrid. Sometimes alcohol will dominate, and warmth will be the primary sensation. Try to re-member the aromas you're smelling now: they make very usable standards for the breed.

Despite the many similarities between these two aromas, people can still be sharply divided on the question of like or dislike. Most will find both wines pleasing, but there will also be extreme parties about both—tasters who will call the Gamay too strong and cloying or the Beaujolais Villages too thin and sweet.

Taste.

Tasting will pretty much bear out what sight and scent have so far established. Most people find both wines as fresh and fruity as advertised, relatively simple, and quite pleasant drinking. The

Beaujolais Villages even reveals some characteristics of what a person who really knew Beaujolais could identify as Fessy's house style (a certain elegance, accentuated by rich fruit and high acidity). It's not possible to say anything that precise of the Gamay because it's not yet clear whether the bright, forward attack this wine shows results from a house style—Buena Vista's particular way of vinifying—or whether it's the gift of that good Carneros soil. House style in wine talk means simply the general way in which a vintner or winery or *négociant* handles wines so as to lend them all a set of distinctive characteristics.

What most people actually taste in the Gamay is pretty much what the aroma led them to expect: intense fruit, tasting initially as if it had to be sweet though it turns out not to be so. Most tasters call it cherry-flavored. Some find it very bright with acid, and some rich and fat with alcohol and extracts. Some take the middle ground and call it balanced. Most people do report a little tongue prickle from acid, though they divide on whether they consider that an attraction or a distraction.

The Beaujolais too gives many tasters an initial impression of sweetness, although it also proves to be completely dry. As with its aroma, this Beaujolais Villages's taste is slightly higher, its body slightly thinner than the Gamay's—though, paradoxically, many people will describe its fruit as being fleshier and more rounded. The particular flavor they most often name is strawberry—ripe, dry, strawberry. It too seems fairly high in acidity.

Despite the fact that they may use much the same words to talk about these two wines, most tasters are quite aware of the very real distinctions between the two. These are very different styles of wine, and taken side by side like this they very nicely point up each other's really defining characteristics. The Beaujolais, for all its acidity, strikes the palate as all soft fruit and good manners, a pleasing, almost genteel, light wine. The Carneros Gamay seems by comparison a bit coarse, but slightly bigger, firmer, almost brambly in flavor, and perhaps better structured. Even their fruit is different—and both are fruity wines. You can learn a lot about style in wine by just taking a few more sips of these two and reflecting a bit longer on the differences you can perceive in the nature of their respective fruitinesses.

Buena Vista is an old name in California winemaking, but its recently developed properties in the Carneros (a hilly transverse valley that intersects the southern ends of both the Napa and Sonoma valleys) have given it a new lease on life. It offers most of the important California varietal wines at very fair value for dollar.

Sylvain Fessy is one of many excellent Beaujolais producers; he sends us everything from simple Beaujolais to a selection of crus.

## Substitutes:

For either wine, the first choice is a younger vintage. For the Gamay Beaujolais, if Buena Vista is not available, try Beaulieu Vineyards, Fetzer, or Pedroncelli. For the Beaujolais Villages, if Sylvain Fessy is not available, try Jean Bedin, Georges Duboeuf, Pierre Ferraud, Louis Tete, or large *négociants* such as Bouchard Père et Fils, Drouhin, Jadot, Latour, Pasquier-Desvignes.

This is the conclusion of the seventh tasting session. There are several ways for you to proceed from here.

*Following the lead of your own preferences:*
   If you liked the first wine better, Buena Vista Carneros Gamay
   Beaujolais, go on to the Ninth Flight.
   If you preferred the second wine, Sylvain Fessy Beaujolais
   Villages, go on to the Eighth Flight.

*Following the kind of grapes:*
   Wine One: There are no more California Gamays in the
   tastings. Try the Eighth Flight.
   Wine Two: Go on to the Eighth Flight.

*Following the wines of the country:*
   Wine One: Go on to the Tenth Flight.
   Wine Two: Go on to the Eighth Flight.

# THE EIGHTH FLIGHT

~~~

*Château de La Chaize
Brouilly 1990
and
Jadot Moulin-à-Vent 1990*

~~~

THIS PAIR MATCHES one of the most esteemed single-estate Beaujolais against one from a highly regarded cru and an excellent shipper. The Jadot firm is one of the most important in Burgundy and one of the most reliable shippers of both Burgundies and Beaujolais to the United States. The purpose of this pair is as much to test your discriminatory powers (since the wines will inevitably have many similarities) as to show the differing possibilities available even within the confines of a single wine like Beaujolais.

Because of its inexpensiveness and abundance, Beaujolais allows us (over this flight and the preceding one) to sample the differences and degrees of refinement possible in three important geographical classes of the same wine: one drawn from the whole region (the simple AOC Beaujolais of the Seventh Flight), one drawn from a single, highly rated township within the region (this flight's Moulin-à-Vent), and one drawn from a single estate within a named township and region (this flight's Château de La Chaize). Nevertheless, all are Beaujolais, and that means your tasting skill will be stretched here, so pay careful attention to the infamous s's. And oh yes—don't forget to enjoy these wines, too. When you're finished, come back here.

## Appearance.

These two wines fall firmly into the true Beaujolais range. Both are a sound, attractive ruby, clear and bright, translucent and light-looking. The Moulin-à-Vent is perhaps a shade lighter than the Brouilly (though that probably wouldn't be true in another vintage). Both are attractive, lively looking wines.

## Aroma.

The distinction between the two wines stands out pretty clearly for most tasters, though there is still a good deal of variety within the reactions to each wine. For instance, almost everybody says that the Château de La Chaize has a very marked fruity aroma, but there are many opinions as to its particulars: berries, some say, especially strawberries, while others say very ripe peaches. Some find the aroma heavy, with an almost caramel note in it; others find it lighter and absolutely unsugary. A few people even smell pepper in it. For all the variety, this is still not a big aroma. The Moulin-à-Vent also has only a small aroma, but it is more heavily floral, with under-tones of things like fresh earth and mushrooms—a heavier, more pungent odor than that of the Brouilly. Both are for most people pleasant and unobtrusive, though a few tasters will probably find the scent of the Château de La Chaize too thin and that of the Moulin-à-Vent too heavy to be really pleasant.

## Taste.

Let's take the Château de La Chaize first. The range of responses to this wine tends to fall into two distinct camps: those who sense it as a rather full wine with a bit of muscle and those who perceive it rather as light and elegant. Both camps remark, with varying em-phases and degrees of pleasure, on its fruit and its acid, but it is almost always the fruit that strikes tasters first. It is usually de-scribed as fresh and clean and dry. The people in the full camp report it as smooth and well balanced, tasting in the strawberry-apricot range of flavors. The light people call it definitely straw-berry, dry and soft and refined, with the acid initially very subdued but showing increasingly strongly with later sips.

Almost everybody feels an acid tingle in the wine. For some it's pleasant, for others excessive, but whatever the subjective reaction to it, it's the acidity that keeps this wine as lively and as pleasing as it is. Ideally, acid should be in balance with other parts of the wine (fruit and alcohol for instance), neither dominating the wine nor disappearing and leaving a flabby corpse behind. The majority of tasters find that kind of balance in this Château de La Chaize, and because of it some may speak of the wine as possessing a degree of complexity unusual in Beaujolais. On the other hand, some of the tasters who describe the wine as light may think that fruit is all it really has.

Finally, almost everybody finds the wine's finish very pleasing: long and dry, so you still taste some of the best of the wine after it's gone. A very pleasant wine, quite easy to drink, and about as polished as Beaujolais is capable of becoming.

Like the Château de La Chaize, this Moulin-à-Vent seems to elicit a fairly uniform range of responses from tasters. Again, fruit is almost the first thing to be remarked upon, and again I urge you to try to taste past the fruit. The taste of the Moulin-à-Vent fruit is markedly different from that of the first wine. It is fuller (there seems to be literally more of it and it seems to fill the mouth more). It is riper, a condition that some people describe as sweeter (though it is not in fact sugar you are tasting but the condition of the fruit). And it is softer; that is, the textural sensation in your mouth is precisely softness (taste sips of the two wines side by side again: you'll see what I mean).

Specific elements don't surface readily in the big, soft fruit of the Moulin-à-Vent's flavor. Most people will sense berries, and a few— particularly if they find the aroma and flavor too strong for their taste—may smell overripeness and taste something like banana in there. Generally, tasters tend to find that this Moulin-à-Vent has more body and more power than the Château de la Chaize. Those who like that combination of elements describe this wine as having more character; those who don't usually dislike some specific element sufficiently to isolate it for criticism.

Tasting two wines comparatively as we are doing of course makes it easier for us to see the virtues and shortcomings of each: that's why we do it. Our Moulin-à-Vent is the bigger wine of the two, but a taste of the Château de la Chaize will show us that for all its size the Moulin-à-Vent is lacking acid, and it would probably be a much more admirable wine if its soft fruit were supported and enlivened by a bigger dose of that. After tasting the Moulin-à-Vent, on the other hand, it's easy to see that the Château de la Chaize, for all its pleasantness, is really a fairly thin wine and could very well use some more body and fruit.

You have to remember in all this that we are dealing here with just about the best that Beaujolais can do. The 1990 vintage was a good one for Beaujolais. That means that you are not here tasting the average for Beaujolais but the standard to which, in most vintages, it rather wistfully aspires. From the point of view of your wine knowledge, that's terrific, because you've really gotten to the heart of the Beaujolais game and can measure every other Beaujolais you'll ever taste by this very valid yardstick. To really cement the lesson, it would be a great idea to rerun this test with the next vintage as soon as it becomes available.

Both in spite of and because of the excellence of the 1990 vintage, the differences you've been tasting between the Brouilly wine and the Moulin-à-Vent are right on target. Moulin-à-Vent is celebrated for being always the biggest and most tannic of Beaujolais, for being the only Beaujolais that really profits from any bottle-age. In a very good vintage, the wines of Moulin-à-Vent may take two or three years to come ready, unlike most other Beaujolais, which is really at its best at about a year old. And the characteristics you noted in the Château de La Chaize are those for which Brouilly wines are famed: freshness, lightness, balance, accessibility.

We were very lucky in our vintage with all these Beaujolais wines, but a mediocre vintage wouldn't necessarily have been a handicap, though it surely would have been less fun. Even in off years (as mediocre vintages are called, no doubt to give the totally untrue impression that they are unusual), carefully made wines will run true to their type. Their qualities may be diluted, but they will still be present. You may be able to judge something of the body from the shadow it throws; that is, you can extrapolate from an off-vintage what a good wine can do in a fine year. Use your taste first about the wine you've got in front of you, and then your imagination about the one you don't have.

Also (and this is in a sense a shopper's tip), it's often possible to buy off-vintages of very fine wines at a very reasonable price. If you're careful enough in your tasting of them and imaginative enough in your projection up the scale, you can make some pretty shrewd guesses from those inexpensive bottles about whether you really want to lay out the megabucks for their big brothers.

This is especially useful to keep in mind in restaurants, by the way, where off-vintages of normally expensive wines can often be the best bargains on the wine list. This is doubly true under restaurant circumstances because most restaurant wines are sold too young. Off-vintages tend to mature more quickly than their better-rated siblings, and you've consequently got at least a fighting chance of getting, at a decent price, a decent wine that's ready to drink.

Aren't you proud of yourself? You learned all that stuff today and you're going to save money, too. Go out and buy a case of wine to celebrate.

Château de La Chaize is imported by Château & Estate Wines Company. Jadot wines are imported by Kobrand.

## Substitutes:

As always, the preferred substitutes would be younger vintages of either wine. Failing that, for the Brouilly you could use Jadot or Maufoux's Brouilly, or Jean Bedin's Côte de Brouilly; for the Moulin-à-Vent, the same wine from Duboeuf or Bedin or Fessy, or from a *négociant* such as Bouchard Père et Fils or Jadot.

This concludes the Eighth Flight. There are several ways for you to proceed from here.

*Following the lead of your own preferences:*
   If you enjoyed either the first wine, Château de La Chaize Brouilly, or the second wine, the Moulin-à-Vent, go on to the Twelfth Flight.

*Following the kind of grapes:*
   There are no more Gamay-based wines in the tastings (see the Third, Fifth, and Seventh flights).

*Following the wines of the country:*
   Go on to the Tenth Flight.

# THE NINTH FLIGHT

❧ ∽๑∾ ❧

## Fenocchio Dolcetto d'Alba Pianpolvere Soprano 1990 and Pio Cesare Barbera d'Alba 1988

∽๑∾

THIS FLIGHT INTRODUCES two different wines from a whole new (to this book's sequence) region, Italy's province of Piedmont, a sub-Alpine region of rolling hills and foggy valleys. Dolcetto and Barbera are the names both of the two grapes and the wines made from them. Italy's DOC laws (legislation governing wine labeling, comparable to France's AOC laws) require specific geographical designations for these, as you see on these two labels: both wines come from the hills around Alba, a sizable township in south-central Piedmont, and a viticultural zone as prized in Italy as the Côte d'Or in France.

Once again, you are dealing with wines normally characterized as fruity. In the area where they are made, most Dolcetto and much Barbera are consumed as young as possible—and as often as possible. Their local popularity is immense: probably half the wine production of the entire Piedmont is Barbera of one zone or another. Both wines accompany food well, and at elaborate dinners they are served with the antipasto and pasta courses, giving place to the bigger Barbaresco and Barolo with the meat course.

Your mission, should you choose to accept it, is to taste these wines to try to determine how you can describe the differences in their fruit. I don't doubt you'll taste the difference readily enough, but putting that perception into words is the tricky part. This tasting is deliberately designed not only to introduce you to two delightful wines but especially to make you feel sympathy for a hardworking wine writer, me.

Oh, yes: one more little item for you to think about. Following the wine traditions of the Piedmont, each of these wines has been exposed to some wood, rather more than would be considered normal in other parts of the world for wines meant to be primarily fruity and to be drunk young. See if you can spot the effects—and the flavors—that arise from wood in these wines.

On your mark; get set; go. Appearance, aroma, taste. Expectorate and expatiate.

Let's talk about one wine at a time, starting with the Dolcetto.

### Appearance.

Its color is a deep, limpid ruby with what appear to be many blue or purple highlights: very pretty and lively looking.

### Aroma.

There should be near unanimity about at least one element of this wine's aroma: just about everybody should smell fruit in abundance here, and most are likely to specify it as berries. But tasters will name other fruits as well, some almost as prominent: cherry, plum, and apricot are all possibilities. Other elements that people are able to pick out in the aroma are alcohol, growing things (stems and fresh-cut grass and sun-baked shrubs), sometimes spice, a slightly bitter element that to some people is reminiscent of peach pits, and a heavier, almost *basso profundo* note that can sometimes be described as clay and sometimes as very intense, very dry fruit. Both the bitter, peach-pit strain and the bass elements of this Dolcetto's aroma are probably traceable to a generous presence of tannin in this wine.

### Taste.

Tasting the wine will bear out and elaborate most of what has been discerned in the aroma. If there is any major difference between the two, it is that in the flavor of this Dolcetto fruit is not as dominant for every taster as it is in its aroma. The fruit is very definitely present, lush and almost sweet, and some tasters will even identify it more specifically here as peaches and plum together, or even as raspberry. Many people will find earthy and woody flavors becoming stronger with subsequent tastes.

Also present in this Dolcetto are generous amounts of acid and tannin. Some tasters in fact may find the acid too strong, though most will think it amply balanced by the full, dry fruit. The tannin especially may have the effect for many people of leaving their mouths a little puckered, a little dried out or chalky-feeling. Others will merely discern a slight and pleasing underlying bitterness— often clearest in the finish—and an underlying, astringent dryness that seems in fact to enhance the quasi-sweetness of the fruit. I say quasi-sweetness because this is a completely dry wine, but—as often happens with wines of this and similar types—the intensity of the fruit creates in the mouth a sensation that we are more used to associating with sweetness.

Let me urge you to pay particular attention to this aspect of the Dolcetto: it is a pretty clear instance of a fairly tricky phenomenon, and it is well worth your while to be able to recognize the difference between sweetness and fruit. Put a bit of this wine "in the hole," as I instructed you before: let a few drops run down below your tongue and behind your front teeth. Let them sit for a few seconds to start drawing out saliva. Taste first with the tip of your tongue (which especially tastes sweetness) and then taste those drops all over your mouth. Was that sugar you tasted? Was that sweetness in any sense you're accustomed to? Not on your tintype: that was the fruit essence of this wine. All its sugar was long ago, in fermentation, converted into alcohol.

Many tasters find that this Dolcetto is not perfectly balanced: depending on their sensitivity, they may find it overly tannic or overly acidic. Nonetheless, it is hardly what you would call a harsh or biting wine. Rather, it has vivid character, lots of fruit, rather full body, and a pleasing bitter finish. In the course of its vinification, a considerable amount of fruit, fruit of a fairly strong character, has been brought into line with other elements that provide spine and structure to make a wine that edges beyond simple fruitiness into a different sort of interest, an interest built around a relation of parts to parts within the overall character of the wine.

That interest goes exactly to the heart of what wine professionals mean by complexity in a wine and shows why they prize it. A complex wine, to put it directly, gives you a lot to taste. This Dolcetto carries the interest and the appeal of simple fruitiness just about as far as it can go in a wine. The Barbera with which it is paired goes one step beyond that.

Now let's turn to that Barbera.

### Appearance.

Its color is a deep, intense garnet, pure and clear; depending on just how old it is when you drink it, this wine may or may not show a bit of youthful purple. It looks heavier than the Dolcetto, though the Dolcetto looks livelier than it. These are quite classic colors for these two wines.

In the Piedmont, Barbera is sometimes (especially in good vintages) allowed to age for a year or two before sale. When slightly older, it may develop some tawny or amber highlights, which in Italian red wines generally and Piedmontese wine in particular are a good indication of maturity.

They emphatically do not mean, as they sometimes do in French or California wine, that the wine is drying out, that is, losing its fruit and often enough its life. In a wine like a Barbera, those tawny highlights indicate a wine past its first flush of youth but by no means over the hill. The expectations a color like that generates about the taste of the wine are that its youthful, intense fruitiness will now be subdued somewhat and that other elements should now be coming forward to create a more complicated total flavor. By those criteria, the Barbera you have in front of you is still a young wine.

### Aroma.

Like the Dolcetto, this Barbera has a fairly generous aroma. Some tasters will think it is like the Dolcetto also in the respect that the biggest component of its aroma is fruit—though they will more than likely describe this fruit as generalized and hard to pin down. If pressed to verbalize the difference, most people will say it is less grapey and less berrylike, more akin to plums. Some tasters will find this particular odor unpleasing and describe it as resiny or barrely.

Beyond fruit, the Barbera contains a whole range of important olfactory elements. Some tasters discern spice, some stems, some alcohol and herbal scents, some tea. It is also possible to pick out in the Barbera's aroma traces that are owing to the barrels in which it rested, particularly stray whiffs of vanilla, which is one of the characteristic odors imparted to wine by oak. By far the most important, however, is a compound of scents that many tasters will detect but find very difficult to describe. Its most frequently mentioned components include tar, tobacco, chocolate, and pepper. Because of this, people who know Italian wine may describe this Barbera's aroma as being like a baby Barolo.

Generally speaking, most people will find that the overall character of the Barbera's aroma, in comparison with the Dolcetto's, is higher and a bit lighter—a tenor voice as opposed to a baritone, if you follow what I mean. The aromas of both, however, ought to be pleasing—intriguing even—to the great majority of tasters.

Taste.

For that same majority of tasters, this Barbera shows a pretty nice balance from the very first taste. There is a slight tannin presence here that is nevertheless clearly discernible to most people: you may feel it as a slight puckering sensation in your mouth or taste it as a hint of vanilla, the barrels' gift to the grape. A few tasters may find this too strong and as a consequence lose track of the wine's fruit flavors and balance.

This Barbera has good acid too, which some tasters may confuse with its tannin. Its fruit is perceptible to most people as cherry, and often specifically black cherry. Despite the clear presence and effect of acid and tannin, the majority of tasters feel the fruit as soft and fresh. As with its aroma, that compound of tar, tobacco, pepper, and chocolate flavors begins to emerge with the second or third taste and starts taking its place right alongside the fruit. Even with all these flavors present, however, most tasters describe the Barbera as round and harmonious.

In comparison with the Dolcetto, this Barbera clearly shows smaller fruit, lacking that intense freshness and concentrated flavor that the Dolcetto has. It does not seem as big or as full a wine, nor as exuberant. On the other hand, the Barbera offers a kind of complexity and elegance the Dolcetto only hints at. This is a very composed wine, a wine that has reined in all of its different parts so that they cooperate to make an integrated whole. To put it briefly, this is what

I would call a borderline noble wine, already crossing over the frontier from fruitiness into complexity.

Many people are not excited by this sort of wine: I most definitely am, and that is something you should know about my taste so you can put my raves and pans in their proper perspective. Lots of other wine fans, professional and amateur alike, would unreservedly prefer the vitality of the Dolcetto to the restraint of the Barbera. But this is very much a question of personal preference. Some people associate the youthful exuberance of a wine like Dolcetto with soft drinks, and some think the more sophisticated style of the Barbera is simply dull. As the philosopher says, you pays your money and you takes your choice.

Just a reminder to you, lest you get a bit bored with all this, that you are now at a point in these tastings where you know a whole lot more about your own taste and why you like what you like than when you started way back there with the Monterey Classic Red and the Banfi Cuvée Placido. You've come a long way, baby—but you've still got a long way to go.

Right here, however, may be about as far as there is any point for us to travel on this particular road. You've now got enough basic information about fruity wines as a class to go out and do more extensive tasting on your own: different brands of Beaujolais, different Gamays, Beaujolais-style Zinfandels, the Loire red wines like Chinon and Saumur, Chiantis from the hills of Siena or Primativo from the Italian south, Merlots and Cabernets from the Italian north. The list is long, and there is plenty there to keep you happy for quite a while.

Most wine drinkers, no matter what more complicated wines they move on to, never really lose their fondness for these charmers. They are wines you can come back to endlessly for straightforward pleasures, renewed and varied every harvest. But there are many more pleasures in the world of wine than these, and where we go from here is out into the deeper vinous waters of the more complex wines—so keep paddling, and keep sipping, and keep on taking notes. *Excelsior.*

Riccardo Fenocchio makes several red Piedmont wines, most with single-vineyard designations, like this textbook Dolcetto (Pianpolvere Soprano is the name of the site from which the grapes originate; it translates roughly as "the high, dusty field"). His wines are imported by Vinifera Imports.

The old family firm of Pio Cesare produces the full line of Alba's red wines, all vinified in a manner judiciously balancing modern technology and profound respect for Alban tradition, just like this classic Barbera. Pio Cesare's wines are imported to the United States by Paterno Imports.

## Substitutes:

As always, first take younger vintages where available. If those fail, we are lucky in that many first-rate Piedmontese producers are represented on the American market, and most of them send us both Barbera and Dolcetto. For the Dolcetto, the following would all make good alternatives: Castello di Neive Dolcetto d'Alba (Vigneto Basarin); Renato Ratti Dolcetto d'Alba (Colombe); Einaudi Dolcetto di Dogliani; Contratto Dolcetto d'Alba. Ceretto's Dolcetto d'Alba Rossana and Vietti's Dolcetto d'Alba Bussia are quite classic. The Dolcettos from Franco Fiorina are a bit lighter than the norm, and those from Oddero and Marchesi di Gresy (Monte Aribaldo) are a bit heavier. The single-vineyard Dolcettos from Prunotto (especially Pian Romualdo) are extremely refined and muscular. The Barberas from most of these same producers will also serve quite well, but consider also the wonderful wines from Batasiolo, Giuseppe Cortese, and especially Ceretto Barbera d'Alba Piana.

Here ends the ninth tasting session. There are several ways for you to proceed from here.

*Following the lead of your own preferences:*
   If you liked the first wine better, the Dolcetto, try the Twelfth Flight.
   If you preferred the second wine, the Barbera, try the Fourteenth Flight.

*Following the kind of grapes:*
   Neither Dolcetto nor Barbera figures in any more of our tastings. You will find other Piedmontese wines in the Eighteenth Flight.

*Following the wines of the country:*
   Go on to the Fourteenth Flight.

# THE TENTH FLIGHT

~~✦✦~~

## B & G St-Emilion 1988
### and
### Glen Ellen Proprietor's
### Reserve California Merlot 1989

~~✦✦~~

T HIS FLIGHT STARTS YOU on the taste trail of the Merlot grape. Extensively cultivated throughout Bordeaux, Merlot is used in the Médoc as a component in the blend of the best red wines, but in lesser percentage than the dominant grape, Cabernet Sauvignon. Across the Gironde River to the east, in St-Emilion and Pomerol, the Merlot grape's contribution to the blend becomes much more important both in quantity and in the qualities it brings to the wine. In California, Merlot has so far been cultivated primarily to produce a varietal wine in its own right, that is to say, to make a wine that contains at least 75 percent and in many cases 100 percent of the Merlot grape.

The first wine you have in front of you in this, your maiden attempt to grapple seriously with the phenomenon of varietal flavor in a noble *vinifera* strain, is a good shipper's St-Emilion. The firm of Barton & Guestier have been wine merchants, specializing in Bordeaux, for over two hundred years. Their wines are imported to the United States by Seagram. The second wine of the pair is an important California firm's blended Merlot—that is, it's made from all Merlot grapes, but the grapes that went into it were grown in different parts of California. Glen Ellen is located in Sonoma but uses all the resources of the state to produce its Proprietor's Reserve

92

series, a line of varietal wines that has succeeded hugely by offering good wine at a good price. Some wag has called the whole idea "fighting varietals": this is one fight we can all join with a clear conscience.

Since this is your first real confrontation with varietal tasting (with a major varietal, that is; depending on how you got here, you may have tasted pairs of Gamay-based wines already), let me spell a few things out for you. It's reasonable to expect to find some similarities between these wines, but don't be at all surprised if the similarities are swamped by the differences.

How can that be, if it's the same grape in both cases? Because of climate and soil, different agricultural techniques, even the way the vines are pruned—the whole package of things that add up to the growing conditions of the vines. These can change the nature of the wine completely. Add to them any differences in the techniques of vinification, and it is possible to completely transform the wine made from Merlot or any other grape into something altogether different from what it makes on its home turf. Vines behave differently in different circumstances, just as people do.

So what do you do now? You know perfectly well: the infamous s's. You've got the tools to handle this job. Now use 'em. Check back here when you're done.

## Appearance.

Color is easily accounted for here: the St-Emilion shows a medium ruby, with some amber or tawny highlights, the Glen Ellen Merlot a slightly deeper, younger-looking ruby with a bit of a purple cast. Both are pleasing, but not remarkable. It's after this that the important differences begin.

## Aroma.

Most tasters find the aroma of the St-Emilion somewhat muffled. You can bring it up somewhat by swirling vigorously (careful! watch out for the rug), or even better by decanting the wine into a carafe or pitcher, but the improvement is only temporary. The aroma remains small and rather elusive, giving suggestions of grass and earth and hints of cedar and black currants: some people may describe it as a slight, pleasing, tarry scent with floral overtones. A few tasters may find an unpleasant, oily scent in it.

### Bordeaux Borders

Bordeaux is one of France's—and the world's—most important fine wine districts. It is subdivided into several zones: Côtes de Blaye, Entre-Deux-Mers, Médoc, Graves, Sauternes, St-Emilion, Pomerol, and Côtes de Bourg. Wines of every conceivable range of quality come from all of them, but the finest red wines—those that have been esteemed for centuries and which have influenced the growth and production of "serious" wines all over the world—come from the Médoc (a stretch of land lying between the west bank of the river Gironde and the sea) and from St-Emilion and Pomerol (a plateau lying east of the Gironde). The Médoc is subdivided into several famous (at least in the wine world) communes or townships: from south to north, Graves (really separate from the Médoc but usually figured with it for red-wine purposes), Margaux, Pauillac, St-Julien, and St-Estèphe. Subsidiary divisions of the other great red wine zones are St-Emilion, St-Georges–St-Emilion, Puisseguin–St-Emilion, Lussac–St-Emilion, Montagne–St-Emilion, Pomerol, and Lalande de Pomerol.

The Merlot, on the other hand, has an aroma that, on first encounter, a few people find objectionable because of its strength. It's larger than the St-Emilion and more forceful. Those who don't much like it talk about a cooked vegetable or olive oil scent. Those who do like it call it fruit, or sometimes *fruit!*, and may even think it smells sweet. When they get more specific, they name elements such as fresh-turned earth or generalized spices or herbs, all of which are pretty normal for Merlot-based wines, and which most people find very attractive.

Taste.

The flavor of the St-Emilion imparts more fruit than its relatively small aroma would lead you to expect: not an abundance, but still a

pleasant surprise. Most tasters detect a slight spiciness in its soft
fruit as well as underlying flavors of tar and/or wood—tannic elements, but definitely soft. The wine is fully dry and medium-
bodied, with a fairly short finish. But the overriding palatal sensation is an unspecific fruit taste combined with soft tannins.

### Wine Build

Structure is a very significant wine term and particularly important to understand when dealing with bigger, more complex wines. Think of it in terms of architecture: the elements
that hit the eye immediately in the facade of the building are
like the flavor components of wine, the things that strike the
palate right away. The internal structure of the building—the
unseen parts, the beams and braces—are what hold that facade up and allow the building to stand in the first place. In the
same way with wine, it is the interactions of the more sub-
merged components, of acid and alcohol and tannin and fruit
and extracts, that structure and support the flavor and make
the wine viable. A wine wherein these different structural
elements are harmoniously fused, so that no one of them is
more conspicuous than the others, is said to be well balanced.
A wine wherein one of them immediately proclaims its presence or absence is unbalanced.

Note well, however, that balanced and unbalanced do not
equal good and bad. A balanced wine can be boring, and an
unbalanced one, if the right element dominates or surrenders,
can be very enjoyable. To make a great wine, another balance is
necessary: the quality of the grapes, the quality of the soil, and
the artistry of the winemaker. Simple formulas never make
superb wines.

Like the St-Emilion, the Merlot's flavor somewhat surprises most
tasters quite pleasantly: it's not as forceful as its aroma, and is in fact
quite readily enjoyable. There is a distinct fruit presence, which
some tasters will perceive as "sweet": it isn't—that's just unadulter-

ated ripe grapes. People usually describe the Merlot's fruit as soft, but not as soft as the St-Emilion. This Merlot has more acid and less tannin than that, though there is still, especially for people sensitive to tannin, a perceptible sourness and astringency in the Merlot. Some tasters may even pick up the faintest hint of tobacco.

Overall, preferences between these two wines will probably divide along the lines of complexity vs. fruit. The B & G St-Emilion, while not a very complicated wine and, at the moment at least, a little unbalanced by its heavy tannin, still offers more components and more structure than the Glen Ellen Merlot—probably because of the presence of at least some Cabernet Sauvignon and perhaps Cabernet Franc in its blend.

The Merlot, on the other hand, gives you a much better idea of what its namesake grape is really all about, which is certainly handy for our purposes at this point. Its almost natural balance, owing to its more discreet tannin and soft fruit, is very characteristic of wines made from Merlot in any part of the world.

### Substitutes:

Younger vintages of the two named wines will work best. After that, for the B & G St-Emilion use another shipper's St-Emilion or, as a last resort, B & G's or another shipper's Pomerol; in place of the Glen Ellen Merlot try other inexpensive California Merlots from makers such as Almadén, Christian Brothers, Gallo, Hawk Crest, or Monterey Vineyards.

This is the conclusion of our tenth red-wine tasting. From here you don't have many choices; all roads lead to the Eleventh Flight and the continuation of your exploration of the Merlot grape.

*Following the lead of your own preferences:*
   If you liked either the first wine, the St-Emilion, or the second
   wine, the California Merlot, go on to the Eleventh Flight.

*Following the kind of grapes:*
   Go on to the Eleventh Flight.

*Following the wines of the country:*
   Go on to the Eleventh Flight.

# THE ELEVENTH FLIGHT

~᷍᷍᷍᷍᷍᷍᷍~

## *Château de Sales Pomerol 1988 and Gundlach-Bundschu Sonoma Valley Merlot 1989*

~᷍᷍᷍᷍᷍᷍᷍~

I N THIS FLIGHT you are dealing with a very respectable Pomerol estate, planted about two thirds in Merlot vines (the remainder is about evenly divided between Cabernet Sauvignon and Cabernet Franc) and an equally respectable California vineyard with a continuous, more-than-one-hundred-year history of grapegrowing (Prohibition interrupted the winemaking). In addition to Merlot, Gundlach-Bundschu also produces a wide selection of other varietals, especially Cabernet, Chardonnay, and Gewürztraminer, plus a few special-label bottlings from its prized Batto Ranch site. Château de Sales is imported by Château & Estate Wine Company.

Even more than the last flight, this pair of wines should demonstrate pretty clearly some of the major differences between French and California styles in winemaking. Also—and by no means to be overlooked—these wines will give you fair examples of the potential of the Merlot grape.

The ball is in your court: it's time for you to do your stuff. Pay particular attention here to the way these wines react to food. And oh, yes, make sure you look this time not just for color but for legs as well—little streamers formed by the wine flowing back down into the glass after you've swirled it.

## Appearance.

In color, these two wines are hard to distinguish. Both are a pretty, clear ruby, the Merlot perhaps a shade darker, moving toward garnet. And oh, yes, for what it's worth, both show lots of legs, quite distinct and persistent.

## Aroma.

When we come to their aromas, most tasters find it quite easy to make distinctions between these two wines, and the distinctions they most often make are essentially typical of the styles of French and California wines. I don't mean just of French and California Merlot-based wines, but French and California fine wines generally.

First and broadest distinction: The majority of tasters, by a wide margin, sense the aroma of the Merlot as heavier than that of the Pomerol. Those who like it call it richer, those who don't call it coarser.

Second distinction: The same large percentage of tasters finds the Merlot's aroma the more deeply fruity of the two, the Pomerol's the more compound bouquet, less dominated by a single element. Some people will call it "cigar-box"—i.e., faint cedar and tobacco scents blended with other, lighter elements.

Whether it results from California's techniques of vinification, which for the most part minimize blends of grapes and maximize single-varietal wines, or whether the California climate simply grows more intensely flavored grapes, California winemaking has up until the present been largely understandable through the idea of varietal intensity. Each wine seems to be striving to become the "perfect expression" of the grape variety from which it is (often exclusively) vinified. California winemakers used to get very mystical when they talked about it, as if there were a Platonic idea of Zinfandel or Chardonnay floating in the ether and waiting to be incarnated by some suitably reverent and devoted Grape Master.

More recently, some winemakers have begun experimenting with blends and modification of varietal wines in the direction of balance, elegance, etc. This is not to say that those qualities are or have been missing in the best California wines. But even with a winery that strives for a kind of European style, as does Gundlach-Bundschu, California winemakers can't help making California wine: wines

*Wine Legs*

Legs, or tears, are the trails formed by the wine as it slips back down the sides of your glass after you have performed the ritual swirl-and-sniff. They have an ambiguous place in wine lore.

Supposedly, they are an indication of richness and body in a wine, because wines higher in extract and glycerine, and theoretically therefore higher in viscosity, will form thicker, slower-moving, longer-lasting legs. Many wines, particularly light-bodied simple wines, make no legs at all when swirled; the wine simply flows back in an even and uniform thin sheet.

But after that, all bets are off. For one thing, there doesn't seem to be any real connection between the small quantities of glycerine present in wines and their viscosity. For another, the formation of legs, and in particular their thickness, probably depends as much on the condition of your glasses as the condition of the wine. Finally, why use so hieroglyphic a sign to read the richness and body of a wine when you can judge both much more directly and accurately by just tasting a mouthful?

Not too many years ago it was believed that some wonderful property of really fine wines caused them to create legs by a kind of bizarre capillary action, the wine actually creeping up the sides of the glass like some sci-fi attack of the killer caterpillars. That particular piece of pseudoscientific mumbo jumbo has quietly died, but the rest of leg lore is still with us and to my way of thinking is just as suspect.

Legs are probably a pure piece of wine-snob hokum—but they'll do as well as anything else to break the conversational ice at a cocktail party. At any rate, you're now armed either to start your own pretentious conversation (and I don't believe you'd do that) or to deflate the next pompous legman (or legwoman) you meet.

that are big, intense, and usually dominated by fruit or (in some cases) oak.

The kind of aroma that you are getting in this Merlot (at least in its gross effects, as we've described them so far) is characteristically California: big, heavy, intensely grapey, with other elements emerging only slowly from behind that overpowering first rush. The first impression that a California wine typically makes upon you is power. Size. Strength. We're not necessarily talking about alcohol here, though alcoholic strength can and does play a part in it. But mostly it's simply an impression of raw, physical bigness, like an overgrown kid who's been working out regularly and has developed a super body but still can't dance, and maybe you wonder if he can really walk down the block without tripping over his own pectorals.

I told you wine tasting was very subjective.

All right, so what else is there to say about these wines? Plenty. We're not even done with the aromas yet.

When you do get past the initial impact of the Merlot, what do you smell? A mix of things, all more or less in minor keys: some woody, oaky aromas (some claim they can even smell charcoal in there); some herbaceous and grassy scents, maybe even hay; and some earthy smells, particularly damp, fresh-turned earth—all very nice.

The Pomerol, by contrast, presents its aroma as very much of a medley right from the start. Most tasters pick up the scent of fruit, but markedly lighter than in the Merlot. You feel as much as smell a sort of alcohol and tannin prickle in the nose. Maybe because of that sensation, some tasters describe the wine as smelling young and lively. After that, some tasters get a whole rush of scents: spice and pepper, earth and grass, wood odors like vanilla and especially cedar. The cedar component even grows as the wine breathes in the glass. In its own very different way, this is all just as pleasing as the Merlot's aroma, but it's an entirely different creature, more restrained, more subtle, more provocative, a courtly old statesman hiding his power rather than flaunting it.

## Taste.

Everything that the aromas of these two wines have suggested to us is borne out by their flavors. Almost everybody reports that the Pomerol is soft, complex, medium-bodied, with a good tannic bite to it. The fruit tastes young, as if it were not yet fully developed. A

### Wine Lungs

Most fine red wines respond well to being allowed to breathe for a while, though just how long that while should be is one of the most arguable—and argued—questions in all of wine lore.

Breathing can take either of two forms: simply pulling the cork and letting the wine stand, opened, for whatever period of time you choose, or pouring the wine into a decanter. Once decanted, some serve it immediately, others let it stand and breathe for a while longer.

The point of either form is to allow the wine to open, to let its aroma and flavor develop, by exposing it to oxygen. Obviously if you decant it, you are exposing all of the wine to oxygen in a short space of time, and a good rule of thumb is that decanting is roughly equivalent to about an hour's simple breathing. Generally speaking, Italian red wines like Barolo and Brunello need several hours' breathing, California's best reds seem to do well with about one hour, and France's finest reds are best served by decanting just before serving. But that is very general advice as well as very subjective opinion. A lot depends on the stage at which you like to drink your wines, so conduct a few experiments of your own and taste a wine at 15- or 20-minute intervals after you open it to see how it changes. Once you think it has opened sufficiently for your pleasure, you can simply push the cork back in if you are not ready to serve it immediately.

good many tasters can pick out traces of cherry and of currants, nice dry fruit hints. It even has a little discernible grassiness and a definite intriguing suggestion of licorice. You could never call this wine crisp, but it is attractive and round, a wine worth paying attention to, though it is too well bred to ever importune your attention.

The Merlot, on the other hand, grabs your lapels and not only introduces itself but gives you its whole medical history to boot. As in its aroma, most tasters find that the prominent element in its flavor is fruit, a big, muscular, ripe, "sweetish" (in quotation marks because this is still a fully dry wine), perhaps berry taste. For most people, tannin is right behind the fruit, however: soft tannins, to be sure, but nevertheless discernible as a major component of this wine. Despite the fact that this Gundlach-Bundschu Merlot is still clearly a medium-bodied wine, most tasters describe it as bigger in most respects than the Château de Sales Pomerol. It seems to have higher alcohol and definitely has more tannin. It even seems to have more fruit, even though the fruit is not now as clearly expressed (it's more muffled) than that of the Pomerol.

The two wines share some very important elements. In both there is a deep undertone of dark, bitter chocolate, which may be the result of their respective vintages (1988 in Bordeaux and 1989 in Sonoma saw some exceptional ripeness and richness). In both there is that fine, pleasing though brief licorice finish. And in both there is a flavor, very hard to describe, that many people discern mostly high in their mouths as a sort of overtaste, straight down the center of the tongue, a kind of high tenor fruit sweetness that in my mind at least is a characteristic of the Merlot grape. I've heard it described as reminding people of everything from currants to licorice to butterscotch. However you perceive it, if you perceive it where I've indicated you are in all likelihood tasting an essential flavor of the Merlot grape, the basic affinity that links these otherwise very different wines.

A few final thoughts for you about these two and the sorts of wines you'll be going on to in the next section. You are here quite literally on the verge of full-bodied wines and already well launched on wines that improve with bottle-age. These two bottles are, by any serious standards, very young wines, and you, thoughtless as ever, have just committed something very close to infanticide in opening them.

If a really knowledgeable drinker had been sipping along with us, he would have been surprised by only one thing: not that the Merlot was somewhat muffled, but that the Pomerol was so drinkable.

Why? Because in wines of this class, where tannin in particular is so important a contributor to both the wine's balance and its longevity, it is normal—expected—that for several years after bottling (these '88s were only bottled at the end of '90) the wine will be harsh, tannic, alcoholic, acidic, or all four. It takes time for all those elements to learn to lie down together peacefully: in a great vintage, it can take decades. So this particular Pomerol is what we call a very forward wine, one ready to drink unusually early. That does not mean that it is now at its peak. Probably far from it, in fact, because wines of this sort commonly go on developing in the bottle for—in a good vintage—five to ten years before reaching a peak and an equilibrium where they may remain, if properly stored, for another ten to twenty years.

No one really knows if California Merlot has that kind of potential for development and longevity, because there just isn't enough of a track record for California wines. But this much is certain: this particular Merlot is still developing, and its real flavor has yet to emerge. It might be one year away or it might be ten, but this is a wine that will go through several changes yet before it reaches adulthood—so don't be surprised if you taste it again in a few months or a year and get a completely different impression from what you received today. That, too, is one of the fascinations and pleasures of wine, as well as being the main reason people put together wine cellars.

Since we are talking here about aging wines, and since you are already well engaged with wines that take well to aging, this is a good place to say a few words to you about a flavor that many connoisseurs regard as peculiar to the taste of quite mature wine. Some don't like it at all and call it the flavor of old and tired wine.

This flavor can be perceived by different individuals as anything from plum to raisin to resin. Usually it is simply called plummy, and it is regarded as more or less characteristic of many older wines. The "more or less," of course, depends on the grapes they are made from. And depending on the grapes and their vinification, the plummy flavor that we are speaking of does not necessarily stand alone or even unmodified. Other fruit flavors may coexist with it, harmonies that were masked by an earlier heavy fruit or heavy tannin may become apparent, overbright acid may subside: any number of changes can go on during the bottle-aging of a fine wine. But all really mature wines show something of this plummy character, and the whole class of clarets—the fine red wines of Bordeaux—does so particularly.

Because of the different grapes and the vinification techniques used, different wines mature at different ages. What is maturity for a Barbera and senility for a Beaujolais is scarcely adolescence for a Barolo or a Bordeaux. But that suggestion of plumminess, whenever

you get a scent or taste of it in a wine, is usually a good clue that the
wine is at or near its mature peak. That doesn't mean it's going to
fall apart and decay in the next twenty-four hours, but it probably
does mean it's not going to get significantly better than it is right
now. So if, for instance, you happen to taste that telltale accent in a
wine you've squirreled away two or three more bottles or cases of,
you'd be wise to start drinking 'em up pretty soon. Some wines may
persevere in exactly this condition for many years, and many of
them can be very lovely indeed in this state of absolute maturity, but
don't plan on keeping them long like that unless you really know the
wine and its staying power, or unless you are content to risk the loss.

   You should know also that many connoisseurs do not like wine in
this condition. For them, this is already too old, and they prefer to
drink their wines, whatever kind they may be, with a flush of
youthful fruit still intact. This is, as are so many things to do with
wine, purely a matter of personal taste.


## Substitutes:

First, younger vintages of the two wines specified; otherwise, Château Bourgneuf (Pomerol) or Château Fonroque (St-Emilion) could
stand in for Château de Sales, and Louis M. Martini Vinedos del Rio
Merlot (Russian River Valley) or Sterling Vineyards Merlot could
substitute for the Gundlach-Bundschu.

Here ends the eleventh tasting session and the section on medium-
bodied wines. There are several ways for you to proceed from here.

*Following the lead of your own preferences:*
   If you liked the first wine better, the Château de Sales Pomerol,
   go on to the Fourteenth Flight.
   If you liked the second wine better, the Gundlach-Bundschu
   Merlot, go on to the Sixteenth Flight.

*Following the kind of grapes:*
   This is the last predominantly Merlot flight. For wines with
   small admixtures of Merlot, go on to the Fifteenth Flight.

*Following the wines of the country:*
   Go on to the Twelfth Flight.

# THE TWELFTH FLIGHT

~ ⚬⚬ ~

## *Prosper Maufoux*
## *Côte de Beaune Villages 1983*
## *and*
## *Yamhill Valley Vineyards*
## *Willamette Valley Pinot Noir 1988*

~ ⚬⚬ ~

YOU STAND RIGHT NOW at the gateway to what is for me the most fascinating and pleasurable stretch of territory on the whole world wine map. The full-bodied red wines are the heavy hitters of wine's biggest league. As a class, these are the wines you select to accompany your best meals and to serve your best friends and to comfort yourself with when everything else is going sour.

Because of their size—and I mean that in the metaphoric sense—these are wines that last, so they are the wines to buy young and relatively inexpensively to lay down until they mature.

These are the wines that I wish every would-be or might-be wine drinker could taste at least a mature mouthful of: they would skin your tongue back and teach you more in a few seconds about why people make a fuss about wine than everything I or anyone else could ever write.

What constitutes the excellence of these wines? What makes them big and full-bodied, and why does that make them capable of age? I'm glad you asked me that.

The answer cannot be given in one word. You have to start with

## Wine Beds

Laying down wine, or cellaring, probably carries a greater freight of romance than any other aspect of wine lore. People inevitably think of cobwebbed racks containing vast numbers of bottles that have slept undisturbed for generations in the ancestral vaults of some decayed aristocrat. The reality is very different. If you've got twelve bottles of your favorite Zinfandel stashed away in the hall closet, you've started a wine cellar.

Anyone can keep wine till maturity, if certain minimal conditions are met: darkness, because sunlight can destroy wine; tranquillity, because motion or vibration can also destroy wine (that's why some wines "can't travel"); consistent moderate temperatures, no higher than 65 to 70 degrees Fahrenheit and no lower than 45, with only gradual alterations within that range, because temperatures too high rush the wine through its life cycle far too fast—cook it, in effect—and because sudden temperature changes can cause wines simply to fall apart. If it meets those conditions, a broom closet, a stairwell, or an ordinary basement can serve as a wine cellar.

Those are the minimal requirements. What are the optimum conditions for wine storage? Most experts agree on dark, tranquillity, a constant temperature of around 55 degrees, and a slight amount of humidity in the atmosphere. And check your corks every fifteen to twenty-five years or so: they might need replacement.

the variety of grapes. Some few red varieties—Cabernet Sauvignon is the best example—seem to produce top-quality wine wherever they are planted. Some, such as Pinot Noir, make superb wine in one location (Burgundy), and in another (California) only grudgingly hint at what they might do. A grape that in one place yields an enormously powerful wine (the Grenache in the southern Rhône) elsewhere gives mostly a mild-mannered rosé (the Grenache in most of California). So at the start, it is a combination of vine and soil and climate that together create the possibility of a big red wine.

After that, a great deal depends on the skill and the methods of the winemaker, on the combination of tradition and innovation each individual brings to each harvest. Normally, for big red wines, wood-aging plays an important role in the wine's development. As the wine rests in the barrels, an intricate exchange between wine and wood takes place, the most marked effects of which are the addition to the wine of wood tannins (different from grape tannins both chemically and in flavor) and flavors from the barrels (new or used barrels can make a tremendous difference in this regard). Also, the wood permits a tightly controlled, indirect contact between wine and air, so a very gradual and limited oxidation goes forward, contributing further to the wine's maturation. Just how long a wine remains in wooden barrels varies incredibly from region to region, even from winemaker to winemaker.

In Burgundy for instance, it used to be routine practice to allow the fresh-pressed juices to ferment on the skins—that is, in direct contact with the crushed grape skins and stems and seeds—for anywhere from two to four weeks. That made a wine high in extracts (dissolved solids), deep in color (leached from the skins: most grape juice is clear), and rich in tannin and acids (tannin particularly from skins, stems, and seeds). Because of the Burgundian climate, the Pinot Noir rarely ripens there to the degree it normally does in California, so in the past young Burgundies were freshened with heartier wines from the south, which were naturally much higher in sugar: now, because of AOC laws, the addition of sugar to the ferment is the norm.

The practice of adding sugar to the fermenting juices is called "chaptalization," after a Count Jean-Antoine Chaptal, an early-nineteenth-century promoter of the virtues of beet sugar. The purpose of the addition is to turn sugar-deficient grapes into wines of adequate alcoholic strength, since during fermentation sugar converts to alcohol.

Chaptalization is probably the simplest and most widely used chemical process in winemaking. It is almost regularly employed in Burgundy, where the grapes often fail to achieve full ripeness, and it is permitted (and seems to be used with increasing frequency) in Bordeaux. In Germany, it is allowed for wines up to the level of Qualitätswein without *Prädikat* (see pp. 184 and 190), but not above that. In Italy it is never permitted. In the United States, it is subject to state law and therefore practices vary considerably. Chaptalization is not permitted in California.

Changes in vinification have made enormous differences in the wines we drink. An old-style Burgundy, drunk young, could be harsh and ungiving, its fruit almost completely masked by tannin. Laid down for ten or more years, a good vintage would ripen into a wine that can only be called opulent: a big, generous wine that opened softly on the palate to reveal depth after depth of flavor. A new-style Burgundy is likely to be much more drinkable young, with more readily appreciable fruit, but it seems unlikely to ever develop the size and resonance those wines used to have. Changed vinification methods have completely changed the wine. They are still great wines, but they are different wines. (Unfortunately, they still command the same prices, among the very highest of all wines. Burgundy may not hit as forcefully as it used to, but economically at least it is still playing in the major leagues.)

In Burgundy, in Bordeaux, in California, and increasingly in Italy, aging the fermented wine in small barrels (called *barriques*) is the normal procedure in setting out to make a fine wine. Sometimes in California the barrels are made of redwood, but most of the time oak is the preferred material, and French oak if you can get it. Even in areas like the Piedmont in Italy, where aging in huge wooden vats has been for centuries the normal procedure, innovators are now finishing their wines in *barriques*. Why? Because the size of the *barrique* ensures optimum exposure of the wine to the wood and thereby the greatest possible interaction between the two. What the oak adds is, once again, tannin, plus some flavor elements: the vanilla or caramel strains in the aromas and tastes of some wines are directly traceable to new oak barrels.

All of these factors contribute ultimately to the longevity of the wine, since the two principal components that keep a wine going are tannin and alcohol.

The latter brings us full circle, back to the grapes again. You can always strengthen the tannin presence in your wine by the way you vinify and age it, but for good alcohol you need good sugar levels to start with. And if you want to end up with high alcohol and big tannin for longevity, you need to have something worth keeping alive, or else you wind up with a zombie wine, a walking corpse animated by alcohol and tannin but with no real spark. So you need a grape that makes a flavorful wine, a flavor capable of standing up to high alcohol and a lot of tannin, and you need good acid to keep that flavor bright and to prevent the wine from going flabby.

This is why the greatest red wines are normally the aged, full-bodied reds: because they simply have more of what makes any wine good, have it in greater concentration, and have it more harmoniously. So what you will be tasting for in this flight and in the flights that follow is, aside from the newly introduced varietal flavor of a few sorts of wine you've not met before, exactly what you've been tasting for all along. The difference is that here you should find all those elements you've been learning about present more abundantly, more precisely, and in better balance. Enjoy.

This and the next flight are devoted to exploring the nuances of the Pinot Noir grape, a variety that has probably broken more vintners' hearts than all the others combined.

In Burgundy, in that narrow stretch of vineyards known as the Côte d'Or—the Golden Slope—Pinot Noir can produce some of the most sinfully luxurious wines your palate will ever have the pleasure to be ravished by. I say "can produce" because even in Burgundy the Pinot Noir is a fickle grape and the climate in addition is tricky; so that for every sensational harvest you get three or four mediocre ones and one or two downright rotten ones. And even in the best harvests, Pinot Noir yields are small, or should be, because a heavy growth of fruit on these vines means flabby, characterless wines. So really fine red Burgundy is scarce and very expensive. Almost certainly, these wines will be the costliest of any this book asks you to buy: Burgundies are pretty much the price leaders in the world of wine.

If the Pinot Noir grape is troublesome on its home turf, it is a complete sociopath everywhere else. In climates less demanding than Burgundy's it grows well and bears good crops and makes, on the whole, dull wine. Winemakers in California and Long Island and South Africa and Australia have tried every conceivable trick of cultivation and vinification, and the end result has been, overall, very forgettable. Only a few really fine bottlings from various makers in scattered vintages have given hints of what the grape might do outside Burgundy, if someone can ever find the magic formula.

The Burgundian example you're going to taste in this flight is a wine blended from the produce of several of the communes of the Côte de Beaune, which is the southern half of the Golden Slope. The domestic example comes from Oregon, which seems to be leading the way in American success with the Pinot Noir. Oregon, like most of the Pacific Northwest, seems destined to be primarily white-wine country, but Pinot Noir typically produces its best results outside the most favored zones of red-wine cultivation: it always seems to do its best as a wine grape in circumstances that are in agricultural terms adverse or at least difficult.

Once again you are being asked to taste as much for similarities as for differences, to try to help you fix in your mind what Pinot Noir tastes like—that is, what is essential to its flavor and what in it can be altered by soil and climate and technology.

Wine apocrypha has it that some fabulous palates can identify in the flavor of a Pinot Noir the forest that the barrels it aged in came from. Feel free to doubt this.

Okay, go ahead and see, swirl, smell, sip, savor, and spit. Be bold, and tread on the aspirations of whole generations of winemakers.

## Appearance.

The Côte de Beaune Villages wine looks its age: it is light garnet, with a telltale orange edge. The Oregon wine shows its youth just as clearly in its lively, translucent ruby tint. Both these wine colors fall into the true Burgundy spectrum.

## Aroma.

Both are rather subdued immediately after pouring, but both open in the glass after a few minutes (long breathing doesn't seem to change these wines very much).

The range of comments people are likely to make about these two wines is large indeed, because both present very complex sets of scent: what are properly, in wine jargon, called "bouquets" rather than "aromas." That is not a distinction without a difference, though the difference is a difficult one for many people to perceive. Aroma, technically speaking, means only those odors that originate from the grapes themselves, while bouquet denotes all those odors arising from the whole process of vinification and bottle-aging. The distinction is essentially a useless one for people who have never had the opportunity to smell freshly pressed Pinot Noir or Gamay or any other grape, and throughout this book, if I make any distinction at all between the words "aroma" and "bouquet," I tend to use them as I do here, employing aroma to mean simpler odors and bouquet more complex ones.

Individual tasters' descriptions of the Beaune's bouquet can run from full, balanced, and fruity on one hand to practically nonexistent on the other. The median position is probably as close to objective truth as we can get with wine: the aroma is of middling strength, but persistent, and it shows good fresh fruit with pleasing leafy and floral overtones and undertones. Most people find it very composed, very balanced, strongly suggesting elegance in the wine to come. The fruit component they seem to find particularly intriguing, describing it as, among other things, rich and attractive and smelling of cherries or plums or currants or cassis.

Perceptions of the Pinot Noir's aroma can range from finding it sweeter, fuller, and more spicy than the Beaune's to smelling a sharpness and acridity in it. Again, about the middle of the spectrum seems closest to target. This Pinot seems to have an aroma somewhat bigger than the Beaune's and decidedly fruity, in fact definitely berrylike, with herbaceous and floral notes in it and a tart or astringent bass tone underneath everything. Both wines' aromas suggest to some tasters a hint of camphor, which is odd—and oddly pleasing.

## Taste.

The polarities of opinion about the bouquets of these wines will probably continue into tasters' reactions to their flavor. Those lining up on the positive side about the Beaune will probably like best its clean fresh fruit, which they will taste as soft, warm, and at least suggesting sweetness. Cherries and plums are the specifics most often mentioned. Many people will also respond very positively to what is usually described as the wine's pleasing complexity. Tasters describe the wine as not exactly crisp, but bright and lively, with decent acid and plenty of tannin contributing to an overall impression of balance, roundness, and some softness. At least some will taste a small but persistent dry finish that ends the wine very nicely. Those who are negative about the Beaune will find it somewhat sour and astringent in the mouth and, in comparison to the Pinot Noir, rather bland.

Those positive for the Pinot Noir will describe it as similar to the Beaune wine, but smoother, perhaps bigger, with more fruit or more enjoyable fruit, and with a bigger finish. They may remark on some attractive quasi-syrupy, quasi-liquory undertones as well, and a pleasing battery of tarry or stemmy flavors. Those feeling negative about this wine may find it a bit thin and too acid, perhaps with an

unpleasant touch of—their words for it will vary—tartness or sourness or bitterness, and with a bitter finish.

What is the objective truth about the two? Well, you should know
by now that when it comes to wine, objective truth is a very elastic
concept. If you pushed me to the wall, I'd say that both the Beaune
and the Pinot Noir are clearly well-made wines and that they share
many similarities, even many specific flavor elements, that derive
directly from their common grape variety. Though both feel rounder
and fuller on the palate than they look in the glass, neither is really
big in body: both are more like middleweights, and that is a real
defect according to my personal ideal of what a Pinot Noir–based
wine ought to be. I like them with more heft and more guts to them:
these two are on the soft-and-charming side rather than the big-
and-impressive side. Nevertheless, both are substantial wines,
round in the mouth and thoroughly enjoyable.

The big difference between them seems to me a perfect illustration of what I think of as the classic Franco-American split. The
Pinot Noir has more fruit—so much more that sometimes it can
seem unbalanced—and the Beaune has more breeding, more
elegance—it is so harmonious and restrained that I sometimes wish
it were more assertive, more aggressive. Those differences, I think,
concisely illustrate what the norms and goals of winemaking are in
the two countries at this time, and they are emphasized—some
would say exaggerated—by the fact that there really do exist such
things as American palates and European palates (even California
palates and French palates), tastes and taste buds that naturally lean
toward one or another of these sets of characteristics. An American-
wine palate relishes the big fruit in the Yamhill Pinot Noir and finds
the Beaune too thin, too small, too unsubstantial. A European
palate delights in the elegance of the Beaune and finds the Pinot
Noir unbalanced, obvious, overstated.

Who is right and who is wrong? Both. Neither. By now you know
as well as I do that the right wine is the wine that is right for you and
right for the occasion (I wouldn't take either of these wines to the
beach, but I could happily drink either of them many other places).
And by now you should also know enough about your own palate
and about at least some kinds of wine to be able to choose the one
you like without feeling at all embarrassed at not liking the other. So
cast your ballot as you please.

Prosper Maufoux is a highly regarded Burgundian *négociant* handling the whole gamut of the region's wines. His wines are imported

to the United States by the House of Burgundy. Yamhill Valley Vineyards is a small, family-owned and -operated winery in Oregon's Willamette Valley, an area many wine professionals hope will at last express the best of Pinot Noir in America. If you wish to explore further the adventures of American Pinot Noir, there are many other first-rate California, Washington, and Oregon vineyards also trying their hands at this difficult grape. Here are the names of some you might want to try: Acacia Winery, or Davis Bynum, or Kenwood, or Joseph Swan (if you can find any), or Carneros Creek, all in California; and in the Pacific Northwest, Adelsheim Vineyard, the Eyrie Vineyards, Knudsen Erath Winery, and Tualatin Vineyards.

**Substitutes:**

First, younger vintages of the two named wines; second, for the Maufoux Côte de Beaune Villages, consider substituting Drouhin's Côte de Beaune Villages (which is usually a lively, fruity wine) or that of another major Burgundian *négociant* (for example, Bouchard Père et Fils, Jadot, Latour); and for the Yamhill Vineyards Pinot Noir, try Louis Martini's Los Carneros Pinot Noir, or Robert Mondavi's Pinot Noir, or Domaine Drouhin Oregon Pinot Noir (very Burgundian in style, actually; it could almost substitute for the Côte de Beaune), or Adelsheim's Elizabeth's Reserve Yamhill County Pinot Noir.

This is the conclusion of the twelfth tasting session. There are several ways for you to proceed from here.

*Following the lead of your own preferences:*
   If you liked the first wine better, the Côte de Beaune Villages, go on to the Thirteenth Flight.
   If you liked the second wine better, the Yamhill Valley Vineyards Pinot Noir, go on to either the Thirteenth Flight or the Fourteenth Flight.

*Following the kind of grapes:*
   Go on to the Thirteenth Flight.

*Following the wines of the country:*
   Wine One: Go on to the Thirteenth Flight.
   Wine Two: Go on to the Sixteenth Flight.

# THE THIRTEENTH FLIGHT

~⦇∽⦈~

## Domaine Dujac
## Morey St-Denis 1988
## and
## Olivier Leflaive Pommard 1988

~⦇∽⦈~

ALLOW ME AT THIS POINT in our tasting together to extend to all of you fledgling Burgundy fans my sincerest condolences. You are probably embarking upon a passion that is going to leave you in financial jeopardy for the rest of your lives. It is a real question whether in economic terms a fondness for Burgundy is more or less costly than playing the horses or playing the stock market. In any event, there is little question that you will drink well, and I'll be happy to come to dinner any time you ask.

Why is Burgundy so costly? For the usual reasons: high quality and low quantity. We've already talked about the balkiness of the Pinot Noir and the iffiness of the Burgundian climate. Multiply those erratic low yields by the fact that the entire Golden Slope is only about thirty miles long and averages only about a half a mile wide. At some spots a strong arm could throw a rock from its western to its eastern limit. That accounts amply for scarcity.

The quality comes from two sources: first, a tradition of cultivating Pinot Noir (and Chardonnay, but that is for another section of this book) that runs back at least as far as the establishment of Cistercian monasteries in the Middle Ages; and second, accidents of soil and sun that have made a few precious plots into the *ne plus ultra* vineyards of the wine world. For devoted oenophiles, La Tache, Romanée Conti, Clos de Vougeot, Clos de Bèze, Le Corton—these are names to conjure with, great red wines that will, sadly, dye your bank book that color, too.

Despite the small size of the Côte d'Or, its topography and its output are quite varied. It is conventionally divided into the Côte de Nuits and the Côte de Beaune. Its northern division, the Côte de Nuits, runs southward from the edge of Dijon to a few miles north of Beaune. The Côte de Beaune continues from that point all the way south to Santenay. The Côte de Nuits is famous for its red wines and the Côte de Beaune for its whites, but the southern division also produces some lovely reds, as you will soon see.

Within these two big divisions exists a series of small townships, some of which are used as official AOC designations and therefore pretty carefully regulated, and some of which are not. In addition, wines may bear the name of individual estates or vineyards, some of which may be shared by several owners, any or all of whom may bottle their wine separately. And to top that, there is a classification of cru in which *premier cru* ("first growth") is actually the second rank and *grand cru* ("great growth") is the first. So the label situation for the consumer is very confusing until you learn exactly what to look for.

Where the AOC is attached is one of the crucial items to keep your eye on: in order of refinement, a wine can be AOC Bourgogne (Burgundy), or AOC village name, or AOC vineyard name. The last category, AOC vineyard name, applies only to *grands crus*, which are the only wines so labeled. So great is their prestige, in fact, that in many cases the villages which contain these *grands crus* have added the wines' names to their own. For instance, the *grand cru* is Le Corton; the village was Aloxe, but on wine labels you will now see Aloxe-Corton—and you will pay for the extra two syllables.

That's enough prologue. If you're not already completely confused and discouraged (it's really not as puzzling as it looks at first), get ready to discriminate between the wine of one of the least-known villages of the Côte de Nuits, Morey St-Denis, and what is probably the best-known red wine of the Côte de Beaune, Pommard. Okay, let's do it. See, swirl, smell, sip, savor. Expectorate and expatiate.

## Appearance.

Both wines are ruby, showing some tawny highlights. If you tilt the wine in the glass you should see in both a faint purple edge, very thin—this will fade with a little more age—succeeded by a narrow band of brownish amber, which is exactly what you ought to see in good young Burgundies like these.

### Aroma.

Neither wine seems yet to have developed a very big aroma, though there is every possibility that it will come for both with time in the bottle.

The scent of the Morey St-Denis will strike most people first with its alcohol and acid—a little peppery prickle in the nose, a sense of warmth—and then with its fruit and some odors related to its vinification. You can pick out herbal scents and fresh wood as well as good, clean earth odors, with a pleasing, generalized fruitiness under everything. Even though this is not a large or particularly strong bouquet, it conveys the impression of a heavier, sturdier wine than its appearance suggests. Most tasters find little to dislike here: even if they are not partisans of Burgundy, they rarely say anything more negative than "it smells too acidic."

Responses to the aroma of the Pommard are likely to be more varied. Some will find it fuller, others thinner, than that of the Morey St-Denis. Most will find it both slightly smaller and slightly more complex, with its fruit elements discernible as fresh, cool, bright, perhaps even apple-y, and backed up by suggestions of mint and flowers. There are some undertones of earth and stems, perhaps even a hint of truffle, all very slight though: the overall impression is smoothness, restraint, a sort of cool, woodsy, moss-on-stones scent. Again, few people find anything to dislike here: at worst, they find it too faint, too insubstantial.

### Taste.

There will no doubt be more diversity of opinion about the actual taste of these wines than about their aromas. Some tasters tend to be thrown off by the acid of the Morey St-Denis and consequently perceive it as a lighter and less substantial wine than it is. This may also be due to the fact that it does seem to need a bit more tannin to structure it. It's very important with this wine to taste it carefully all over your mouth to sort out these niceties of balance, because they can tell you a lot about the possible longevity or long-term pleasure potential of the wine.

In any event, most tasters will probably respond very favorably to the fruit of the Morey: it's soft, with definite berry and currant flavors in it, and completely dry. Some will taste a flavor hard to describe but most like the wininess of a good Winesap apple: whatever you call it, it is a positive attraction of this wine's taste. Overall, the Morey strikes most tasters as round, soft, with good acid, and a nice astringent finish.

Most tasters will also respond very favorably to the Pommard: if there are reservations or negatives, they will probably center on the wine's tannin, which for some palates will mask or at least partially obscure the wine's other components. But tannin to the degree this Pommard has it is only to be expected in a young Burgundy, and it in fact bodes well for the wine's future.

Those not bothered by the tannin will find the Pommard smooth and weighty on the tongue, clean and full, as if it were delivering simply more of whatever it has than did the Morey. It shows a remarkable balance for so young a wine, and its various components—acid, fruit, tannin, alcohol—and flavor elements are already so intertwined that it is very difficult for most people to separate them even verbally. The impression the wine creates in the mouth is at once more uniform and more complicated than that of the Morey, a kind of robustness wrapped up with elegance. Most tasters discern a rather nice finish as well.

Looked at from the point of view of an ideal red Burgundy, or at least my ideal red Burgundy, the worst thing I can find to say about these wines is that they are about twenty years too young. I'd love to open a bottle of each on New Year's Eve, 2000, and see how they've grown up. Both are very forward for Burgundies, but of course more and more of them are now being vinified precisely for that, to become drinkable sooner. Whether or not that affects their ability to age remains an open question—another reason I'm curious to try one of these again at the turn of the century.

By the way, and just for the record: the relatively greater body and robustness of the Pommard upsets completely one piece of conventional wine wisdom, that the reds of the Côte de Nuits are bigger and gutsier than those of the Côte de Beaune. So much for wine wisdom.

A final word about these wines: If you are going to begin seriously exploring Burgundies, try to find yourself a really knowledgeable wine dealer to help you out. Everybody needs guidance with these wines, especially because of their cost. My general advice is:

Until you know your way around, stick with wines from reputable shippers—Prosper Maufoux, Bouchard Père et Fils, Louis Latour, Drouhin, Jadot, Bouchard Aîné, Faiveley, etc. And good luck.

Domaine Dujac and Olivier Leflaive are among the most respected of Burgundy's middle-sized *négociants*. Both their wines are imported by Frederick Wildman.

## Substitutes:

Younger vintages of the two named wines are the preferred substitutes. If they are not available, look for a Morey St-Denis from other traditional Burgundian *négociants*, such as Bouchard Père et Fils or Jadot, or from some of the smaller importers such as Robert Haas or Chadderdon, and Pommard from similar *négociants* or from worthy but not preposterously expensive growers such as the Prince de Merode (for example, Merode's Pommard Clos de la Platiere).

This is the conclusion of the Thirteenth Flight. There are several ways for you to proceed from here.

*Following the lead of your own preferences:*
    If you liked either the first wine, the Morey St-Denis, or the second wine, the Pommard, go on to the Eighteenth Flight.

*Following the kind of grapes:*
    These are the last Pinot Noirs in the tastings.

*Following the wines of the country:*
    Go on to the Fifteenth Flight.

# THE FOURTEENTH FLIGHT

❧

*Barbi Rosso di Montalcino 1989*
*and*
*Badia a Coltibuono*
*Chianti Classico Riserva 1986*

❧

IF YOU CAN MANAGE to pull the corks of these wines thirty minutes to an hour before your tasting, do so: the reasons will be given below.

In this flight you are tasting wines made from different clones of the Sangiovese grape, one of Italy's two or three most important red wine varieties. Both clones are cultivated in Tuscany, but in different geographical areas. Although not far apart as the crow flies, these districts are quite distinct from each other, since the topography of Tuscany is so broken that every kilometer north or south, east or west, up- or downhill can mean a new soil composition and a separate microclimate. Add to that the variations in vinification sanctioned by Tuscan tradition and you wind up with a major viticultural region where even neighboring wineries can turn out radically differing wines.

You may be surprised to find a Chianti among the full-bodied wines. The common stereotype of Chianti as a light-bodied spaghetti red in a wicker-covered flask has been outdated for some time now, but this is one of those classic cases where perception lags behind reality—which, by the way, creates some nice bargains for you, you canny fox, since it has caused the prices of many less well-known Chiantis to trail well behind their real worth.

119

The basic grape in all Chiantis (yes, Virginia, there is more than one kind of Chianti) is the Sangiovese: it comprises 60 percent and upward of any wine bearing the Chianti name. The remaining 40 percent (often much less) is made up of another red grape, the Canaiolo, and, in the traditional formula, two white grapes, Trebbiano and Malvasia. In Chianti destined to be aged for *riserva*, these last two grapes figure less and less importantly.

Chianti is labeled for the zone in which it is grown as well as for the aging it receives. The zones are Colli Aretini (the hills near Arezzo), Colli Fiorentini (the hills north of Florence), Colline Pisane (the hills around Pisa), Colli Senesi (the hills south of Siena), Montalbano (northeast Tuscany), Rufina (farther east), and Classico (the traditional heart of Chianti, lying between Florence and Siena). The age designations are *vecchia* and *riserva*, indicating two and three years of barrel- and bottle-aging. Wines from any zone may be made into *riserva*, but it is most commonly and most successfully done in the Classico and the Rufina.

A Chianti becomes a *riserva* by receiving its education in wood: it must be aged in barrel and in bottle for three years before it can be labeled *riserva*. That is the legal requirement, but most Chianti makers (at least most of those whose wines you will find on sale in America) previously exercise a rigorous selection process, starting with the grapes at harvest time, to set aside only the very best of their wines for *riserva*. So for all practical purposes, the *riserva* designation indicates not only barrel-aging but quality control as well.

It also indicates an important difference in the handling of the young wine. Chiantis intended to be drunk young—non-*riserva* Chianti—are often treated with the *governo Toscano*, the introduction to already fermented wine of new musts from reserved, partially raisined grapes. This brings on a second fermentation, which raises the alcohol level, deepens color, intensifies fruit, and sometimes leaves the wine lightly fizzy—what Italians call *frizzante*. It may also leave the wine somewhat unstable, with too much volatile acidity, and therefore unsuitable for any lengthy keeping. But it makes, par excellence, a fresh, fruity wine for immediate drinking, which is the appropriate fate of most simple Chianti. Chianti earmarked for *riserva* status never undergoes the *governo Toscano* but is instead vinified and aged in the conventional manner of all fine wines.

Badia a Coltibuono is an old wine estate (actually an ancient abbey: *badia* = *abbazzia*) near the southern end of the Chianti Classico zone. They make several different Chianti Classico and Classico *riserva* as well as a much-appreciated 100 percent Sangiovese wine they call Sangioveto. All their wines are noted for the ability to age well. They are imported to the United States by William Grant & Company.

Vintners in the area around the hill town of Montalcino, south of the Chianti Classico district, cultivate a special clone of the Sangiovese, known as the Sangiovese Grosso or the Brunello. In this very restricted zone, and under very rigorously controlled conditions of viticulture and vinification, these grapes, unblended, yield what is perhaps Italy's finest and certainly its most expensive wine, Brunello di Montalcino. It is also one of Italy's newer wines, with a history of little more than a hundred years (as opposed, for instance, to Chianti's documented 600 plus). Great as Brunello can be, it is often ungiving in its youth and may take years to develop. Rosso di Montalcino, a wine made from younger vines in the same zone and aged less than Brunello, offers a glimpse at the quality and character of this Tuscan giant, at a fraction of its cost.

The Barbi firm, one of the most important producers in the Montalcino area, makes both Rosso di Montalcino and a highly esteemed Brunello, as well as a special proprietary wine called Brusco dei Barbi, made with the Brunello grape but vinified like a non-*riserva* Chianti, and designed to be drunk young and fresh.

So you are now about to taste the Sangiovese in its two forms and treated by two different methods. Be prepared to pay attention both to similarities and to differences: what you taste in these two wines can be a complete capsule education in the variables of wine-making.

All right, swirl away, and read on when you're ready.


## Appearance.

Both wines are a deep ruby, with the older Chianti Classico *riserva* showing tawny or amber highlights. The latter, in Italian wines, do not necessarily indicate complete maturity, though they do show a wine that is, as this one ought to be, past its first youth. Generally speaking, fine Italian red wines show more amber/orangey highlighting at every stage of their development than do French or California wines of comparable age and quality.

Aroma.

Depending on how long these wines have been uncorked, their
aromas will be more or less pronounced. Not, as you might expect,
that they will dissipate after uncorking, but rather that their aromas
will grow over a substantial period of time. Both of these wines—
and this is true of fine Italian wines generally—benefit greatly from
being allowed to breathe for about an hour before they are served. If
you have just a few minutes ago uncorked them, arrange to leave
them on the table for a while if you can: they will change and open
even in the glass. Or decant them to provide a little instant aeration.
Alternatively, leave a little wine in your glasses, taste it again in half
an hour, and match the notes you take then with those you've
already taken. I can promise you the differences will be very instructive: the wine really improves—literally seems to open up—
with breathing.

Back to work. To most tasters, the Badia Chianti smells vinous in
the best sense of the word: a satisfying, winey aroma in which you
can identify an alcohol warmth and fruit-sweet scents, with other
smaller elements occasionally surfacing (a little salt-air tang, a bit of
grass, perhaps a hint of vanilla). Most people agree that the Rosso di
Montalcino has a slightly more abundant and more immediately
evident aroma, but it is also simpler, lighter, more acid, seemingly
dominated mostly by a soft fruit scent (berries perhaps?) and an
alcoholic tingle, with earthy undertones and some fresh-sawed-
wood notes. Those who don't like this sort of wine are likely to find
either or both aromas too alcoholic on one hand or too insubstantial
on the other, but most tasters seem to find them quite pleasing.


Taste.

The first impression the Badia Chianti creates on most people's
palates is a combined sensation of roundness, warmth, and fruit-
and-tannin together. Even if you find the tannin initially a little too
strong and perhaps masking the fruit (the tannin will soften in the
glass and the fruit will come forward in a short while), you should
nevertheless be able to discern this ensemble of characteristics,
because the wine presents itself complexly from the outset.

If you are really having trouble picking out the fruit, put a little
wine "in the hole" behind your front teeth and under your tongue as
I told you about earlier. After a few seconds, the tip of your tongue

ought to be able to pick up a distinct sweetish, grapey flavor there. The feel of the wine in your mouth is smooth and slightly chewy. To many tasters it gives the impression of a substantial presence, even though in fact this particular vintage strikes me at least as inclining more toward what I would describe as medium body rather than full. It also has a very attractive bitterness to it that is particularly discernible in its long, dry finish. Overall, the impression it leaves you with is a compound of complexity (from the various elements of flavor) and elegance (primarily from what you feel in the texture and finish of the wine). I piously trust that by this stage of the game you can easily see just how far this is from what you used to think Chianti was.

The Barbi Rosso di Montalcino usually sets tasters up to sense that complexity in the Chianti by being in itself a more direct and straightforward sort of wine. It strikes most tasters as fuller and less subtle—the latter quality a result of its youth, the former the gift of the Brunello grape. The Barbi Rosso's most prominent feature, in fact the feature that in most tasters' opinions really dominates the wine, is very soft, sweet fruit—nut-sweet—with a small underlying tannic bitterness: pure Sangiovese flavor. This wine may seem to some tasters bigger than the Chianti, fruitier and more full-bodied, but it may also strike some as less balanced. While some tasters may find this Rosso di Montalcino too big and alcoholic for their pleasure, most will enjoy the pronounced character of its soft fruit and will drink it happily with the simple foods for which it cries.

It is a fact of life that almost any wine will bloom when you match it with the right food, but one of the great advantages of many Italian wines is that they partner so well with such a diverse range of foods, often in the process revealing flavors and nuances hidden before. This is particularly true of Sangiovese-based wines like these. Rosso di Montalcino responds very well to simpler foods like plainly broiled chops, omelettes, cheeses, charcuterie. The Badia di Coltibuono Chianti Classico *riserva* and other wines of its kind—particularly older specimens—marry quite well with roast meats or elaborately sauced meats and fowl or excellent cheeses. Really fine vintages would accompany game wonderfully.

If this range of wines pleases you, there are many more examples of it to try. Look into the Chianti Classico *riserva* from houses like Ruffino, Brolio, Frescobaldi, Fossi, and Antinori, as well as smaller estates like Castellare, Monsanto, Monte Vertine, Villa Cerna, and Spalletti. And don't forget Chianti's kissing cousin, Vino Nobile di

Montepulciano, a very elegant wine in the same style as the Chianti Classico *riserva* you've just liked.

If on the other hand you prefer what you tasted in the Barbi Rosso di Montalcino, then try some of the other Montalcino wines, starting with other Rossos and working your way palatally and fiscally up to the esteemed and expensive Brunellos. Altesino, Banfi's Poggio all'Oro estate, Caparzo, Castelgiocondo, Col d'Orcia, Costanti, Il Poggione, and last but not least, the inventor of Brunello, Biondi-Santi, all make fine specimens. Be warned, however: a real Brunello can be very, very hard in its youth, and it can take a long time to come around. A decent vintage will normally not be drinkable until it is at least ten years old, and as a class these wines are famous for their longevity. They are supreme examples of wines worth buying young—and relatively inexpensively—and laying down for the days of their fabulous maturity. Chianti Classico *riserva* also rewards such treatment, though to a lesser degree than Brunello.

## Substitutes:

As always, the best substitute is a younger vintage of the wines named here. Otherwise, Chianti Classico *riserva* and Rosso di Montalcino from any of the estates named above will serve, though Antinori's or Castellare's or Monsanto's Chianti Classico *riserva* and Banfi's or Altesino's Rosso would be optimal.

Here ends the fourteenth tasting session. There are several ways for you to proceed from here.

*Following the lead of your own preferences:*
If you liked the first wine better, the Rosso di Montalcino, go on to the Sixteenth Flight or the Seventeenth Flight.
If you liked the second wine better, the Chianti Classico Riserva, go on to the Fifteenth Flight.

*Following the kind of grapes:*
These are the last Sangiovese wines in our tastings (earlier example in the Fourth Flight).

*Following the wines of the country:*
Go on to the Eighteenth Flight.

# THE FIFTEENTH FLIGHT

❧

## *Château Les Ormes de Pez 1988 (St-Estèphe) and Château Smith Haut Lafitte 1988 (Graves)*

❧

Y OU ARE ABOUT TO EMBARK on what might for some of you turn out to be a lifelong journey of exploration amongst the thickets, forests, and peaks of Cabernet Sauvignon. Cabernet is probably right now *the* international glamour varietal, but don't hold that against it. Despite all of its current swank, it makes great wine, and it does so in a wide variety of soils and climates. For centuries it has been the basic constituent of claret, a lovely red wine in which, according to Bordelais tradition, it blends with varying amounts of Merlot and/or Cabernet Franc. Now it also makes fine straight varietal wine (i.e., 100 percent Cabernet) in California and Long Island and South America and Australia and is beginning to respond well in experimental plantings in Italy and Spain.

Cabernet possesses one of the most readily identifiable aromas and flavors of any great varietal grape. Once you have tasted a few good specimens, you should be able to recognize its characteristics even when you come across them diluted or subdued. So here is your chance to add an important volume to your palatal library. This flight matches two clarets from different communes of Bordeaux,

125

### Clearing Up Claret

Claret is the traditional—though completely unofficial—name for the fine red wines of Bordeaux and especially, if not exclusively, those of the region called the Médoc, along the Gironde north of the city of Bordeaux. The Médoc is divided into communes: Margaux, St-Julien, Pauillac, and St-Estèphe. Although Graves and Sauternes lie south of the city of Bordeaux and are not part of the Médoc, their wines are of as high a quality and they are often placed in the same category with them.

The wines from all these communes have long been prized by connoisseurs. Their most prestigious productions are always the wines of single estates or châteaux. In 1855 the various châteaux were ranked into five growths, or crus. This ranking, although in many particulars now inaccurate, still greatly influences the prestige and prices of Bordeaux wines. The most famous—and expensive—of Bordeaux's wines are the handful of *premiers crus*: Château Lafite, Château Latour, Château Mouton Rothschild, Château Margaux, and Château Haut Brion.

and the next will expose you to two different styles and regions of California Cabernet. Cabernet is, by general consent, the most important and perhaps the most rewarding red grape variety in the world, so taste very, very carefully.

Ready? Okay: see, swirl, smell, sip, etc.

### Appearance.

The Château Les Ormes de Pez shows the classic color of a young claret: claret-colored, in fact. It is, simply, a clear, pretty garnet. The Smith Haut Lafitte is slightly lighter, what I would call dark ruby, with a few amber lights. Generally in clarets this is regarded as a color typical of a more mature wine, though the wines of the Graves do show it earlier than the wines of the other communes. Clarets are generally regarded as real *vins de garde*, that is to say perfect wines for cellaring until they mature fully, whenever that may be; this vintage is thought to be better than average for that purpose, so both of these wines can be expected in their maturity to show a pronounced amber rim.

### Aroma.

You will probably find that the Château Les Ormes de Pez seems to have a distinctly big, two-stage aroma. The first thing that strikes most tasters is a composite of wood and fruit and growing things. You can get quite a range of descriptions for this—grassy, sunny, a warm orchard scent, flowers—but generally speaking, we can call it pleasing growing things. The Les Ormes de Pez's big, tannic, alcoholic aroma opens further in the glass—some will say deepens or intensifies—to climax in a scent of cedar that many connoisseurs regard as a hallmark of Cabernet Sauvignon.

Most tasters will describe the Smith Haut Lafitte as smelling very much like the Les Ormes de Pez, but smaller, less emphatic, less alcoholic. Tannin is a bit more prominent in its odor, and the cedar comes out sooner, accompanied by a pepper and spice aroma that many experts also consider characteristic of Cabernet. Both wines are giving a pretty good show of the range of typical Cabernet Sauvignon scents.

### Taste.

On the palate, the Les Ormes de Pez usually makes a very clear impression, first and foremost, of fruit—fine, sweet, intense fruit—followed by wood. The fruit is berrylike and only suggests sweetness, because it is in actuality fully dry. The wood flavors have a definite tang that suggests fresh oak to most people. Most tasters are also aware of a lot of tannin—you can feel it especially on your cheeks—but it by no means fully masks the fruit. The sensations on the tongue are likely to be of weight and richness: this is a complex wine, not yet full-bodied wine but clearly growing toward it. It ends with a long, elegant finish in which some people will perceive the flavor of currants, yet another hallmark (so expert opinion has it) of the Cabernet grape.

The flavor of the Smith Haut Lafitte, most people will find, parallels the Les Ormes de Pez's in many respects. These similarities are where you should look to learn the essential nature of red Bordeaux: the quality of freshness of the fruit and its special accents, the particular interplay of tannin and acid and alcohol with that fruit, and the wood or oak elements overlaid on it. Those are really the keys to understanding and appreciating any claret, and these two wines are doing a lovely job of laying them out before you.

Most tasters will locate the differences between the Smith Haut Lafitte and the Les Ormes de Pez primarily in two areas: body, and the relation of tannin and fruit. Most people find the Graves the less full, slightly thinner yet more elegant wine of the two, and they will describe its fruit as softer, less intense (some will say less sweet), with the taste of tannin more prominent, for a few tasters even muffling the fruit a little. Most of the flavors that we spoke of in the Les Ormes de Pez can also be found in this Graves, but a bit more muted. There are also in here hints of licorice or tobacco, and some people describe this wine as more vinous and more mellow than the St-Estèphe. It also has a long finish, pleasing and astringent.

These are both lovely wines, and most of the differences between them are attributable to the geology and the geography of their respective communes. That slightly licorice suggestion and the vinosity of the Smith Haut Lafitte seem to me definitely characteristic of the red wines of the Graves, while the whole attack of the Les Ormes de Pez, its opulence of bouquet and flavor and abundance of tannin and fruit, seems to me representative of the best qualities of the wines of St-Estèphe. (That, by the way, is a distinction many wine professionals might argue with.) Both wines share a particular kind of elegance that serves to distinguish them from the style of California Cabernet, which you will be tasting in the next flight.

Although Château Les Ormes de Pez is not a classified growth, most connoisseurs rate it in that league. Château Smith Haut Lafitte is a well-esteemed classified growth, the property of the Eschenauer firm.

**Substitutes:**

If you can't get younger vintages of these wines, try other small châteaux in their communes: for Les Ormes de Pez, substitute Calon Segur, or Lafon-Rochet, or de Pez; for Smith Haut Lafitte, try Carbonnieux, or Haut Bailly, or Malartic Lagravière, or Olivier.

This is the conclusion of the fifteenth tasting session. There are a few ways for you to proceed from here.

*Following the lead of your own preferences:*
    If you enjoyed either the first wine, Château Les Ormes de Pez,
    or the second wine, Château Smith Haut Lafitte, go on to the
    Sixteenth Flight.

*Following the kind of grapes:*
    Go on to the Sixteenth Flight.

*Following the wines of the country:*
    Go on to the Nineteenth Flight.

# THE SIXTEENTH FLIGHT

~~✦~~

## Martini Napa Valley
## Reserve Cabernet Sauvignon 1987
## and
## Ridge York Creek
## Cabernet Sauvignon 1986

~~✦~~

WHAT YOU ARE CONFRONTING in this round should be two excellent examples of the California approach to Cabernet Sauvignon. Both are from prime Cabernet country in the Napa Valley, which has effectively set the pace for Cabernet cultivation and vinification in California. The Martini winery began turning out stylish Cabernet long before California Cabernet became stylish, and the family-owned firm—now in its third generation—shows no sign of stopping. Ridge and its winemaker Paul Draper, although they have tamed their wines considerably from the exuberance of some of their first bottlings, are still producing what many think of as classic California style in Cabernet—big, robust, and muscular wines.

Once more you will be tasting for a number of things: the similarities and differences in the styles of the wines as well as for yet more information about the essence of Cabernet Sauvignon. In the previous pair of wines, if you paid close attention, you should have really been able to taste the character of French Cabernet. Here, if you work just as hard and enjoy just as thoroughly, you should really be able to pick out the character of California Cabernet.

Okay, enough prologue: hop to it. Seeswirlsmellsipsavorspit!

## Appearance.

We have clearly distinguishable differences in color here. These are among the darkest wines, and the densest in appearance, that we have dealt with. The Martini is the lighter of the two, a very deep ruby to the Ridge's emphatic garnet. If you tilt your glass to about a 45-degree angle and hold it against a white background, you should be able to see very clearly that both wines still show the purple rim that indicates their youth. Both probably still have a lot of maturing to do.

## Aroma.

Both these wines have big aromas, though the Ridge seems much more assertive. Almost every taster is struck by the Martini's young, powerful fruit, a deeply grapey smell carried by alcohol and tannin. Some people may describe the latter as a slight oakiness or perceive it as an astringent quality in the aroma. Behind that initial fruit wallop comes what are usually sensed as a battery of peppery, herbaceous odors. Descriptions of these can vary considerably, but most experts consider scents in this range typical of California Cabernet.

A few people respond to the tannin in the Ridge Cabernet's aroma before anything else, and indeed can sometimes find that almost everything is masked for them by the tannin. Most, however, find that the Ridge's aroma literally jumps out of the glass at them, and if they find themselves overwhelmed it is by fruit and flowers. Some even identify the specific scent of raspberries here. Most will describe the aroma as heady because of its high alcohol. And most will discern grassy, tannic elements as well as herbal notes, with pronounced smells of pepper and cedar following after (cedar too is thought of as typical for the aroma of California Cabernet).

## Taste.

For most people, the Martini presents three successive waves of flavor. The first impression it makes is of a soft fruitiness, which some describe as grapey and others berrylike. The second occurs when the tannin and acids bite in, creating for some people an unpleasing sort of scrubbing sensation on the tongue; most perceive it as a dry, austere, tannic follow-through from the initial flavor. The third stage is the wine's true finish, a strong, lingering aftertaste that mixes fruit and tannin in about equal quantities, though different palates will probably perceive it as inclining to one side or the other. Overall, the wine presents a package of flavors utterly representative of Napa Cabernet: cherry, bell peppers, and herbs, with earth and tea in the finish.

With the Ridge Cabernet, a few people again are going to be overwhelmed by the tannin and simply not taste anything else: they'll have to wait until the wine is a few years older before they are able to appreciate this or any other Californians in this style. Most tasters are going to be surprised, however, by how much of the fruit they can actually enjoy despite all the tannin they discerned in the aroma. The tannin is still there—many will taste it right behind the fruit—but the fruit itself is very forward, soft, and deep. Some even taste in it a specifically flowery quality, almost a delicate honey taste. Behind or underneath all these overt sensations lurk what are sensed at this stage as more than suggestions but less than full-fledged presences: pepper and licorice and other deep tones are among the possibilities that you may taste. Most people find the wine has an exceptionally big, dry finish.

These two provide marvelous illustrations of the California way with Cabernet. If you are able to taste them right along with or immediately after the two Bordeaux, you will see that by comparison the Martini looks big and very, very fruity and the Ridge looks simply massive. By the same token, the two clarets taste incredibly elegant and polished alongside the muscular and bumptious Californians. By themselves, the Ridge seems the bigger, more robust wine, the Martini the more polished. If you want to make analogies with Bordeaux wines, the Martini Cabernet is molded in the suave style of Margaux and the Ridge in the powerhouse style of Pauillac (try that comparison with some wine snobs and see how your stock rises). Both seem to have a long and quite interesting bottle life in front of them: you can look forward to their tannins mellowing and their fruit maturing and a lot of those just-perceptible undertones emerging into prominence. These too would not be a bad pair of wines to sample again on New Year 2000, if you can manage to keep yourself from drinking them for that long. In fact, these two will be very interesting to try again in just a few years—and surely you can restrain your impatience that long?

If you have enjoyed either or both of these wines, you've really got the whole state of California and its now over five hundred (I think) wineries before you, since most of them make a Cabernet and many of them make several (labeled for different locations, usually). Best bets? Try some of the more highly reputed ones, like Mondavi, or Heitz, Beaulieu, Stag's Leap, Burgess, Conn Creek, Château Montelena . . . the list could go on and on. And don't forget some of the bigger makers, like Almadén and Gallo, who can produce a surprisingly good Cabernet at a surprisingly reasonable price. Happy hunting.

## Substitutes:

As you well know by now, the best substitutes for these two wines will always be their younger vintages. Failing that, try Beaulieu Vineyard's Georges de Latour Private Reserve Napa Valley Cabernet Sauvignon or Clos du Val's Napa Valley Stags Leap District Cabernet as alternatives to the Martini, and Cabernets from Château Montelena, Conn Creek, Gundlach-Bundschu, or Trefethen as alternatives for the Ridge York Creek.

This is the conclusion of the sixteenth tasting session. Paths are beginning to converge.

*Following the lead of your own preferences:*
  If you liked either the first wine, the Martini Cabernet, or the
  second wine, the Ridge Cabernet, go on to the Seventeenth
  Flight or back to the Sixth, Tenth, Eleventh, Fourteenth, and
  Fifteenth if you have missed any of those.

*Following the kind of grapes:*
  These are the last Cabernet Sauvignon wines in the tasting.
  Earlier Cabernet flights are the Sixth and the Fifteenth.

*Following the wines of the country:*
  Go on to the Seventeenth Flight.

# THE SEVENTEENTH FLIGHT

~~~∘⌒∘~~~

## Clos du Val Napa Valley Stags Leap District Zinfandel 1988 and Sutter Home Amador County Reserve Zinfandel 1988

~~~∘⌒∘~~~

IF THERE IS ANY SUCH THING as California's very own grape, the Zinfandel is it. Like the Etruscans and the hula hoop, its origins are shrouded in mystery. The latest theory has it that it is a clone of the Italian Primativo, a robust and early-ripening vine from Puglia that was brought to California in the nineteenth century by the near-legendary Agoston Haraszthy, who is blamed or credited for almost everything in California viticulture. Dissidents from this theory claim to be able to prove that Zinfandel was already being cultivated on Long Island in the eighteenth century.

Whatever its secret origin may be, Zinfandel in California is Supervine, producing three distinct types of wine. The best known is the style you've already tasted (in the Third Flight), a fresh, relatively light, and definitely fruity wine. This is usually loosely referred to as a Beaujolais-style Zinfandel.

At the other extreme, Zinfandel yields an enormous wine of 15 or 16 and occasionally more degrees of alcohol and some residual sweetness. This is the late-harvest style, vinified from extremely ripe grapes that have produced very high concentrations of sugar. In the fermentation of such a wine, the yeasts that convert sugar into alcohol are themselves often killed by the concentrations of alcohol they have made before they completely convert all the sugar. It's a thankless job, being a yeast. But what their heroic little deaths produce, in this case, is a powerhouse wine that blows away the competition at juried tastings. Unfortunately, it's also a useless wine if you normally take your wine with food, because its sweetness and alcohol won't let you taste anything else. You have to treat a late-harvest Zinfandel as if it were a port or a similar fortified dessert wine.

Between these two extremes, Zinfandel also produces a more claret-like wine that preserves some of the live fruit of the Beaujolais style and borrows some of the body and authority of the late-harvest style. For many wine drinkers this is the most interesting and rewarding of Zinfandel's incarnations. There is no absolute orthodoxy about this kind of Zinfandel, so you get different emphases from different growers, ranging from a stress on freshness and vitality to a concentration on strength and power to an accent on elegance and breeding. And there is certainly no unanimity about how those stylistic goals are to be achieved: different makers will produce wines of anything from 100 percent Zinfandel to blends of (the legally required 75 percent) Zinfandel and one, two, or three other grape varieties, which may include Cabernet Sauvignon, Cabernet Franc, Merlot, Petite Sirah, Pinot Noir, Syrah, or Carignane, depending on the maker's preference and/or field mix. This variety is in fact one of Zinfandel's attractions, and while most of the world's attention has been diverted by white Zinfandel, a usually sweet party wine of little interest but large sales, California winemakers have been quietly sharpening their skills and producing claret-style Zinfandels of great polish and depth. Within this style, all the variations show some aging potential and a real capacity to accompany the kind of meal that Doctor Johnson thought you could ask a man to. The wines you have in front of you are examples of this kind of Zinfandel.

Okay, perform your ritual. Sniff as you have never sniffed before, because there should be more than ever for you to recognize here. And remember to taste the wine both with and without a bite of cheese or some such, to see how food does or doesn't change it. Then talk the wines over among yourselves and read on.

Appearance.

Both the Clos du Val Napa Zinfandel and the Sutter Home Amador Zin are dark ruby in color, bordering on garnet, translucent and brilliant. You can get marked color variation in this kind of Zinfandel, however, both because of stylistic differences and because of age. Younger Zinfandels usually show a very dark ruby or garnet, almost opaque, heavy looking, with some very youthful purple highlights: the wine can on occasion look almost murky. Older Zins will lighten somewhat in color and begin to show amber highlights.

Aroma.

Here there are readily observable differences between these two wines. Almost every taster will describe both aromas as strong, distinctive, and marked by fruit scents, but after that, consensus ends.

Most people like the scent of the Clos du Val, though they also frequently describe it as complex and difficult to pin down. They often say it has a fresh quality, but not like the fresh fruit of a Beaujolais-style Zinfandel—more balanced than that, and containing lots of individual odors simultaneously, and overall marked by a blackberry-bramble aroma that is supposedly definitive of Zinfandel. The specific things that tasters most often name are plums and alcohol and tannin and pepper—black pepper, not green bell peppers—followed for some tasters by a suggestion of tea, then a composite of rich scents like berries and peaches and chocolate and fresh wood or cedar. That cedar scent, by the way, is one I strongly associate with maturing California wine, Cabernet as well as Zinfandel.

Just about every taster uses the word "intense" to describe the Sutter Home's aroma. To most people it smells deeply of very dry fruit: some people will even say prunes. This fruit smells different from the Clos du Val's, however. It does not seem as fresh: in fact, to some people it suggests thick, heavy, fruit jam. Most people mean by that a strong compliment to the wine, though a few find that scent simply too strong for comfort. Like the Clos du Val, this wine too has a medley of specific odors merged in its bouquet— herbaceous scents and chocolate and tobacco and a strong scent of tea, as well as a kind of forest-floor scent along with cedar. Many people find that as the wine sits a rather strong tannic odor, a blend of tobacco and strong tea, comes up.

Those who don't like this style of wine often find either the earth/tannin odor elements too strong (in which case they probably call the aroma musty) or the fruit/alcohol odor too powerful (in which case they are likely to talk about an acetone or overripe banana scent).

Neither this Clos du Val nor this Sutter Home Zinfandel is yet what you could call a fully mature wine. A more developed nose would in all likelihood show considerably less tannin than either of these wines do right now, and its fruit would be of a different quality and timbre, plummier, more rounded. By and large, however, these are very fair representatives of the aromas characteristic of this claret style of Zinfandel at this age.

Just for the record, "a developed nose" is a legitimate piece of wine jargon, no matter how grotesque the image it conjures up. Try very hard not to think of a bottle with a proboscis like an elephant's trunk, and resist wondering about the condition of its eyes and ears. "Nose" is simply a bit of professional shorthand (now there's an image) for the whole olfactory attack of a wine, aroma and bouquet altogether. "Developed" means only that the scents have evolved from a youthful condition toward what connoisseurs consider a more mature state. After you smell a few older wines, you'll as readily identify the characteristics of a mature bouquet as you now spot those telltale tawny highlights that reveal maturity in a wine's color.

## Taste.

Most people are surprised by how claretlike the Clos du Val tastes to them: they tend to use words like smooth, soft, and balanced to express the quality of restraint they sense in it. Most describe the fruit as light, fresh, and dry, and tasting of plums and berries. A very few may call the fruit bland, especially by comparison with the Sutter Home's, but most find it well in scale with the wine's unobtrusive acid, alcohol, and tannin. Many people report a lingering dry finish that they find very attractive. Some will call that finish chocolaty, while others will find it tannic. Overall, most tasters will tend to evaluate this wine as quite elegant, especially for their expectations (if they had any) of a Zinfandel.

The Sutter Home strikes most people as much more like what they anticipated in Zinfandel. Some may even say that it strikes them as tasting the way the Clos du Val smells. This 1988 vintage is possibly still a little muffled (do *not* think of little children wrapped up for winter in their down coats), but its essential elements are all in place and need only a bit more bottle-age to bring them out very clearly. The first thing almost everyone tastes in this wine is good fruit, fat and almost sweet, a full, berrylike fruit that for some people specifically recalls blackberries. This flavor is almost the hallmark of Zinfandel: it is as close as you can come to pinning down a varietal flavor in a single word. Sometimes you'll see it referred to as "brambly" or "like blackberry," but this is still the flavor that's meant. In this particular wine it arrives packaged with other flavors as well. Different tasters may name tar, chocolate, tobacco, spice (even camphor), tannin, acid, or alcohol as part or parts of what they discern in here.

Along with that batch of fine flavors, and definitely contributing to the "brambly" quality, comes a nice tannic bite on the top of the tongue and on the cheeks. The sensation may feel as if your tongue was getting a good, vigorous scratching. The wine finishes quite pleasingly, with a long, dry, fruity aftertaste.

Put side by side like this, these two wines give you what is practically a paradigm of the styles available in Zinfandel. The Sutter Home is big and not quite burly, but intense. The Clos du Val, while not Little Lord Fauntleroy by any means, is more restrained, less vivid, but more complex and more seductive. Both wines provide clear examples of the progress of California Zinfandel toward distinctiveness and distinction. Both wines have years yet to grow and round out, to judge by the quality of their fruit, the quantity of their alcohol and acid, and the vigor of their tannins. It would be very interesting and instructive—and no small bit of fun as well—to clock the development of these two baby Paul Bunyans over the next five or ten years. You could roast a lot of ducks and nibble a lot of goat cheese very happily with either of these as accompaniment.

Clos du Val is a smallish Napa Valley enterprise with a French winemaker (if you thought you spotted a Continental hand in that Zinfandel, you were right, you clever devil). Clos du Val makes Cabernet, Chardonnay, and Merlot as well as Zinfandel.

Sutter Home has grown with the white Zinfandel boom, but while the white stuff may pay the bills, the red Zins are the measure of Sutter Home's worth. It recently acquired the Montevina estates, which continue to produce fine Zinfandels under its own label.

If you enjoy the Zinfandel flavor, you've got lots of territory to explore: hardly a winemaker in California doesn't make at least one Zinfandel. Many issue several different Zins, either vinified in different styles or made from grapes grown in special locations that lend a particular character to their wine. A good many Zinfandels, especially those in the more intensely colored and flavored style, profit from five or more years of bottle-age. And of course nobody really knows just how long a well-made Zinfandel of a great year will last.

If you like the grape, you might want to think about a long-term experiment to see which expires first, you or your pet Zinfandels. After all, everybody should have a goal in life, and that one at least will keep you out of trouble. Besides, there is strong empirical evidence that people with the patience to wait for their wines to mature are not very likely, in the meanwhile, to bomb other people for disagreeing with them. Wine helps you take the long view.

**Substitutes:**

Younger vintages of these two wines, of course. Failing that, seek out a good Martini Zinfandel to stand in for the Clos du Val, and any of Ridge's Zins to fill in for the Sutter Home.

This concludes the Seventeenth Flight. There are only a few ways for you to proceed from here.

*Following the lead of your own preferences:*
  If you enjoyed either the first wine, the Clos du Val Zinfandel, or the second wine, the Sutter Home Zinfandel, go on to the Eighteenth Flight.

*Following the kind of grapes:*
  This is the last Zinfandel tasting. There was an earlier Zinfandel in the Third Flight.

*Following the wines of the country:*
  This is the last flight of California wines. Go back to any of these flights you may have missed: First, Third, Fifth, Sixth, Seventh, Tenth, Eleventh, Twelfth, or Sixteenth.

# THE EIGHTEENTH FLIGHT

∼୬ᧇ∼

## Vietti Barbaresco Masseria 1986
## and
## Ceretto Barolo Brunate
## Bricco Rocche 1986

∼ᧇᧇ∼

THIS PAIR OF WINES will dramatically show the importance of allowing Italian wines to breathe. You should draw their corks at least a half hour before you plan to use them: a full hour would be better. You can also always decant them if you prefer. Even with that breathing time, they will continue to change and open in your glasses. They can progress from an initial condition that is almost mute to the olfactory equivalent of eloquence.

Among Italy's winegrowing provinces—and that means all of them—Piedmont is perhaps the most esteemed for the quality of its red wines. Like its great rival Tuscany, Piedmont builds its finest reds around a single noble grape variety. In this case it is the Nebbiolo grape, which in the Piedmont produces three related but different wines: Nebbiolo, Barbaresco, and Barolo. They are all 100 percent Nebbiolo wines—that is, unblended varietal wines—and all made in a series of interlocking DOC zones in the southern Piedmont around the town of Alba.

The major differences among them arise from the soils in which and the altitudes at which they are cultivated and from the amount of barrel-aging they receive before bottling. Wines labeled Nebbiolo are generally grown on lower and less desirable fields than either Barbaresco or Barolo and receive the least barrel-age of all three wines. Barbaresco is grown on soils similar to and at the same altitude as Barolo, but it receives a year less of barrel-aging.

Nebbiolo is invariably the lightest wine of the three, but this doesn't mean it's a weakling: not by a long shot. Most Nebbiolo should be drunk within five or six years of harvest, but some very fine vintages produce a wine that stays live and muscular for up to ten years. With Barbaresco and Barolo, your normal expectation should be to only start drinking them about ten years from harvest. It used to be impossible to do so: except in very light vintages, old-style vinification left these two wines hard and tannic for a few years after bottling, and they normally only started rounding out to show their true character at about six years of age. Modern vinification techniques have made Barolo and Barbaresco drinkable younger than ever: some can be enjoyed even within months of bottling— but unless fruit is all you prize in a wine, there's little reason to broach them before their time. A first-class Barbaresco or Barolo from a first-class vintage is capable of developing in the bottle for ten to fifteen years and then remaining healthy and enjoyable for another ten or fifteen years.

In the Piedmont they distinguish between these two wines in terms of classic sexual stereotypes: Barolo is big, assertive, robust, masculine, while Barbaresco is soft, more elegant, more polished, feminine. Fortunately or unfortunately, the stereotypes are as inaccurate about the wines as they are about people, and in some vintages not even the winemakers can distinguish between the two, so if you were starting to think of them as brother and sister wines you're going to have to accept them as occasional transsexuals as well.

Both of these very big, austere red wines are appropriate accompaniments to the most important dinners, particularly to what are called in Italy *carni nobili* (the great roasts and furred game).

Okay, get to it—sniff, savor, etc.—and file your report. Then read on.

## Appearance.

Once again, an easy question to answer. Both these wines are the classic garnet with amber highlights that is almost the hallmark of a maturing Nebbiolo-based wine.

## What's Up, Doc?

Italy's DOC (*Denominazione d'Origine Controllata*) laws correspond roughly to France's AOC laws—they control labeling, geographic designations, grape varieties, and other related matters. Italy has also introduced a new category, DOCG, which so far has been granted to only a few wines (among them Brunello, Vino Nobile di Montepulciano, Barbaresco, Barolo, and Chianti Classico). The "G" stands for guaranteed, and what the Italian government is trying to guarantee is quality. The wines so designated must be tasted—each vintage, at several stages—by a panel of experts who certify that they are sufficiently fine and typical to be called by their prestigious names. Any wine not measuring up is supposed to be declassified and can then be sold only as simple red table wine. If it works, this will be a great protection for consumers. If it doesn't, it will be ranked as one of wine's most high-minded experiments.

### Aroma.

Although the aroma of the Barbaresco is nowhere near as big as it will be when the wine is mature, it nevertheless is already displaying on a smaller scale most of the components that connoisseurs identify as characteristic of the Nebbiolo grape. If you've really been exercising your nose as you ought up to this point, you should be able to pick out, in the bouquet of this wine, at least traces of some of these: delicate fruit, alcohol, a general herby scent, fennel or licorice, tea, and tobacco (sometimes described as a pleasing cigar-box aroma). In a fully mature Barbaresco, some of those elements would be very powerful: with this young wine you may have to hunt a bit to find them, but they should all be there.

The aroma of this Barolo is similar to that of the Barbaresco—no surprise there—but more forthright—again no surprise. That is as it should be with these two wines. The Barolo's scent seems prominently marked by alcohol at this stage of its maturation, a warm heady overtone that in effect colors the whole bouquet. Fruit and spice also seem more to the fore than in the Barbaresco: berries, spearmint or peppermint, a salt or even saltwater tang, tea, some suggestions of tobacco—you could detect any or all of those within the general framework of this Barolo's rich, vinous, almost pruney bouquet. You'll have to take my word for it that this too is still essentially a small aroma compared to what a properly aged and properly aerated Barolo will hit you with.


**Taste.**

The taste of the Barbaresco at this stage doesn't really live up to the promises made by its provocative aroma. The fruit is present, and you can even pick hints of berries and especially cherries from it, but it is nevertheless somewhat muffled: the wine is still what is called in the jargon of the trade "closed," meaning that its various components are still masking each other rather than supporting and revealing each other. There's nothing unpleasant about it—far from it—but it's just not yet showing all it has to give.

In this particular case, the tannin is partially masking the other components: you can really feel its presence in this wine's big, chewy texture. In fact, tasters with a particular sensitivity to tannin may very well find that it almost completely hides the fruit from them at this time and they perceive only a bland, somewhat astringent flavor. Given the relative youth of this Barbaresco, that is not surprising: indeed, the surprise is that the wine is this drinkable already.

Listen up now, because this is important and difficult. I've got you drinking immature wines for two very real reasons: money and availability (this whole discussion, by the way, applies as much to any other of the wines we're tasting in the previous half-dozen flights as it does to this one). If you could get a mature Barbaresco or Barolo, it would cost you considerably more than these infants did—and that "if" is the real rub. Presuming I were hardhearted enough to make you pawn your progeny to buy a really mature wine, and presuming you were by now sufficiently hooked on the joy of wine to be willing to part even with the dog and the parakeet if necessary to taste some really good stuff—even with all that, you might not be able to buy a mature bottle.

The facts of business being what they are—costs of overhead, storage, problems of cash flow—and the facts of agriculture being what they are—supply of any wine, but especially a fine one, is very, very limited—wines just don't stay in the shops for the length of time it takes them to mature. If they do, *you*—understandably, from the maker's and the retailer's point of view—have to pay a hefty premium not simply for the years and years of storage but for the money each of them has tied up in that bottle. It's an investment that pays no dividends and no interest until you decide you want that particular wine.

If I could be sure you all had access to older wines, I wouldn't hesitate to send you out to get them. After all, what's money? Especially when it's yours we're spending. If you had the older wines in front of you now, your tasting task would be simple, and my writing chore a breeze—in fact, I'd probably have to spend more time restraining your enthusiasm than instructing you what to taste for. But alas! What you have to do with these two and the other big wines we are tasting is extrapolate—imagine what you taste here in bits and pieces and traces to be magnified and harmonized. You have to intellectually intensify your experience of these wines along the lines I suggest to you: the tannin diminishing its direct impact, the fruit coming forward and its flavor maturing, growing a bit liquory, the whole of the flavor and the aroma, too, expanding so that when you pull the cork people halfway across the room know it by scent alone.

If you ever have the opportunity to taste any one of these wines at its maturity, by all means grab it and render all this prose super-fluous. If you don't have that opportunity but already like what you're tasting in these young wines, by all means buy some now and keep them for a few years. There are no better rewards for patience that I know of.

Enough of this long digression: we haven't yet talked about the taste of the Barolo. And after all that talk about young wines and mature wines, an irony: this Barolo, of the same age as our Barbaresco, is very forward and come-to-ish. It quite kindly makes itself available to you in a way that young Barolos most often do not. It is, first of all, extraordinarily well balanced for its age, quite complex and rich already. There is a big, concentrated fruit flavor right up front in the wine, hardly obscured at all by tannin even though there is plenty of that still in evidence: most tasters get distinct suggestions of plums and berries and cherries and currants all through it. The finish is long, with an almost licorice tang, and the overall palatal impression for most people is velvety and live. Comparatively speaking, in addition to being somewhat more accessible than the Barbaresco (which is definitely uncharacteristic), this Barolo is bigger, with more powerful fruit (which is what the clichés about these wines predict). It gives you a genuine and very useful preview of the way these wines normally develop. And remember: they both have years to go yet.

I can conceive of the possibility that some people somewhere might dislike these wines, but I'd rather not know about them, thank you. It would destroy my faith in the human race.

If you are interested in the further adventures of the Nebbiolo grape, there is a whole world for you to explore. Other fine makers of Barolo and Barbaresco range from big firms like Fontanafredda and Granduca, which make a whole line of Piedmontese wines, to smaller producers like Gaja and Pio Cesare, Ratti and Marcarini and Prunotto, Conterno and Giacosa and Roagna. In addition, in a different DOC zone in the northeastern Piedmont, the Nebbiolo is vinified into another group of wines, generally lighter in body and sometimes more elegant than the two you've just tried: Gattinara (from Antoniolo and Monsecco) and Spanna (from Vallana) are particularly fine, but also look for Carema, Ghemme, and Boca.

## Substitutes:

If you can't get younger vintages of either of these two wines, you could try Di Gresy's Gaiun Martinenga or Pio Cesare, or Produttori di Barbaresco (especially one of their cru wines) in place of the Vietti Barbaresco. For the Ceretto Barolo you could try substituting a Barolo from Bruno Giacosa, Giacomo Conterno, or Prunotto.

This is the conclusion of the eighteenth tasting session. There is only one way for you to proceed from here.

*Following the lead of your own preferences:*
   If you enjoyed either the Barbaresco or the Barolo, go on to the Nineteenth Flight.

*Following the kind of grapes:*
   This is the only Nebbiolo flight among our tastings.

*Following the wines of the country:*
   Go on to the Nineteenth Flight.

# THE NINETEENTH FLIGHT

❧ ⟅๑๑⟆ ❧

## *Château Fortia*
## *Châteauneuf du Pape 1985*
## *and*
## *Masi Amarone 1986*

⟅๑๑⟆

I F AT ALL POSSIBLE, let these two wines breathe for an hour before tasting them.

This final pair of red wines (yes, you've made it that far: graduation is at hand!) is distinctive in several respects. It's the only pair in this grouping that doesn't share the same grape as its base, or the same method of vinification, or even the same country of origin.

So what have these wines got in common that justifies lumping them together, you ask, half-expecting I can't answer that?

Hah, I say: size.

Size? Size.

These are among the biggest fully dry dinner wines in captivity. They have high alcohol (13.5 percent is about as low as they ever get), high tannin, high acid, and often enormous fruit—big, mouth-filling wines, with great, flavorful intensity. In the most literal sense, they stand in a class by themselves—which is why I have put them in a class by themselves.

Châteauneuf du Pape is produced near the city of Avignon, on the banks of the Rhône in southern France. It is perhaps the finest hot-climate wine made anywhere. Contrary to what you probably think, the best wines do not come from those climes where the grapes grow most prolifically. Usually the opposite is true; in wine lore a hot climate usually equates with flabby, unstructured wines, too high in sugar and/or alcohol to make anything other than picnic wines at best. At worst, you can use them in a your car's radiator.

To make even decent table wine in a really hot climate requires great care in growing and harvesting the grapes and great skill and control in their vinification. In Sicily, for instance, the production of some light white wines pleasing to modern tastes required unlearning two thousand years of viticultural techniques plus wholesale importation of a brand-new technology: stainless-steel tanks, reduced-temperature fermentation, glass-lined holding tanks (also temperature controlled), and anoxygenic bottling. In Châteauneuf du Pape and other locations on the Rhône (notably Hermitage), the skills of French vintners go well beyond that to create a wine not merely drinkable but outstanding by any criteria.

Amarone is another case entirely. The product of a far more benign climate, Amarone derives from grapes grown on the tranquil hillsides near Verona, not far from Lake Garda in Italy. Except for Amarone, Veronese vines do not produce big wines but rather light, smiling ones like the popular white, Soave, and the red Valpolicella and Bardolino (in the Second Flight). In fact, the real surprise I have been saving up for you—if you will be good enough to cast your mind all the way back to that second tasting—is that the huge wine you are about to taste, Amarone, is made from exactly the same grapes as that pleasant, light Bardolino you drank then. In fact Amarone is grown in exactly the same fields as the almost-as-light Valpolicella. Its full name is Recioto di Valpolicella Amarone— Amarone for short, though it is the only thing short about this wine.

I will explain all in a little while. For now, see, swirl, sniff, sip, savor, spit—especially spit, given the alcoholic strength of these two musclemen. I want you sober enough to be able to follow my golden prose right to the end.

## Appearance.

No problem. Château Fortia is a lovely clear garnet, and the Masi Amarone is the same garnet with some tawny or amber highlights, which, I remind you for the last time, is a sign of a maturing Italian wine (though as Amarone runs, this one is quite an infant yet).

Aroma.

Like the Nebbiolo-based wines, these two demand a bit of breathing time—about a week, one of my tasters suggested. Both wines have very deep aromas that will increase and complicate with age, and both wines, because of their concentrations of alcohol and tannin, are not easily harmed by oxidation. I have left half-empty bottles of Amarone standing for a week with the cork only loosely reinserted (and obviously half the bottle filled with air), and they have at the end of that time not only been perfectly drinkable but a few of them had actually improved. I don't really recommend that as a way to treat wines, not even wines like these, but it certainly does tell you something about them.

The first element of the Châteauneuf's aroma to strike you is likely to be its alcohol, a warm, heady rush that bears the rest of the scents on its back. There are many of those. Most people usually detect fruit first—a rich, plummy scent that some will think smacks of overripeness, though to my mind that is the characteristic sunbaked smell of southern grapes. After that they tend to pick up a cluster of perfumes—violets, cinnamon, stems and grass, a truffly/earthy smell. The overall impression is of strength, of graceful power.

The Amarone is not utterly different from that. The big, richly plummy alcoholic rush is present in it too, though some tasters can discern a pleasing, almost apple scent as well. Flowery perfumes are present too, though they are harder to identify specifically here than in the Châteauneuf. Many people also pick up what they identify as a smell of yeast or bread dough—a fresh, live scent that might be attributable either to an unfinished malolactic fermentation (unlikely, but possible, and a small defect if present) or to the presence of *Botrytis* on the grapes (less unlikely and more possible, and a big plus for the wine if present).

For most tasters, however, the predominant sensation here is a very characteristic Amarone bouquet, a kind of heady compound of resin and raisin that, in a way very different from the Châteauneuf, nevertheless calls up images of sun on the vines and bright, hot afternoons. If the overall impression created by the aroma of the Châteauneuf du Pape is graceful power, Amarone creates a sense of powerful grace—and I am not just playing with words here; where the emphasis falls makes a very big difference in the wine.

*Tech Talk*

Two technical terms here deserve special attention: malolactic fermentation and *Botrytis.* They are very different from each other. Malolactic fermentation is a second, smaller fermentation that occurs (or should occur) in most red wines. *Botrytis* is the name of a mold that forms on ripe grapes. It rarely has any role in the making of red wines.

Immediately after the crushing of the grapes, all wines, red or white, go through what is called a violent or tumultuous fermentation. During this fermentation the grapes' sugars are converted to alcohol by the action of yeasts. Malolactic fermentation is a smaller, less violent fermentation caused by naturally occurring bacteria. This fermentation will happen naturally in most wines unless it is deliberately forestalled. It usually comes hard on the heels of the first fermentation, and it converts malic acid to milder lactic acid. Its effect on red wine is usually to smooth it and advance its maturation. Consequently, almost all red wines undergo malolactic fermentation, but very few whites are allowed to go through it. This is because malic acid conveys a greater sensation of live acidity to the tongue than does lactic acid, and in most white wines the kind and degree of acidity contributes importantly to your tasting a fresh fruit flavor that would be lost or seriously diminished by malolactic fermentation.

Wine jargon often shortens the phrase "malolactic fermentation" to simply "malo."

*Botrytis* (in full, *Botrytis cinerea*) is a mold that causes grapes to lose water, shrivel slightly, and concentrate their sugars. It also imparts a distinctive, honeyed flavor of its own which with practice you can learn to identify in wines made with grapes that have been visited by *Botrytis cinerea.* Any kind of mold is usually a disaster in the vineyard, but *Botrytis* at harvest time can be a blessing. The French call it the *pourriture noble*, the noble rot. It is responsible for the magnificent sweetness of some of the world's most famous dessert wines—France's Sauternes and Barsac; Germany's Auslese, Beerenauslese, and Trockenbeerenauslese; and the Hungarian Tokay.

In the Verona area, sweet dessert wines are made with grapes partially affected by *Botrytis*; the wines are called simply Recioto di Valpolicella or di Soave, depending on the zone. Recioto di Valpolicella is already unusual in being a red wine made from such grapes; the word Amarone added to that name indicates the same sort of grapes vinified to full dryness, a very, very unusual condition. Grapes affected by *Botrytis* give a dry wine an intense fruitiness that is absolutely necessary to balance the very high alcohol resulting from the conversion of all those concentrated sugars.

Taste.

Almost every taster describes both these wines as presenting truly complex tastes. The structural elements (tannin, acids, alcohol, fruit) and a whole range of flavor elements intertwine quite differently in each, though the overall effect of both is remarkably similar. Any largish group of tasters is likely to divide right down the middle as to which of these wines is bigger and more complex than the other.

Some people, however, are going to find both of these wines just too much and be put off by everything about them, describing them as too sweet, too strong, too astringent, too assertive, too sour. But if you have been really bitten by the red-wine bug (and you'd have to be a supreme masochist to travel this far with me if you haven't been), you should thoroughly enjoy the smoothness and authority, the iron-fist-in-the-velvet-glove character of these two wines.

The Châteauneuf fills your mouth with soft, "sweet" fruit. Various people taste in it berries and plums and nuts as well as herbal flavors. There is strong tannin discernible too, as well as some vanilla notes contributed (no doubt) by the barrels, all of which makes for a pleasing, slightly bitter (some find a definite taste of almond) finish. With its high alcohol and abundance of acid added to these flavor elements, this wine makes a total impression of richness and variety that defines opulence in a red wine. Considering that this is a mere babe in arms as the fine Rhône wines go, I would say that the prognosis for its future health and long life is excellent. I would also say that I wouldn't at all mind being around for its twenty-first-birthday party.

Not that the Amarone is any slouch, either. It, too, is very smooth and balanced, with deep flavor and velvety texture. It, too, tastes of plums, but there are other fruit and herb suggestions as well—anise and peaches, for instance, and apples, and raisins (the last particularly noticeable in the finish). The Châteauneuf du Pape is probably a fractionally bigger wine (on the scale of two such wines as these, small differences are hard to gauge, and individual responses will vary widely) and the Amarone a better balanced, more elegant wine. Rather than do anything as commonplace as leave you with an overall impression, it lingers with you. Its finish is remarkably long and full, so the ghost of the wine continues to haunt your mouth after you've emptied your glass. Even smell the empty glass, and see how persistent its bouquet is. This is a very complete wine—and once again it is little more than an infant. Can you imagine what this lady will be like when she makes her debut?

For all their overt differences, the Châteauneuf du Pape and the Amarone make remarkably compatible partners. They share one striking similarity in their origins as well, and it makes the wonder of their bigness and grace all the more remarkable: both are made from grapes that grown in other places, treated in other ways, yield only ordinary wines at best. The grape that makes up almost 75 percent of this Château Fortia is the Grenache, which outside of the Châteauneuf du Pape zone gives little better than a pusillanimous rosé. It is only one of thirteen generally undistinguished grapes (the Syrah is the only exception, and it is not often a large component) that may be blended into Châteauneuf. Amarone is made from grapes unknown outside Verona, the Corvina, the Rondinella, the Molinara, and the Negrara, which otherwise produce only the light and relatively low alcohol Valpolicella and Bardolino.

So what turns Châteauneuf and Amarone into great wines?

In the case of Châteauneuf, it appears to be the peculiar combination of soil and climate along the southern Rhône that works the magic. If so, there is hope that many other regions may yet stumble on the vine that in their particular conditions will make a wine as good and as special.

In the case of Amarone, the magic seems to lie more in the skills of the winemaker and the unusual process of vinification that Amarone undergoes. If that is the case, there is hope that craftsmen will yet happen on the special techniques that will enable them to transform yet more ordinary wines into causes for celebration.

Amarone is made by a process akin to that which normally yields dessert wines. Selective picking of very ripe bunches and parts of bunches begins the process. Then those grapes are arranged on straw mats or on special frames in bright, airy conditions and allowed to dry about halfway to raisinhood before being pressed. Their fermentation is very slow—it may continue most of the winter—and, unlike the fermentation of most sweet wines, it takes place in contact with the skins, so in addition to concentrated fruit and high alcohol, the wine also draws all of the available tannin and extracts from its grapes. And again unlike most sweet wines, the fermentation is never interrupted until all the grape sugars have been converted to alcohol, leaving a fully dry wine.

If the style of either of these wines appeals to you, there is ample room to explore yet ahead of you. Other good makers of Châteauneuf are Château de Beaucastel, Domaine de Mont-Redon, and Domaine du Vieux Télégraphe. There are also the scarcer and more expensive northern Rhône wines, from Hermitage and the Côte Roti. Other good producers of Amarone are Allegrini, Bertani, Bolla, Santa Sophia, Tommasi, and Quintarelli (a smaller maker: his wines are hard to find).

Masi is a long-established Veronese firm, a quality producer of all of the traditional wines of the region.

Château Fortia is one of the most prized estates of the Châteauneuf du Pape region. Its wines are imported to the United States by Banfi Vintners.

## Substitutes:

As always, first try to get younger vintages of these two wines. If that is not possible, consider using Chapoutier's La Bernardine Châteauneuf du Pape, Domaine Chante-Cigale, Jaboulet's Les Cedres, or Château Vieux Télégraphe in place of Château Fortia, and an Amarone from Allegrini, Tommasi, or Zenato in place of the Masi Amarone. Bolla's Amarone will also serve, though it is not as distinctive as any of these others.

This concludes the red-wine tastings. You made it. Congratulations! You now know all about a better red. If you're up for it, you might look back over the flights containing Italian wines (the First, Second, Fourth, Ninth, Fourteenth, and Eighteenth) and those containing French wines (the Second, Third, Fourth, Sixth, Seventh, Eighth, Tenth, Eleventh, Twelfth, Thirteenth, and Fifteenth) and taste any of them you may have missed on your way here. After that, you can tackle the white wines. And then the rosés. And then the sparkling wines, including champagnes. Meanwhile, I'll be working on the sequel to this book, *Son of Mastering Wine Entertains Count Dracula*. Look for it wherever books are sold.

# WHITE
# WINES

# THE FIRST FLIGHT

~⚬⚬~

## *Sichel Blue Nun Liebfraumilch 1987 and The Monterey Vineyard Classic Chenin Blanc 1989*

~⚬⚬~

WHITE WINE IS THE CHAMELEON of the wine world: it comes in every conceivable degree of dryness and sweetness, every style from completely still through *frizzante* and *pétillant* and crackling to fully sparkling, and every shade of color from the palest straw to almost deep amber. In fact, if you lump together rosé wine with white, as for all practical purposes you can, white wine comes in just about every color except white—a moral I leave the world to reflect on in its own time.

The uses of white wine vary as much as its guises. It's drunk as a light refresher, as a cocktail, as an appetite teaser or palate cleanser before dinner, as an accompaniment to dinner, as a partner to dessert, or as dessert itself. There's no mystery to its popularity: the only real question to be asked about the current white-wine boom is why it was so long in coming.

For all its popularity, however, white wine remains for most people at least as great an unknown as red. Maybe greater. My hunch is that a high percentage of the folks who order simply a glass of white wine in a bar or restaurant do so for one of several reasons:

157

- They can't be more exact because they don't know the names of any specific white wines.
- They do know some names but can't remember whether they remember them because they love them or because they hate them.
- They think all white wines taste alike.
- All the white wines they have so far tried *do* taste alike.
- They have been told that, past the most basic level, white wine gets very expensive.
- It's all been just too much trouble to learn about, and besides, why take a chance embarrassing yourself with a mistake?

If any of those describes your state, let me assure you right off the bat that white wine is a much less complicated subject than red wine. It's a lot easier to sort out, and once you've grasped a small handful of key distinctions there is a considerably smaller field of variations to keep in mind. In fact, in most wine courses and most wine books, just as in wine service at a dinner, white wines customarily precede reds and thus serve, because they are more accessible, as an introduction to red wines.

So, shrewd observer that you are, you are now asking yourself "What then is this madman doing placing white wines after red wines in this supposedly logical book? What kind of sense does that make? Let's see him get out of this one."

Easy. Not only easy, but once again proof that I have nothing but your best interests at heart, that nothing but concern for your ease and pleasure guides my writing; and you'd have to be a churl and a scoundrel to doubt that, after all we've been through together.

The fact is (or at least the fact as I see it is) that white wines are *intellectually* easier to learn than red wines, but palatally more difficult.

Why? Because white wines are more similar to each other than are red wines. The flavor differences among white wines are more subtle, more delicate, and often more fleeting than those that divide reds. The gradations of intensity, of sweetness and dryness, shade more imperceptibly into each other. Even the noblest white-grape varieties are so subject to the influences of soil and climate and vinification that they can and do produce everything from the most frivolous quaffing wine right across the spectrum to the most serious dinner wine. No white grape is so austere and so distinct that, like the red Cabernet Sauvignon, it is essentially unusable for light wines.

So while white wines as a class are fairly easily understandable, and while generally speaking white wines are readily pleasing and palatable (accessible in that sense and to that degree), forming a knowing taste for white wines is, I think, a more difficult process than developing a knowledgeable palate for reds, because the distinctions from wine to wine are so much finer. That is why I have positioned the white wines here, after red wines, so you will approach them after you've had some pretty vigorous practice tasting and distinguishing tastes. So limber up your nose and taste buds, because they are really in for a workout.

The basic equipment you need to taste white wines is exactly the same as that you used for tasting reds. The only change you might want to consider is trading in your piece of cheese (I sincerely hope it hasn't been the same one throughout) for some toasted almonds or a simple unsalted cracker: those flavors are a bit more congenial with white wine for most people, though heaven knows the right cheese and the right white wine make a lovely combination too.

Tasting procedures are exactly the same; the ritual of the infamous s's remains intact. (If you're being a stubbornly independent soul and are beginning your wine tasting here, please take a look back at pages 15–22 for the basic tasting technique.) The variation I'd counsel here is to urge you to concentrate even more on sniffing out the nuances of aroma, not only because they are more delicate in white wines, but also because the pleasing aromas of white wines are so large a component of the pleasure they give and so often an accurate indicator of the flavors to follow. I guess this amounts to saying that aroma in white wine relates to flavor and to overall pleasure just as it does in red wine, only more so.

One note: Most white wines are best served chilled, not icy. There are exceptions to this in both directions, and I will try to call your attention to them at appropriate times. However, if you should encounter a wine that is simply giving you nothing—no scent, no taste, absolute zero—try letting it sit in the glass for a while to warm before retasting it. Overchilling can completely smother a wine and cause it to go absolutely dumb, and different wines overchill at different points. If it is only overchilling that's wrong, the wine will relax and release scent and flavor as it warms. If you take it all the way up to room temperature and you still don't smell or taste anything, first make sure it's not just you coming down with a cold, and then return the bottle to your wine dealer. White-wine sensations may be delicate, but they shouldn't be undiscernible.

And one last piece of what should be welcome news to you: At the level with which we begin these tastings—the level of simple, everyday table wine—the quality and accessibility of white wines are a good jump higher than those of red wines of comparable cost. This probably arises from the major innovations that have been introduced into the making of white wines over the past twenty-five years; technology has taken hold there to such an extent that even a mediocre harvest can usually be made to yield palatable light and fruity wines. Why the same or related technology hasn't yet had the same effect on inexpensive red wine I don't know, but there seems to be more badly made red *vin ordinaire* than white. So rejoice! You're starting off at a very respectable level of winemaking here.

As with the red wines, each tasting session of whites concludes with a set of alternative paths for you to follow. Just as with the reds, I once again strongly urge you to taste straight through the first four flights before you start branching out—there is basic information in those first four pairs that will stand you in good stead through all the subsequent tastings.

I think you will find that white wines pretty readily offer themselves for your understanding in varietal clusters. At any rate, the number of paths and options available to the white-wine taster are fewer than those through reds, and you will find that a fair number of the tastings that follow are going to involve you in a straightforward sequence of flights built around the same grape. This is especially true with Riesling, Sauvignon Blanc, and Chardonnay, and it is part of the reason why white wines are so easy to come to terms with intellectually and often so difficult to distinguish palatally.

Happy hunting!

If you have no sweet tooth, be warned about these two wines.

If you do have a weakness for sweets, you probably already know these wines or others like them, since wines of this and greater degrees of sweetness comprise one of the largest-selling groups of wine on the U.S. market. They are here at the beginning of your plunge into white wines because for many people they form the bridge from what they have been drinking, be it soft drinks or pop wine or mixed drinks, to the world of drier dinner wines.

Even if you already have a dry palate, it's still worth your while to taste these wines carefully, because the flavor components that we're going to be talking about in them will be basic to most white wines.

Whereas in red wine the interplay of fruit and tannin became the basic building block on which you built your knowledge and preferences, in white wine you'll find the interplay of acid and sugar forming much the same base.

Acid and sugar will condition your perception of a wine's fruit, its liveliness, and its body. Their proportions relative to each other in a wine will determine whether you taste that wine as sweet or dry, fruity or austere, flabby or thin. It is quite possible, for instance, that wine A will taste to you sweeter than wine B, which may in fact have more sugar in it. How can that be? Wine B could have either much more pronounced flavor and fruit to mask the sugar, or much higher acid to balance it, or a combination of both factors.

Certain levels of sugar are commonly regarded as above or below the perceptible level, which is usually estimated to be 1 percent sugar by weight. That figure should be taken only as a very loose average, subject to variation by the presence and absence of other elements in a wine and subject also to the varying sensitivity of individual palates. Some people seem able to taste even minuscule traces of sugar, while others are relatively unconscious of amounts that are well above that so-called threshold level.

Of course, the same is true of other elements in wine (notably tannin), but with white wines sugar is generally the first flavor factor to be dealt with. By the way, the presence of tannin in a wine seems to raise the sugar threshold—that is, in the presence of tannin more sugar is needed for a taster to perceive sweetness. Because of the way most white wines are vinified, however—with little or no contact between musts and skins—they are normally quite low in tannin, so that is a complication you won't often encounter.

Some wines have so much sugar (many pop wines are in this class) that no natural flavor is perceptible other than sugar. These are wines that there is no point talking about because there can be only one thing to say about them—how sweet they are. A wine like that is unsuitable for use at a meal because all that sugar masks every other flavor; you cannot taste foods, and you certainly cannot taste other wines, after a sugary drink. As far as I am concerned, a wine that you can't drink with food is unfit for human consumption.

Most people who have become used to such wines find it very hard to retrain their palates to accommodate dry wines (which is one reason I'm trying to break you in gradually with moderately sweet wines in this first flight). I don't know whether it is scientific fact or not, but sugar seems to be an addictive substance; at least it can be as hard to kick the sugar habit as any other. The one reward I can hold out to you is that once you do make the effort to dry out your palate, you'll discover a whole range of wonderful flavors you never imagined before—and that is as true of foods as it is of wines.

In most circumstances, a wine's label or back label will give sufficient though sometimes coded information about its approximate degree of sweetness. If either label uses the word "sweet," you can be sure it's good and sweet. "Luscious" and similar words mean very sweet; wines so labeled properly belong with or as dessert. The euphemisms by which more modestly sweet wines present themselves are words such as "semisweet," which always means sweet; "semidry," which still means sweet; and "soft," which usually means sweet.

Got all that straight? Get ready then to taste two moderately sweet wines, one a Liebfraumilch and one of the most popular German wines in the United States, the other a California wine vinified from a grape variety that produces both dry and sweet wines. They are paired here because both are commonly described as soft, fruity, lightly sweet wines. They are that, and yet there are striking differences between them. You can see you've got your work cut out for you; once again, you're going to be tasting to see if you can discern sameness and difference.

All right, go to it. Perform the full operation, as directed at the beginning of this book: see, swirl, smell, sip/slurp, savor/slosh, and spit. Take good notes, and if there are several of you tasting together, talk over your reactions when you are finished tasting but before you read any more about these wines. Just for the record, it's better for you to taste first and read later because it is much too easy to be coerced by the printed word. What matters in these tastings is not what I say but what you sense. The descriptions are given as grids against which you can match your own perceptions and your own taste. Ideally they should serve as a sort of doublecheck for you, to prompt you to react with

"Hey, I didn't taste that at all: let me go back and taste that one again," or

"Well, I see what he means by that," or

"I think he's describing the same thing we tasted but he's calling it something different than we did," or

### Sweet Talk

The name Liebfraumilch designates a German white wine, always semisweet, from the growing areas along the Rhine. Riesling (one of the truly great grapes), Sylvaner, and Müller-Thurgau grapes may go into it, and normally it is blended from the produce of several (if not many) vineyards. Connoisseurs tend to sneer at Liebfraumilch, but it has retained its international popularity for many years.

Chenin Blanc is a grape variety that keeps threatening nobility. In France, along the middle Loire, it is a staple white-wine grape and makes wines that range in sweetness from fully dry to luscious and in style from the charming Vouvray to the impressive Savennières. In California it is mostly vinified with light sweetness, though every year a few interesting fully dry Chenin Blanc wines appear on the market.

"Well, I've tasted this wine a couple of times now and I still think he's crazy."

That's a whole lot of prologue, I realize. My apologies if you've been bored. Drink on.


### Appearance.

Neither of these wines should present any difficulty as far as appearance is concerned. Both ought to be clear, pale straw colored, very clean-looking—almost textbook cases of a color that you're going to see is characteristic of a whole class of young, fresh white wines. There may be the slightest degree of difference in shading between these two wines—either could be the tiniest bit darker than the other—but any such difference should be very slight. A bright lemony or brassy or urine color (it does happen) in wines like this is ninety-nine times out of a hundred an indication that the wine is too old. But pay attention to that phrase "wines like this," because there are some wines where a bright golden shade is perfectly normal.

## Aroma.

Most people are going to perceive the aromas of these two wines as having areas both of similarity and of distinction. The balance between likeness and difference for an individual taster is going to tilt in the direction of his or her individual sensitivities. Let's take the Blue Nun first.

Most people are struck right away by a sweet scent, which they describe as a sweet fruit scent or a flowery aroma. Some will also pick out citrus smells and leafy or herbal elements: often mint is named. Some profess to find the specific smell of dried apricots in the aroma of this particular wine. Those who don't like this style of wine will describe all these same things as excessive, cloying, sickly-sweet; those who like it will call it delicate and pleasant.

Whichever side of that taste divide you fall on, you ought to know that this is very close to a classic German wine aroma. Indeed, many of the elements you are smelling here (again, whether they please you or not) are directly traceable to the Riesling grape, which is responsible for Germany's greatest wines. Those flowery, sweet-fruit notes in the aroma (the latter are often spoken of as "honeyed"), the leafy elements, and the overall clean and lively character of the aroma: all these you will find too in the Riesling grape, whether it is vinified in Germany or New York, France or Italy, Washington or California. What percentage of this wine is actually Riesling would be difficult to say; nevertheless, Riesling is certainly present in its bouquet.

By contrast, the aroma of the Chenin Blanc will strike most people as drier—that is, there is a less marked sweet-fruit aroma, though fruit of one sort or another is still prominent. Like the Blue Nun's, the Chenin Blanc's aroma is clean and refreshing, though most people perceive it as a bit coarser—the fruit seems wilder, the herbal elements less delicate (woodruff is one sometimes named). Many people discern one dominant sweet-fruit tone (melon is what most call it) balanced by a sharper, more acidic element such as lime or pineapple. Once again, the question of whether you like this or hate it, whether you find these aromas pleasing or repellent, is purely a matter of personal taste. For the record, however, you should note that this is a very typical aroma for Chenin Blanc; allowing for variations in vinification, this is more or less what Chenin Blanc ought to smell like all the time.

Okay, you're working on two new grapes for your repertoire in your first tasting of white wines. They're rather disproportionate: the Chenin Blanc only rarely reaches greatness, while the Riesling is regarded by most connoisseurs as one of the two noblest white grapes in the world. Nevertheless, both are capable of making accessible wines in a style that pleases multitudes of nonconnoisseurs.

On to their flavors, then.

### Taste.

It's fair to say that 99 percent of the people tasting these two wines are going to find their flavors absolutely consistent with their aromas, whether those individuals liked the aromas or not.

The Blue Nun is sweet, of course, though some tasters are surprised to find that it is not as sweet as they feared. The reason for that is twofold.

First, this Liebfraumilch possesses a very definite fruitiness which is perceptible by everybody except those whose sugar threshold is so low that every other flavor is masked for them. (If you are one of those, you are probably not going to find much to please you in German wine, though you may respond better to other nations' versions of the Riesling grape.) Some will perceive this fruitiness only as a generalized fresh flavor, others will describe touches of pineapple or peach, and some will even find a slight tartness lurking deep in the wine. In any event, the presence of this good fruit works to domesticate, as it were, a certain quantity of the wine's sugars: our palates incorporate them into those fruit flavors, where they seem natural and appropriate.

Second, the Riesling grape naturally possesses a great deal of acidity, and the presence of that acidity in the wine works somewhat to hold the sugar in balance, or at least to partially restrain it. Most people taste the acidity in several ways: most specifically, perhaps, in that touch of tartness in the wine or in those bright and biting pineapple flavors, but most importantly in the general liveliness, freshness, and vitality of the wine. Without sufficient acid this wine would be limp, flabby, dead—a sucrose corpse.

The acid animates it, and in that respect this wine reinforces a very valuable lesson at the start of these white-wine sessions. The trinity of fruit and sugar and acid is the key to understanding most white wines. Acid and fruit and sugar don't explain everything about white wine by a long shot—but you can use them as reference points to triangulate to where your own taste lies, and you can use them to chart your own path through white wines. What the interplay of tannin and acid and fruit was to your understanding of red wines, the relation of sugar and acid and fruit can be to your grasp of whites.

Compared to the Liebfraumilch, the Chenin Blanc seems to most people simultaneously drier, fuller, and less vivid. It feels a bit bigger and weightier in the mouth, but less lively, so that some tasters perceive it as a bit flabby. Others will find that its lesser sweetness, greater roundness, and the more subdued taste of its fruit (tasters frequently discern a slightly tart apple flavor) make it for them a better-structured, more satisfying wine, especially with food.

You can learn a lot about your own palate from this wine in this particular tasting. In this setting (that is, tasted after the Blue Nun), did this Chenin Blanc strike you as an essentially sweet or an essentially dry wine?

Mind now, I'm talking about the flavor in the mouth as separate from the aroma; if you're in doubt, take a little taste of the Blue Nun, wait a minute or two, then taste the Chenin again. Ask some of your friends to make the same test; I think you'll find the results very interesting. Perceptions will run from totally sweet to totally dry, with a lot of mixed reports about sweet starts and dry finishes, and vice versa. By paying very close attention to your own reactions to this Chenin Blanc, you can learn a lot about just how much sugar you can tolerate, how much you enjoy, how much or how little sugar masks other flavors for you, or how well you are able to discern other flavors despite the presence of sugar. Unlikely as it may seem, the two wines of this flight can constitute a full-scale seminar in tasting if you give them the proper time and attention.

Blue Nun is the largest-selling German wine in the United States. It is produced by Sichel, a major dealer in quality German wines, and imported into the United States by Schieffelin & Company.

The Monterey Vineyard is a very large, very modern winemaking firm now owned by the Seagram interests. It makes large quantities of impressive quality wine from a full range of California's best varieties, and it sells them at quite reasonable prices.

**Substitutes:**

Younger vintages of either of these wines are the best choices, but there are other possibilities. Robert Mondavi Napa Valley Chenin

Blanc 1989, for instance, possesses the same essential Chenin Blanc character, though it is a bit more complex and Vouvray-like. Other Liebfraumilchs tend to be slightly sweeter than Blue Nun but nevertheless fit the general description.

This is the conclusion of the first tasting session. It would be very useful to you to go straight on through the next three flights, but if you wish there are several other ways for you to proceed from here.

*Following the lead of your own preferences:*
Whether you liked the first wine better, the Blue Nun, or the second wine, the Chenin Blanc, go on to the Fifth Flight.

*Following the kind of grapes:*
Wine One: Go on to the Fifth Flight.
Wine Two: There are no other Chenin Blanc tastings.
Try the Seventh Flight.

*Following the wines of the country:*
Wine One: Go on to the Fifth Flight.
Wine Two: Go on to the Second Flight.

# THE SECOND FLIGHT

*Moreau Blanc*
*and*
*Trefethen Napa Valley*
*Eschol White*

I F YOU ARE PROCEEDING directly on from the first pair of wines to this tasting, make sure you take at least a bite of cracker and a large drink of water to wipe the sweetness from your mouth. Better yet, get up and walk around for five or ten minutes to let your palate clear so you can give these next two wines a fair trial. We're the victims of the logic of our program here: in moving from simple and accessible wines to more complex ones, we've been forced to start white wines with a fair dose of sugar, which runs dead counter to the logic of a tasting sequence. Normal tasting sequence places white wines before red wines, young wines before old, light wines before full-bodied, and dry wines before sweet. That is the usual pattern for serving wines at dinner, too. So try to scrape off as much of the sweetness as you can before you start sampling the next wines.

Ready? This pair of wines matches examples of two styles of very popular dry whites, one a French import, the other a Californian. Both are blends of several grapes—the Trefethen predominantly Chardonnay, the Moreau in all likelihood with a good percentage of that grape—from diverse but respectable growing areas. Neither is vintage-dated, so it is important to try to buy this wine from a shop that handles it regularly. White wines of this type are not built for bottle-aging, and you don't want to get stuck with one that has been sitting on somebody's shelf with its cork drying out for two years. On the other hand, you don't have to worry about vintage variation, since these are both wines that are blended to preserve a consistent style and flavor from year to year.

Presuming you've done your shopping well, you should be ready now to pour the wines—well chilled but not icy cold—and perform your ritual eye, nose, and throat examination. So go to it, and check back here after you've registered all your comments.

### Appearance.

If you have by any chance gotten a bottle of either of these wines that is either too old or has been badly stored, the color should give you the first clue. Both the Moreau and the Trefethen Eschol White should be pale straw in color, the Trefethen perhaps a slight bit deeper in color than the Moreau Blanc. Any deeper shade of yellow, especially anything edging into bright yellow, brassy, or golden, will almost certainly mean that the wine has oxidized and will have no flavor left.

I know I've told you this before, but it is important. If you ask for a young white wine in a restaurant and it comes out of the bottle lemon yellow, don't even bother tasting unless it is a sweet wine like Sauternes; just send it back. If one of the two in front of you now is a color like that, taste it only if you are curious to know what oxidized wine tastes like; otherwise just bring it back to your dealer and get a fresher bottle.

Remember: Pale straw and slight variations from it are going to be the normal colors for the great majority of the white wines we'll be tasting together. Only a few, older dry white wines of superior stature can handle the kind of bottle-age that darkens them beyond that.

### Aroma.

Well, you may have had to work pretty hard here, because no one ever accused either of these wines of being intensely aromatic. Many people in fact have trouble picking out any aroma at all, a condition that can result from everything from bottle variation in the wine to bad sinuses in the wine taster. If your wines are even a fraction too cold, the aroma of the Moreau Blanc particularly may disappear, so if you didn't get any scent initially, warm the glass in your hands a little—cradle it as you would a brandy glass—and swirl and sniff once more. But don't expect a whole lot.

### Through a Glass Brightly

As you cup that wine glass to warm its contents, you are presenting yourself with a perfect illustration of the logic of wine-glass shapes. Why do all the experts insist on stemware for wine glasses? Precisely to keep hands away from the wine.

Every quality a wine glass should have relates to a quality of wine. You want to be able to see the wine clearly; hence, uncolored glass and crystal. You want to keep its temperature as constant as possible; hence, stems to keep hands from heating it. You want to be able to release the wine's aroma; hence, wide bowls. But you don't want to dissipate that aroma; hence, incurving rims or tulip shapes. The bigger aromas of red wines indicate that larger glasses are in order for them, just as champagne's attractive bubbles want a tall, narrow glass to show them off best.

What most tasters report they smell in the Moreau Blanc is a slight, clean aroma, dry and refreshing. Specific scents are difficult to isolate because the overall impression is faint, but some people do detect a bit of generalized fruit, or acidity, or a delicate wheatlike scent. Don't worry if you didn't smell any of that; the aroma is small at best. Besides, let me remind you once again that this is not a test, and you are not graded—nor should you grade yourself—by how closely what you smelled matches what's on the page. I'm just trying to give you a range of typical responses, and if you smelled something completely different, it may mean that my range doesn't go far enough. What you smell is what you smell, and the important thing is for you to try to remember the scent and the wine and just how much they pleased or displeased you. In case you've forgotten, your taste is what counts.

The Trefethen makes life a little (but not much) easier for your poor overworked sniffer. Its aroma is stronger than that of the Moreau Blanc, though it is still small by any objective standards. Smelling it right after the Moreau seems to lead to two opposite responses in tasters. One group reports a dominant aroma of damp earth and wet straw; the other a complex of slightly sweetish, fruity aromas—anything from honey and simple fruit to pears, pineapple, even canned grapefruit. A taster familiar with white wines might be able to pick out a hint of an aromatic grape—a vague suggestion of the sort of floral or minty aromas associated with Riesling, for instance.

Once again, however, we are not dealing with a big aroma here, and these are not blockbuster, attention-grabbing scents, but very slight, fleeting impressions, so don't give up on white wine if these scents are not coming through to you. I told you at the start, white wines are difficult precisely because they're so often delicate and their impressions subtle, so stick with them and keep tasting.

## Taste.

This leads us logically to the taste of these two whites. If you are tasting with others, you may be surprised by how much disagreement there can be about the flavors of what are, in the final analysis, two simple table wines. People can perceive these wines as polar opposites—which is surprising enough—and different tasters may very well reverse each other's poles and find fruity what the other found sour, pleasing what the other found blah, and so on. I wish I could tell you why this is, but nothing I know about these wines explains that extreme range of opinion. If I didn't know it were so, I'd say it couldn't happen. At any rate, it means I can't really give you a majority opinion on either of these wines, so I'll just let you have the perimeters and some of the high and low points of each range of response and you can see if your reaction falls anywhere on this map or if you're charting your own Northwest Passage to connoisseurship.

Of the Moreau Blanc, opinions run from sour and flabby up through soft and inoffensive all the way to pleasant and crisp and a little fruity with a nice touch of tartness. Everybody agrees that it is dry and light. Even those who don't think much of it agree that it makes a decent quaffing wine; as one taster put it, fine for outside on a warm day. The things that you clearly won't taste in this wine are big, full body and pronounced flavors. The tastes you will find fall into a broad range of delicate suggestions and nuances, which you will like or dislike according to your own sensitivity in discerning them—exactly as it was with the Moreau Blanc's aroma. This is a consistent wine, made to a small, but to many people very pleasing, scale.

Of the Trefethen Eschol White, opinions run from discerning in it an overly aggressive fruit taste, through finding it a little too fruity, all the way to tasting in it soft, very light fruit. Again, everybody agrees that it has a bit more body than the Moreau (though it is still light) and that it is dry. They agree, too, that the flavor doesn't really follow through on the various hints and suggestions of the aroma, that the wine doesn't seem to have the kind of complexity its nose half-promised. It has what you may later in these tastings come to recognize as a subdued Chardonnay character, but not a lot of it. Again, the general consensus is that this is acceptable quaffing wine, useful with simple, everyday meals—which is exactly what it's designed to be.

Pretty obviously, the average wine drinker is going to respond to these wines as the unaffected, straightforward wines they are, and our scrutinizing them as we've just done may look like putting a private on the rack for information only a general can provide. But these two whites, and many others like them, are drunk with pleasure every day in America. They appear on home tables with dinner. They're poured as house wines in restaurants and bars. They're probably even slugged from the bottle at picnics and ball parks. If by pushing them as hard as we've just done you can begin to recognize and isolate what you like and don't like in them, then you can use them for the starting gate they should be rather than the dead end they too often are.

Once they get you off and running, the makers of these two wines can also accompany you a good way down the track. Moreau is one of France's largest dealers in the white wines of Chablis, and he handles just about every conceivable gradation of Burgundian white wine.

The Trefethens took over the old Eschol vineyard in 1973 and have since then made a name for quality and value in everything from their basic Eschol red and white wines through their much-admired Cabernets, Chardonnays, and Pinot Noirs, to their very Burgundy-like, late-released "Library" wines.

**Substitutes:**

Maufoux Blanc de Blancs can stand in quite adequately for Moreau Blanc, as can Oliver Leflaive Bourgogne Chardonnay Les Setilles 1989 (the latter, however, has some slight wood elements in its taste—vanilla, oak, etc.). If Eschol White is not available, try Monterey Classic White or Mondavi Woodbridge Chardonnay.

Here then ends the second white-wine tasting. You would do well to go straight on through the Third and Fourth flights, but, if you wish, there are alternatives.

*Following the lead of your own preferences:*
   Whether you liked the first wine better, the Moreau Blanc, or the second wine, the Trefethen Eschol White, go on to the Third Flight.

*Following the kind of grapes:*
   Wine One: Go on to the Twelfth Flight.
   Wine Two: Go on to the Twelfth Flight.

*Following the wines of the country:*
   Wine One: Go on to the Third Flight.
   Wine Two: Go on to the Seventh Flight.

# THE THIRD FLIGHT

❧

## Soave Bolla 1990
### and
## B & G 1725 Bordeaux Blanc 1990

❧

I F THERE IS a universally known imported wine in the United States that is *not* Lambrusco, it must be Soave, and if it's Soave, in most people's minds it must be Soave Bolla. The Bolla firm, maker of the classic wines of Verona (Soave for white, Bardolino, Valpolicella, and Amarone for red), has so successfully identified its name with the wine that many people seem to think it's one word—which is perfectly okay, since Bolla's is a good, representative Soave.

The other half of this pairing is an equally sound and representative white Bordeaux (*Appellation Controllée Bordeaux Blanc*) from a long-established Bordeaux *négociant*. B & G handles a rather complete line of traditional Bordeaux wines, from simple reds and whites like this one (which bears the firm's proprietary name) up to classified châteaux.

All you really need know by way of preliminary beyond that is that at the level of production you are about to taste, both these firms can be relied upon for a sound, well-made wine that will be reasonably consistent in flavor and style from year to year.

Now the ball is in your court: see, swirl, smell, sip, savor, and spit. Talk the wines over if you're tasting in a group, and then check back here for explanations, consolations, and advice to the winelorn.

### Appearance.

Once again the colors of these wines present no problems. Both are (or should be) pale straw, clear and clean. They are almost identical in shading: perhaps if you strain a bit you could see that the Soave is a hint paler than the Bordeaux Blanc, but the difference falls somewhere between negligible and invisible.


Aroma.

Their aromas, however, will probably strike most people as markedly different.

For one thing, this particular vintage of Soave offers little in the way of bouquet. Most people will find its aroma insignificant, almost nonexistent. Some, by dint of real effort and perhaps a lot of imagination, will catch faint whiffs of fruit and of light floral, herbaceous scents. You should regard such absence of aroma as a real though not fatal defect in the wine. It's obviously not serious enough to ruin your enjoyment of it, but it does deprive you of one of the wine's attractions. Soave should have a delicate—not hallucinatory—aroma that mixes fruit and flower and herb. It should definitely smell clean and fresh. This particular vintage doesn't smell unclean; it has scarcely any scent at all.

Comparatively speaking, the Bordeaux Blanc appears to have the more forceful and distinctive aroma. It may seem sharper and to some people, perhaps because of their remembrances of dinners with wines of this type, to have a kind of salt-air tang, like the clean, fresh aroma that comes from a plate of freshly shucked clams or oysters. That's imaginative, of course, but why not? It points you in a right direction for the use of wines like these. By the way, it also means that people who dislike clams and oysters and whose associations with salt-air tang are low tide in Newark Bay may very well find the aroma of the B & G 1725 unpleasant. For them its comparatively greater presence is not a plus but a minus.

More conventionally, however, most people tend to describe the scent of the Bordeaux Blanc as a composite of grassy, herby, fruity, and/or earthy tones. That covers a lot of ground, and few tasters seem to find anything more specific to put a label to, unless it is a small but discernible lemon scent. That is probably because most Bordeaux Blanc is a blend, the most important parts of which are two distinctly different grapes, Sémillon and Sauvignon Blanc. Generally speaking, the grassy, herbaceous elements in Bordeaux Blanc are probably traceable to Sauvignon Blanc, and the earthy, fruity components to Sémillon. In wines of this caliber those two grapes may well be blended with several others of less note, but their aromas and flavors should still be pronounced in the final harmony.

### Taste.

You should be able to distinguish the flavors of the Soave and the Bordeaux Blanc equally clearly.

For most people, the Bolla moves: it seems sprightly, lively. This is because of the relatively high acidity of this Soave, which some people taste directly as a kind of bright tingling on the tongue. Those less tolerant of acidity may find the flavor veering into the sour range, even to the extent of outright unpleasantness. The majority of tasters, however, are probably going to find Soave Bolla pleasingly light, tart, and acidic, with a fruit component in its flavor that suggests citrus to some and apples to others. Among those who like this wine, a great number discern a small but pleasing aftertaste that they describe variously as tart, nicely bitter, or almondy. Such a finish usually is thought of as a hallmark of a well-made Soave.

The B & G 1725 Bordeaux Blanc distinguishes itself from the Soave in most key respects. Almost everybody feels it in the mouth as a less lively, slightly more weighty wine: fuller but less sprightly. At its worst, this apparently lower acidity in the Bordeaux can be sensed as not simply softness but flabbiness, though that is likely to be a minority opinion. For most people, the wine shows round and soft. On first taste it releases a little burst of fruit sweetness (distinctly not sugariness) and then follows it with what some people describe as a pleasing citric fruit flavor; most people simply taste fruit, period. The wine has a small but nice dry finish.

Both are well-made wines it is not unfair to think of as having been carefully designed to respond to two slightly different tastes in white wines. Neither is it unfair to think of them as good examples of differing national styles in making white wines.

The Soave and Italian white wines generally (with some conspicuous exceptions) favor the bright, light, acidic style. Most of them, particularly the varietal white wines from the hyphenated Italian areas of Trentino–Alto Adige and Friuli–Venezia Giulia, display more fruitiness, more clear taste of the grape variety, than Soave does, but they tend to be every bit as acidic and lively. Because of that, they are preeminently wines for drinking chilled and young—within a year or two of harvest.

The Bordeaux Blanc and other French wines from the most esteemed growing areas—Bordeaux, Burgundy, Alsace, parts of the Loire valley—predominantly favor the fuller style, with lower acid levels and more complex fruit flavors. Their greater body permits them to develop over time in the bottle, so they are characteristically (once you have moved beyond the simple shipper's wines such as the Bordeaux Blanc we have just tasted) wines for drinking at a few years of age and only lightly chilled in order to reveal their best bouquet and flavor.

There is, obviously, no good or bad at issue here. As always, it is at bottom a question of which style pleases you more—or even better, which style pleases you more under what circumstances or with what food. You can have a lot of fun and absorb a lot of calories working out a complete answer to that one.

## Substitutes:

Younger vintages of either wine will always make acceptable substitutes. For the Bordeaux, you could also try Maître d'Estournel Blanc. Instead of Bolla, you could try simple Soave from other makers, such as Anselmi, Folonari, Pieropan, Santa Sofia, or Zenato. A cru Soave (one from a single vineyard) will be more expensive and probably very different—much more distinctive and elegant—than a simple DOC Soave.

Here ends the third white-wine tasting. It would be best if you went right on to the Fourth Flight, but if you wish alternatives, there are several ways for you to proceed from here.

*Following the lead of your own preferences:*
   If you liked the first wine better, the Soave Bolla, go on to the
   Fifth Flight.
   If you liked the second wine better, the B & G 1725 Bordeaux
   Blanc, go on to the Ninth Flight.

*Following the kind of grapes:*
   Wine One: There are no other grapes like this in our tastings.
   Wine Two: Go on to the Ninth Flight.

*Following the wines of the country:*
   Go on to the Fourth Flight.

# THE FOURTH FLIGHT

❧

## *Cavit Pinot Grigio 1990*
## *and*
## *Barré Muscadet 1990*

❧

**T**HESE TWO KINDS OF WINE normally both have pretty high acid levels coupled with complete dryness, which makes them very versatile dinner wines with uncomplicated foods. Italians would use a wine like Pinot Grigio to accompany antipasto, while the French think of Muscadet as a classic wine with fresh shellfish, especially oysters. Within their basic structural similarities, you should be tasting for differing kinds and styles of fruitiness, body, and balance. I don't think that anyone who has tasted several of these wines would ever, even in a blind tasting, mistake a Muscadet for a Pinot Grigio. What you should be looking for in this tasting is the reason why that is so.

Good luck: swirl away.

Finished already? Made all your notes and talked everything over? Tasted everything with and without a little nibble? Then let's get on with it.

Appearance.

Yet once more, pale straw. Either one of these wines could well be the palest wine you've yet seen. In this particular vintage, the Pinot Grigio is ever so slightly paler than the Muscadet; in another vintage the reverse might easily be true. And either of these wines, in another vintage, might be a touch darker than this, but there is nothing at all abnormal about this degree of paleness.

**Aroma.**

Here the differences start showing themselves. Though neither wine has a big aroma, each is distinctive.

The Cavit is fruity and fresh. You may pick up a sort of leafy scent and suggestions of mint in it. You will sometimes come across more forceful versions of it, but this aroma gives you a very faithful rendition of the scent of the Pinot Grigio grape (in French, *Pinot gris*: the gray Pinot).

The Muscadet smells crisp and clean. Some people sense a kind of tartness and acidity in it, a scent like crisp apples. It may give the impression of being drier—less sweet—than the Pinot Grigio's aroma. It too is a single grape scent, though the Muscadet is usually much less intense in aroma than the Pinot Grigio. Neither is considered an aromatic grape.

The great majority of tasters find the bouquet of both wines lively, or pleasing, or refreshing, and they tend to summarize the differences between them by describing the Pinot Grigio as more delicate, the Muscadet as more complex, or the Pinot Grigio as having more fruit and the Muscadet more personality. That last word is vague; what people seem to mean by it is some combination of complexity and charm.

**Taste.**

First of all, the Pinot Grigio strikes the tongue as lively, nervous, sometimes even a bit *frizzante* (fizzy). Sometimes it can be felt as a little prickly; that's the good, bright acid at work, animating the fruit.

Different people taste that combination of fruit and acid in markedly different ways. At one extreme, a taster may describe it as sharp, or bitter. Most are likely to be at the other end of the spectrum and taste it as fruit and spice—a nice white-grape flavor, perhaps mixed with some suggestions of apple or of citrus or of clove, maybe even a hint of sweetness (if people taste that at all, it's usually right at the start, before the acid really asserts itself). The acid persists into the finish, which—depending on whether they like it or not—people will call everything from pleasantly astringent to sharp, sour, bitter. Overall, however, most tasters find this Pinot Grigio bright, crisp, and very pleasing—perhaps a bit light (1990 was a light-bodied vintage), but pleasing nevertheless.

Responses to the Muscadet can be very paradoxical. Objectively speaking, the wine seems to be rounder and to have a bit less acid and less fruit than the Pinot Grigio, but that dual reduction hits individual palates quite differently. A few tasters can really feel the absence of the fruit and as a consequence find the wine too acid, almost sour. At the opposite extreme, others sense the lower acid and find the wine softer and blander than the Cavit. The great majority of tasters, however, seem to fall in the middle range and find the Muscadet quite pleasant. They describe a wine that is slightly fuller in body, a little less crisp, and a little less acidic than the Pinot Grigio, a wine that is very dry—almost austere—with interesting but subdued fruit and a completely dry finish. Most people take that greater fullness and total dryness to indicate that this is a great wine with seafood, and experience almost always shows they are right.

There you have it: very different wines, though because of the limits of our language for sensory description, the words and phrases we have to use to talk about them are uncomfortably similar.

Accounting for their differences is no easy task either. Sure, the basic flavor of their grapes differs—the Muscadet is normally a more neutral grape—but what makes the fruit so much more prominent in the Cavit than in the Barré? I don't know for certain, but I'll risk a guess. There may be more residual sugar—naturally occurring unfermented grape sugar—in the Pinot Grigio than in the Muscadet.

In the course of fermentation, sugar is normally converted into alcohol by the yeasts on the grapes. Dry wines are the result of converting all the available sugar to alcohol. Sweet wines are produced when the fermentation either naturally halts before all the sugar is converted, or when the fermentation is stopped by raising or lowering the temperature to kill the yeast. Preserving a small trace of sugar in a wine of high acidity would help to reinforce the strength of its fruit and bring it more to the fore, perhaps even make it more full.

Because of the high acid in these two wines, you really wouldn't taste a trace amount of sugar as sweetness, but it would contribute toward fleshing out the fruit flavors and raising them up a notch or two on the flavor scale. If I'm right, these two wines make a fine illustration of just what an impact small adjustments in our trinity of sugar and acid and fruit can have on the final taste of a wine.

**Substitutes:**

For either wine, a younger vintage is the best choice. Lacking that, Clos de Beauregard and Domaine du Château de l'Hyvernière will quite adequately stand in for the Barré Muscadet; Domaine de la Batardière and Domaine du Verger are also possible, but they are exceptionally fruity for their kind. Collavini Borgo Armenti Pinot Grigio, EnoFriulia Pinot Grigio, Peter Zemmer Pinot Grigio (Alto Adige), Pasqua Grigio della Luna (Valdadige), and Castello Banfi Pinot Grigio (Tuscany) will serve well as alternatives, though all are more distinctive and refined than the Cavit.

And that, class, concludes your lesson for today, and with it the fourth white-wine tasting session. There are several ways for you to proceed from here.

*Following the lead of your own preferences:*
   If you liked the first wine better, the Cavit Pinot Grigio, go on to the Fifth Flight.
   If you liked the second wine better, the Barré Muscadet, go on to the Ninth Flight.

*Following the kind of grapes:*
   This is the only tasting of either of these kinds of grapes.

*Following the wines of the country:*
   Wine One: Go on to the Fifth Flight.
   Wine Two: Go on to the Seventh Flight.

# THE FIFTH FLIGHT

∿ ◠◟◞◠ ∿

*Livio Felluga
Tocai Friulano 1989
and
Sichel Bereich
Bernkastel Qualitätswein 1989*

◡◠◟◞◡

YOUR MISSION, should you chose to accept it, is to taste these two wines, decide which you like, and then figure out why.

Here are a few of the key elements that could play a part in your preference. First of all, one of these wines is markedly less alcoholic than the other. There should be differences in body between the two wines. Their grapes are different and ought to taste markedly distinct. Aromas too—one is usually called spicy, the other floral. And there are differences in dryness and sweetness to be taken into account here. Finally, there should be a very perceptible stylistic difference between them, a distinction in what you could call their whole attack.

Other items may strike you as well: this is not meant to be an exhaustive list, just a set of reminders of what you can try to be aware of while you are performing your ritual sighting, swirling, sniffing, sipping, savoring, and spitting. So go to it, and take good notes. And just in case you've forgotten again, this is not like an examination in school. There are no wrong answers, unless you're really perverse and lie to yourself about what you like, or let yourself be bullied into something you think you ought to like. Even then, that's wrong only because it's wrong for you, not because there is anything objectively wrong with any choice you make.

Got that? Okay, stop that nauseating display of gratitude and go taste.

All right, let's talk about these wines, taking the second first because you've had a wine somewhat similar to this before—Blue Nun, in the very first flight of white wines. Bereich Bernkastel is, as the name and the shape of the bottle indicate, a German wine. Bereich simply means district or area and is a word in common use on German wine labels. Bernkastel is the name of the particular wine-making district, in this case a very large and famous one on the Mosel River. Qualitätswein indicates approximately the middle level of the German wine-ranking system. So this wine is a cousin of the Liebfraumilch of your first flight, which is also a Qualitätswein, though it originated from a much larger viticultural area or group of areas, along the banks of the Rhine. This Bernkastel is made predominantly if not exclusively from Riesling grapes.

The Bernkastel's companion wine in this flight comes from a very different part of the world: Friuli, in Italy's extreme northeastern corner—a region that formed a part of the Austro-Hungarian Empire and its successor states until well into this century. Tocai is the most popular white wine in the region, where it is drunk with almost every conceivable sort of food on every sort of occasion. It is always vinified dry and should not be confused with the Hungarian Tokay, a sweet dessert wine, or Alsatian Tokay, which is made from another grape altogether (the *Pinot gris*, in fact). Just for the record, our wine is pronounced Toe-kigh (to rhyme with "high"); the other two wines are pronounced Toe-kay to rhyme with "hay."

## Appearance.

In appearance, this Bernkastel looks very much like the Blue Nun of the first white-wine pair. It has the same light, pale straw color with just a suggestion of a few greenish highlights that is the hallmark of young Riesling-based wines. If your bottle is showing darker than that, it is possibly too old to drink, in which case it should taste rather flat and tired—something akin to stale ginger ale.

In appearance, the Tocai is very like the Bernkastel—a clean, pale straw color, definitely a shade darker or more golden than the German wine, but still light and clear. Here, too, very dark colors

## German Wine Geography

German wine labels can be very confusing to the uninstructed eye, and they aren't helped much in clarity by the abundance of Gothic script that squiggles across and around and up and down them. Under all that baroque camouflage, however, there is a wealth of very exact information.

Vintage of course is prominently and unambiguously displayed. After that, look for the level of the wine: Tafelwein, which is rightly not often exported; Qualitätswein, often abbreviated QbA; and Qualitätswein mit Prädikat (QmP). Under German wine law, the wines of the first two classifications may be fermented with added sugar (chaptalization), but Qualitätswein mit Prädikat can be made only with the grape's own natural sugars.

After that, look for the large geographical region from which the wine comes: Ahr, Hessische Bergstrasse, Mittelrhein, Nahe, Rheingau, Rheinhessen, Rheinpfalz, Mosel-Saar-Ruwer, Franken, Württemberg, and Baden. The most important on the American market are Mosel-Saar-Ruwer (usually just called Mosel, and often spelled the French way, Moselle) and the three Rhine areas, Rheingau, Rheinhessen, and Rheinpfalz.

Finally, look for more precise geographical or vineyard information: a town name (usually ending in "er"—for example, Bernkasteler, a wine from Bernkastel) and/or a vineyard name (for example, Bernkasteler Doktor). If you want to get yet more precise, check the name of the vineyard owner/winemaker, since many vineyards (like Bernkasteler Doktor) are divided among several owners, any or all of whom may bottle wine under their own label—which will, if you hunt hard enough among the squiggles, give you all this information.

would indicate a wine oxidized or oxidizing. Tocai should be drunk relatively young, but it can take some bottle-age with advantage.

## Aroma.

If all is well with your wine, the odds are very strong that most of you found the Bernkastel's aroma very pleasant. Different tasters will report different degrees of intensity, of course, ranging from very faint to strong, but most use similar words to describe what they are smelling. "Flowery" and "floral" head the list, usually followed by "fruity" or "sweet." Some tasters may discern more specific scents: peach, mango, and citrus are not unusual candidates among the fruits, and cinnamon, mint, and even camphor appear among the spices.

Normally a minority dislikes the aroma of this wine (though in any random group it might well be a majority). Those who find it unpleasing frequently describe it as smelling musty to them, or smelling of wet woolens, or similar phenomena. What they seem to object to is the fruit odor, which they find overpowering or cloying. Whether they like it or dislike it, however, what this wine gives them is a classic Riesling scent.

Don't be surprised by great diversity of opinion about either the intensity or the quality of the Tocai's aroma. Especially in a comparison with the Bernkastel, it is possible for some tasters to discern little more than a strong presence of alcohol—not because the Tocai has so much alcohol, but because the Bernkastel has so little: 8.5 percent as opposed to the Tocai's 12.5 percent.

But most tasters pick up a range of different scents in this wine. The one most commonly noted is a bittersweet nuttiness, which some tasters specifically discern as bitter almonds. Fruit, too, appears often in people's descriptions, and they tend to emphasize its ripeness or spiciness: comparing the Tocai's odor to spiced pears, for instance, is one possibility. Equally common descriptions cite the odors of flowers and spice and earth, the latter (for those who aren't happy with this wine) often shading over into the oppressively musky.

## Taste.

Opinions tend to be more evenly divided about the taste of the Bernkastel. Usually a small minority actively dislikes it. Sugarphobes, of course, taste nothing in it but sweetness and hate it for that reason: they are balanced out by sugarphiles, who agree with them about the taste but love it for that reason. Others don't feel as strongly but simply find it uninteresting; they will describe it as too light, or watery, or flaccid, or dull. Those who like it praise its light fruitiness and moderate sweetness, which they taste as complementing each other. They may specifically taste peach or pear or even crabapple in it. Almost all tasters perceive a definite sweet finish to the wine and an apparent increase in sweetness as the wine opens in the glass. Some of both the likers and the dislikers will call this Bernkastel soft: that perception results from the wine's relatively low acidity. Some vintages of these wines will be even lower in acid and will actually taste flabby, while others may be higher in acid and consequently taste drier. This particular vintage of Bernkastel has achieved a lovely balance on a delicate, small scale.

The Tocai often feels slightly prickly or fizzy on the tongue, giving it a bit of an edge that different tasters sense as either a pleasing liveliness or an annoying sharpness. Those who dislike that aspect of the wine may also find it a bit on the sour side, overall. Most tasters tend to remark on the wine's nice bright fruit or its spiciness. Hazelnuts and pears are two specific flavors that many people taste in Tocai. Many also report tasting a good, somewhat almondy finish.

Whichever of these wines you may have preferred, tasting them side by side should have helped you to smell and taste more clearly important aspects of both.

Aromas, for instance: you should (if neither alcohol nor sugar interferes for you) be able to place the Tocai definitely in the spicy category and the Bernkastel definitely in the floral, even though one may have some flowery tones and the other some spicy ones. Also, you should be able to perceive that the bouquet of the Bernkastel is comparatively delicate and slight, while that of the Tocai is bigger and more assertive, but somewhat coarser.

The taste comparisons work in similar directions. The Bernkastel allows you to see the good acid in the Tocai, which you might otherwise miss, while the Tocai underlines the charm of the Bernkastel's softness. You are, I think, also made more aware than you might otherwise be of the heft of the Tocai—not that it is a big wine, but its roundness and more aggressive fruit make its medium body feel more substantial on the tongue, especially when counterpoised by a low-alcohol, light-bodied wine like the Bernkastel.

Overall, those things should add up to two wholly different styles, two distinctive modes of attack. The Bernkastel succeeds by charm and delicacy, reinforced by a touch of sweetness. The net effect is of lightness and grace, a wine that promises refreshment.

The Tocai on the other hand is a bigger wine, fully dry, and more forward: not what you would call muscular (you wouldn't say anything like that, would you?), but definitely more energetic—bracing rather than refreshing. Your preference among wines as interestingly different as these should be beginning to blaze a pretty clear trail for you through the white-wine jungle.

A word about the makers of these two wines. Sichel is an old and highly respected shipper of German wines. Now a part of the Schieffelin Company, it exports to the United States the whole gamut of German wine, from Liebfraumilch up to estate-bottled rarities. Livio Felluga is a family firm rooted in Friuli. Felluga vinifies most of the important grapes of Friuli and is particularly notable for its white wines, especially those made from the traditional vines of the region. These are now imported to the United States by Palace Brands, a division of Heublein.

## Substitutes:

Younger vintages of either wine are the first line of substitutes. Failing that, the Bernkastel Qualitätswein from Deinhard & Company makes an excellent stand-in for the Sichel wine: it tends to be a bit drier and slightly more acid, but otherwise conforms quite nicely to our description. For the Tocai, try versions of the same wine from other producers in the Collio or Colli Orientali area of Friuli— Russiz Superiore, for instance, or Borgo Conventi, or EnoFriulia. Also possible, though a touch less distinctive, is Angoris Tocai Friulano (Isonzo del Friuli).

This is the conclusion of the fifth flight. There are several ways for you to proceed from here.

*Following the lead of your own preferences:*
   If you liked the first wine better, the Felluga Tocai, go on to the Eighth Flight.
   If you liked the second wine better, the Sichel Bernkastel, go on to the Sixth Flight.

*Following the kind of grapes:*
   Wine One: This is the only Tocai tasting.
   Wine Two: Go on to the Sixth Flight.

*Following the wines of the country:*
   Wine One: Go on to the Eleventh Flight.
   Wine Two: Go on to the Sixth Flight.

# THE SIXTH FLIGHT

～❦～

*Rudolf Müller Piesporter*
*Goldtropfchen Riesling*
*Kabinett 1989*
*and*
*Deinhard Deidesheimer*
*Herrgottsacker Riesling*
*Spätlese 1988*

～❦～

THIS FLIGHT SHOULD certainly stretch your new skills, so taste carefully—especially those of you who have been pluming yourselves on your abilities to discern flavors even in the presence of residual sugar. These two are only lightly sweet wines, one of the Kabinett classification and the other a Spätlese, but they embody the two broadest divisions in top-quality German wines. In the first place, representing the wines of the River Mosel, in the traditional long-necked green bottle, is a single-estate (Goldtropfchen) wine from the town of Piesport. And in the second column, representing the wines of the River Rhine, is a single-estate (Herrgottsacker) wine from the town of Deidesheim, in the equally traditional Rhine bottle of long-necked brown glass. The differences between the wines of the Mosel and the Rhine are significant, but they are also subtle, as are the differences between Kabinett wines and the slightly later harvested Spätlese wines. You will have to concentrate to register all the significant differences among so many family similarities.

Okay, you've been warned: now do the ritual, and report back after you've talked over your findings.

## Appearance.

As usual, the appearance of these two wines presents no problems: both are the classic pale straw color, with occasional—and attractive—green or gold highlights.

## Aroma.

The first impression most people form of the scent of the Piesporter in some way or other reflects its freshness: they may call it fresh, or clean, or refreshing, but almost all find it pleasing. Most also find it of delicate to moderate strength, and a great majority of tasters also detect in it distinct flowery tones. Fruit, too, appears often in descriptions of this aroma—peaches or, more often, pears—often with an exotic spicy element attached: woodruff or pepper, for instance, are both possibilities. Some people also report green tones as well—grass, or herbaceous odors, or green grapes. For most, this elaborate combination of elements is still delicate; but for others it is just too sweet and too perfumed to be truly pleasurable.

The Deidesheimer strikes most people as having the more pronounced aroma of the two. Some tasters describe it as deep and pungent, somewhat reminiscent of a red wine's aroma (that's what they say if they like it) or almost cheesey or like damp wool (that sort of description usually comes from those who don't like it). As it sits in the glass, the Deidesheimer opens up to release more floral aromas and eventually fruit scents—bananas and especially the lemon smells that are commonly associated with the Riesling grape, though other fruits may well be named. In a Spätlese like this those scents, which are typical of this kind of wine, tend to be especially forceful. Again, those who don't care for this wine will find those fruit odors too strong: they will probably call them overripe.

## Taste.

The flavors of the Piesporter and Deidesheimer distinguish themselves from each other in much the same way. Most people taste the Mosel wine as delicate and light, fruity and pleasingly acidic.

### German Wine Grades

Kabinett is one of the grades of Qualitätswein mit Prädikat, wines which must be vinified only with their own natural sugars. Since the German wine-growing areas are very northerly and the Riesling grape is a late ripener, the amount of QmP wine produced varies tremendously from harvest to harvest. In good years, grapes intended for QmP are left on the vines as late as possible to concentrate their sugars and acids, and sometimes there is help from *Botrytis*. Repeated hand pickings, often selecting individual grapes from a bunch, are the key to the greatest German wines. On the label, the varying degrees of sweetness achieved are indicated by the particular *Prädikat* (descriptive word or phrase): in ascending order of sweetness and of lateness of harvest, Kabinett, Spätlese, Auslese, Beerenauslese, and Trockenbeerenauslese. The last two are usually referred to simply as BA and TBA, respectively, for obvious reasons. All these gradations sweeter than Kabinett and Spätlese are usually regarded as dessert wines, and some examples of them are among the very greatest wines of that category.

Different tasters, of course, will detect different fruit flavors, though pears and citrus—especially lemon—are the most common. But don't be surprised if you or one of your fellow tasters also pick up a hint of strawberry or black currant or a more floral element in there. A great many people find to their surprise and pleasure that this Mosel is drier than they expected, especially in the finish—probably the effect of its good acid balance. The possible objections to this wine are as varied as ever. For some it is too acidic, for others too sweet, for others too delicate—they taste nothing at all. But the majority of tasters seem to find it modestly sweet, light, fruity, and delicate, all within a small but pleasing range; "charming" is a word they will often use to sum it up.

The biggest impressions the Deidesheimer makes, after its initial rush of fruit and sweetness, are of liveliness and intensity: it seems to most people more forceful and more aggressive, a bit bigger and more mouthfilling than the Piesporter. It too has a fine bright acidity that balances its residual sugar, so that this Rhine wine actually seems to dry somewhat in your mouth before it ends with a beautifully long, honeyed finish. Some people describe it as tasting of pears and especially of apricots as well, with hints of thyme and lemon mixed in—a whole fruit stand of flavors mingling together. Its balance of sweetness and acidity and its sort of modulation or alternation in the mouth of sweetness and dryness are prominent features of this wine, and most tasters comment on them in one way or another, though their language for doing so can run anywhere from confusion and frustration at being unable to pin this wine down, to real satisfaction with its complexity.

Congratulations! You've now figured out the broad distinction between wines of the Mosel and wines of the Rhine.

No, I'm not kidding, and no, it's not simply that Mosels come in green bottles and Rhines in brown (though it doesn't hurt to know that for quick identification at a distance). But the delicacy, and the lightness, and the floral qualities that we talked about are all traditionally regarded as hallmarks of Mosel wines, which are probably among the world's lightest "serious" wines. And the greater liveliness and force, the bigger body and richer flavor of the Deidesheimer are precisely the characteristics that distinguish Rhine wines from Mosels. So you did it—you're capable of tasting that kind of quite subtle distinction; and if you can do that, the world of white wine holds very few problems for you. You're well on your way to getting a workable handle on it already.

Just to give you a little better idea of what you've been drinking, here is a little extra information about these wines and their makers.

Piesport is one of the most esteemed wine towns in the district known as the Middle Mosel, and Goldtropfchen is the most prized vineyard within the denomination. Rudolf Müller is a very reputable *négociant*, with a particular expertise in the wines of the Mosel. Its wine is imported to the United States by Heublein's Palace Brands.

Deidesheim is one of the most esteemed wine towns in the Mittelhaardt district of the Rheinpfalz, the part of Germany bordering on Alsace. It is commonly known in English as the Palatinate. Its wines have long been popular in Germany and abroad. Herrgottsacker is one of several top-rated vineyards within the limits of Deidesheim. Deinhard is a long-established (since the 1700s) firm of German winemakers and wine dealers: it owns excellent properties in several of Germany's best wine regions. Its wines are imported to the United States by Kobrand.

**Substitutes:**

As always, younger vintages of the two primary wines should be your first choice. Otherwise, Deinhard also exports a Piesporter Goldtropfchen Riesling Kabinett, and Rudolf Müller exports a Deidesheimer Holfstuck Riesling Qualitätswein roughly comparable to this Herrgottsacker. Other major exporters—Sichel, for instance—also send us wines of the same villages, if not of exactly the same vineyards.

This concludes the Sixth Flight. There are several ways for you to proceed from here.

*Following the lead of your own preferences:*
Whether you liked the first wine better, the Piesporter, or the second wine, the Deidesheimer, go on to the Seventh Flight.

*Following the kind of grapes:*
Go on to the Seventh Flight.

*Following the wines of the country:*
This concludes the German wines in these tastings.

# THE SEVENTH FLIGHT

~◈~

## Trimbach Alsace Riesling 1988
### and
## Trefethen Napa Valley
## White Riesling 1989

~◈~

YOU'RE NOT DONE with Riesling yet. This is a grape variety that rivals—many would say surpasses—Chardonnay as the premier white-wine grape of the world, and like the Chardonnay it is cultivated and vinified just about everywhere in the globe that serious winemaking is possible. And like Chardonnay, too, Riesling responds so sensitively to different soils and vinification techniques that it is possible to distinguish, in broad terms at least, what can genuinely be called national styles. So far you've been dealing with the classic German style in Riesling: in this flight you're going to be tasting to find out what France and the United States make of this grape.

Pour the wines, see, swirl away, then smell, sip, savor, and spit.

Appearance.

In color, both these Rieslings are a clear straw yellow, a tone darker than any of the German Rieslings you've been drinking. This is a characteristic color range for non-German Rieslings other than late-harvest wines, which would normally be considerably darker and more golden than any wine we've yet dealt with.

Despite the fact that the Alsatian wine zone directly touches on the German and in geographical and climatic terms has to be considered as virtually identical to it, most tasters find that the Riesling wines of Alsace differ quite markedly from those of Germany. So great is the difference, in fact, that Alsatian Riesling and Rhine Riesling (even though Alsatian Riesling grows along the banks of the Rhine, Rhine Riesling by universal practice always refers to German wine) are routinely cited by wine professionals as a textbook case of exactly the kinds of difference vinification techniques can make in a wine.

I think you can see this clearly right from the beginning, in that slight difference in color. The drier German Rieslings (the Kabinett classification) are usually paler, more delicate looking; these two wines are comparatively more robust in appearance.

### Aroma.

Most tasters also notice big differences in the Alsatian Riesling's aroma. It smells drier, for one thing, and a bit deeper. Most people still smell fruit in it, but often now compounded with a whole range of other odors in the leafy-herbal-spicy group: mint and pepper and grass, for instance, and sometimes even woodruff. The Trimbach's aroma is still not a big one, however, and for many people those specific elements are just too elusive. All they will report smelling is a general sense of dryness and depth, and their reactions to it can run from mildly pleased to neutral to mild dislike of its blandness.

As a handy reminder to you of previous flights, the California Riesling turns out to be a wine much more in the Germanic style. Most people still find its aroma noticeably stronger and heavier than that of German Riesling (and in fact heavier than this Alsatian example), but they also tend to find a lot of the same components in its scent that they found in German Riesling. Most describe it as soft and fresh and mildly sweet-smelling, for instance. Many discern the same sort of fruitiness and spiciness they found in German Riesling: pears and apples and even mangoes are often mentioned, along with leafy odors and mint and pepper. For some tasters, of course, these odors are either indistinguishable (they are in that case likely simply to call the wine flowery or perfumed) or indiscernible (they're likely to call it dull) or over-strong (they'll probably call it cloying), but most of those who have been responding pleasurably to Riesling will find the Trefethen wine's aroma typical and enjoyable.

**Taste.**

People tend to react in rather polar ways to the Trimbach Riesling. Those who dislike it usually say it has too much acid, which causes it to taste tart or sour or bitter to them. Those who like it tend to admire its balancing of dry fruit and acid. They find strong citrus elements—especially grapefruit—and other, more subdued, fruit flavors—peach or pear, plum or apple—and a very slight spicy flavor in it, with a finish that they describe as dry or astringent (those who don't like it call it bitter).

The Trefethen Napa Riesling strikes most tasters as a heavier wine, with more body and fruit. The specific flavors most likely to be mentioned fall into the by now familiar Riesling range—apple, peach, plum, spice. It may seem slightly *pétillant*, a little fizzy on the tongue. Its acidity catches almost everyone's attention: because of it, people will differ surprisingly on just how much sugar they taste— or think they taste—in this wine, and their finding it sweet or dry doesn't seem to correlate with whether they like it or not. Those who do like it frequently describe it as bright, or live, or balanced. Those who don't say the fruit fades out too fast or that it finishes too bitterly or that it is badly structured.

These two wines as a pair are a fair example of the styles of their respective countries in vinifying Riesling. Both are bigger and fuller than German Riesling. Alsatian Rieslings, like this Trimbach wine, tend to be fully dry and medium-bodied, with a slightly steely quality that differs markedly from the German soft touch. The American dry style in Riesling, of which this Trefethen is a very fair example, runs toward greater fruit and higher alcohol than either Alsatian or German Riesling, and it has a rather full body that possesses neither the steeliness of Alsace nor the softness of Rhine. There is also a sweet or lightly sweet American style in Riesling that in most key respects follows the pattern of German Riesling, so in shopping for American Riesling (whether East Coast or West Coast, New York, New Jersey, California, or Washington) make sure you read the label carefully for information about the total or only relative dryness of the wine. Both the United States and Alsace also make dessert wines from late-picked, very ripe, and sometimes botrytized Riesling grapes, just as Germany does. All of these very sweet wines are capable of reaching levels of extraordinary succulence, and they are never inexpensive.

Because of their expense, and because also their extreme sweetness makes it impossible to taste anything else after them, we won't be dealing directly with the great dessert wines. You shouldn't hesitate to try them on your own, however. At their proper place in a meal, with—or better, as—dessert, they can be incomparable. All of the German QmP classifications of Auslese or sweeter are eminently qualified to serve as dessert wines. Equivalent classifications elsewhere bear designations like Vendange Tardive or Sélections des Grains Nobles (Alsace) or Late Harvest (California). All should be deep gold in color, richly scented, lusciously sweet, but also with a wealth of flavors and nuances beyond simple sugar.

Trimbach is an old family firm whose participation in the Alsatian wine trade began in the seventeenth century. They produce the full range of Alsatian white wines—Riesling, Gewürztraminer, Sylvaner, Pinot Gris, Pinot Blanc. Trefethen Vineyards is a highly respected, family-run Napa Valley winery. Trefethen also makes a very Burgundian-tasting Chardonnay as well as a handful of red wines.

**Substitutes:**

Younger vintages of these two wines are the best option. Otherwise, use young Riesling from such important Alsace houses as Dopff "au Moulin," Dopff & Irion, Hugel, Muré (especially Muré's Clos St-Landelin), and Willm; and young, dry Riesling from other California or Pacific Northwest growers (e.g., Château Ste-Michelle).

Here ends the Seventh Flight. There are several ways for you to proceed from here.

*Following the lead of your own preferences:*
   If you enjoyed either the first wine, the Trimbach Riesling, or the second wine, the Trefethen Napa White Riesling, go on to the Eighth Flight.

*Following the kind of grapes:*
   This is the last Riesling tasting. Make sure you haven't missed the First, Fifth, and Sixth flights.

*Following the wines of the country:*
   Go on to the Eighth Flight.

# THE EIGHTH FLIGHT

~~~~~

*Hugel Alsace*
*Gewürztraminer 1989*
*and*
*Parducci Mendocino County*
*Gewürztraminer 1990*

~~~~~

THESE TWO WINES mark the transition between medium-bodied and full-bodied white wines. Depending on how they are vinified, Gewürztraminers will range from medium-bodied and highly aromatic to full-bodied and more restrained, from fully dry through lightly sweet to lusciously sweet, late-harvest-type dessert wines that can rival the finest Rieslings for succulence.

For our purposes, the Gewürztraminer qualifies as an almost perfect grape: it has a distinctive, quite easily rememberable aroma and flavor, and almost everybody likes it. I'm not trying to prejudice your opinion, but the Gewürztraminer—from the consumer's point of view if not the winemaker's—is a user-friendly grape. Its clumsy name is its only consumer problem, and most people get around that by either shortening it to Gewürz or abbreviating it to GT.

The two wines you are about to taste have been chosen as fair representatives of the dominant styles of Gewürztraminer from its two currently most interesting areas of production, Alsace and California. The Alsace wine is fully dry, as is traditional there; the California example is lightly sweet, the style currently most popular there.

Enough preamble: taste the wines. Remember your full ritual—
see, swirl, smell, sip, savor, and spit. And don't forget to try tasting
both with and without a bite of food to see how it affects the wine.
Go to it now.

### Appearance.

For the first time in quite a while, we have some color variation to
deal with here. The Alsatian Gewürz is straw colored, perhaps a bit
deeper than you've been seeing among the Rieslings, with greenish
gold highlights. The California Gewürztraminer is still darker
straw, a bit more golden perhaps, with a definite pinkish tinge to it,
at least in this vintage: in some lights it will look like an onionskin
tinge. Both wines should be attractive, clear, and bright.

### Aroma.

As far as aroma is concerned, both these wines ought to give you
something you can really grapple with: most people think of Gewürztraminer as an aromatic grape, and rightly so. A Gewürz
without odor is a crippled wine.

Most tasters describe the aroma of the Hugel as clean and fresh.
They find that it is made up of both fruit and floral elements, but
when you search for more specifics, you wind up with a whole fruit
stand. The possibilities include apples, figs, grapefruit, raisins,
anise, grass, mint, pepper, and just generalized spices.

Many people have real difficulty pinning down specific components of this aroma, though they find the whole thing quite distinctive. Most tasters like it: they call it pleasant, intriguing, appetizing,
and other words to the same effect. For some people, however, it is
all a bit too much, and they find this aroma somewhat foxy or
musky or musty, cloying or overperfumed. Very few ever describe it
as insignificant or delicate: when such a thing happens with a
Gewürztraminer, it almost always means either nasal troubles or
bottle troubles.

Most of the broader categories of things that people discern in the
Hugel Gewürztraminer they will also find in the Parducci's aroma. It
is similarly fresh, clean, and fruity, though most tasters report its
scent as less forceful and slightly more fruity than the first wine's.
That is, it is *comparatively* more delicate and less intense; some will
call it weaker. If you really press yourself and your fellow tasters and

smell for all you're worth, you might pick up some specific aroma elements that distinguish this wine a bit further from the Alsatian. For instance, people sometimes discern scents of pear and citrus or almond in the California wine, as well as those scents it shares with the Alsatian GT, scents such as flower and fruit and grass and mint (you might even find that the Parducci has a specifically spearmint odor). Objections and negative comments are usually pretty much the same here as for Wine One.

## Taste.

The fruit, vegetable, and flower stand stays open for business during tasting as well as smelling, and the same cornucopia of specific elements usually appears here. Those who don't like this sort of wine tend to respond to the totality rather than to components, and they may simply call the taste of Gewürztraminer peculiar, or unpleasant, or strange, or—more rarely—too sweet.

What that last comment usually reflects, when it is made of dry Gewürztraminers like the first of these and lightly sweet wines like the second, is a confusion of the flavor of intense fruit with sweetness. If you pay close attention, you can really see that it is actually fruit flavor and not sugar you are tasting. This phenomenon happens occasionally with any number of different kinds of white wine. I've always wondered whether we're not the victims here of a bit of Pavlovian palatal conditioning: because our routine experience of intense fruit flavor is almost always in association with sugars as well, does it mean that the one taste automatically calls up the other for us?

Whatever the truth of that matter, it remains a fact that some tasters have trouble—especially with a spicy grape like this one— distinguishing between strong fruit and sweetness. There is not much one can do about that other than to be aware of the possibility and to practice making the distinction by drinking lots of dry, fruity white wine.

I warned you this was going to be a rigorous discipline.

Tasters who like this kind of wine spot a whole range of flavors at work in it. Of the Hugel version, for instance, in addition to simple, generalized fruit, they may report tangy fruit, licorice, pears, pepper, and spice, while the Parducci rendition of Gewürztraminer may elicit responses that include the omnipresent simple fruit, apples, grapefruit, pears, cinnamon, and spice. Most people find the Hugel very crisp and acidic and tasting somewhat less fruity on the whole than its aroma led them to expect. The Parducci, on the other hand, usually surprises people by being—comparatively—very fruity, more so than its smaller aroma promised, and also—again comparatively—less acidic. Both these impressions probably derive from its little bit of residual sugar, which heightens the fruit flavors even as it tones down the acidity. Both GT's fit the definition of wines at the upper end of the medium-bodied spectrum, and both consequently feel like substantial presences on the palate. Depending on your reaction to their acid/fruit or acid/sugar balance, you may find the Hugel too biting, perhaps verging on sour, or the Parducci too soft, lacking in bite, or perhaps verging on flabby. Or either one of them may strike you as a wine in perfect equilibrium, with just the right amount of acid and body to support a lively and distinct varietal flavor.

Characteristic varietal flavor is, in fact, what you're tasting in these two wines. No matter what words you've used to describe it, that conglomeration of fruit and spice that we've been talking about in the aroma and the taste is typical of the Gewürztraminer grape. It may vary in intensity (as it does slightly in these two wines), and individual wines may vary considerably in the sweetness or dryness they partner it with, but that spectrum of sensations is what Gewürztraminer yields everywhere it is vinified.

Regional differences do occur, of course. For instance, the Hugel Gewürztraminer seems measurably more acidic than the Parducci, which has a fuller and richer, though softer and less bright, fruit flavor. That, I think, owes to the respective climates in which these grapes were grown. California grapes just routinely reach greater ripeness than Alsatian grapes. As a consequence, they possess more developed flavors, higher sugars (which means higher alcohol in a completely dry wine), and lower acid. So the firmer, brighter style is typically Alsatian, and the softer, fuller style is Californian.

If you pay careful attention to the finish of these two wines, you'll probably notice that the Alsatian Gewürztraminer finishes drier and somewhat longer than the Californian, and that it plants a little barb at the back of your throat before it goes down. For some people that finish is a little too bitter and raspy. For others it is pleasantly astringent. But whether it is enjoyed or deplored, it too is characteristic of the Alsatian style of slightly austere, acidic attack. Neither style, obviously, is objectively better than the other; it just depends on which pleases you, or which you're in the mood for at the moment. There is a time for steel and a time for velvet.

The name of the Gewürztraminer grape derives from the German word for spicy ( *gewürz* ) and the name of the town where it is believed this vine originated, Tramin, now Termeno, in what used to be the Sud Tirol but is now the hyphenated Italian region of Trentino–Alto Adige. The grape is still cultivated there, where it produces for the most part rather light-bodied but intensely aromatic wines. Gewürztraminer is also vinified in Austria and Germany and several parts of the United States in addition to California.

The Hugel firm is one of the oldest and most respected in Alsace. It makes the full line of Alsatian white wines and is particularly famed for its late-harvest dessert wines. Its wines are imported to the United States by Dreyfus, Ashby & Company, a division of Schenley.

Parducci is a good-sized, family-run winery producing an almost bewildering array of California wines at invariably fair prices. Quality levels are sound, and the wines are made with integrity throughout the line, so good value for your money is the norm with most of their bottlings.

## Substitutes:

Younger vintages of these two wines are the best option. Otherwise, use young Gewürztraminer from such important Alsace houses as Dopff & Irion, Hugel, Muré (especially Muré's Clos St-Landelin), and Willm; and young Gewürztraminer from other California or Pacific Northwest growers (e.g., Babcock Vineyard, Deloach Vineyards, Thomas Fogarty Winery, Hidden Cellars, Husch Vineyards, Martini, Mirassou, Navarro Vineyards, and Wente)—but be aware that sugar levels vary greatly. Gundlach-Bundschu's Sonoma Valley Gewürztraminer, a lovely dry wine, is about midway in style between Alsace and the California norm.

This concludes the eighth white-wine tasting session. There are several ways for you to proceed from here.

*Following the lead of your own preferences:*
   If you liked the first wine better, the Hugel Gewürztraminer, go on to the Eleventh Flight.

If you liked the second wine better, the Parducci
Gewürztraminer, go on to the Ninth Flight.

*Following the kind of grapes:*
This is the only flight of Gewürztraminer.

*Following the wines of the country:*
Go on to the Ninth Flight.

# THE NINTH FLIGHT

~~∽୨୧∾~~

*Schyler Graves 1989
and
Gallo Reserve
California Sauvignon Blanc 1989*

~~∽୨୧∾~~

WITH THIS FLIGHT you are starting to explore the fuller-
bodied white wines. These sorts of wines are almost invariably vinified fully dry. Most of the wines you've tasted before this
could be drunk equally happily as aperitifs or as dinner wines; most
of the wines you are about to taste simply have too much substance
to make a satisfactory cocktail. These are dinner wines par excellence, designed to accompany food of all sorts. Not that the greatest
of them can't be enjoyed all by themselves: some of them in fact
deserve to be enshrined in a kind of splendid isolation and savored
alone, as what in Italy is called a *vino da meditazione*, a wine for
thinking both with and about. But that's getting more than a little
ahead of ourselves: we're going to start a bit less exaltedly than all
that.

Your focus of attention for the next two flights is going to be the
Sauvignon Blanc grape. Let me underline that this is a distinct and
important white-grape variety. Many people have the false impression that wines labeled Sauvignon Blanc are just white-wine versions of Cabernet Sauvignon, but that is not so, and you are now
going to be able to one-up all such poor ignorants whenever the
opportunity presents itself. There are in fact some white versions
of Cabernet Sauvignon, just as there are from time to time rosé

versions of it—why I will never understand, since it wastes a perfectly fine red grape. To my palate they are usually dreadful, but
you can decide that for yourself if you are curious about them. They
are always clearly labeled Blanc de Cabernet or White Wine from
Cabernet Grapes, so there should be no reason ever to confuse them
with the true white wine from the white grape Sauvignon Blanc.

### Bordeaux Blancs

The Bordeaux region rests its vinous fame on its great red
wines (from the Médoc, St. Emilion, and Pomerol) and on its
sweet white wines (from Sauternes and Barsac). It also produces enormous quantities of dry white wine, ranging in quality from dismal to quite extraordinary.

The largest AOC category, Bordeaux Blanc, is made up
mostly of decent everyday wines, but it can include as well (as
can any class of wine made anywhere) wines that are extraordinary for their price and wines that would be poor at any
price. Entre-Deux-Mers is another large category of reliable
white table wines. They are named for the specific place they
are produced, the fat tongue of land lying between the con-
verging rivers Garonne and Dordogne, the "two seas" of the
name.

It is generally agreed that the finest dry whites of the region
come from the area called Graves, southeast of the city of
Bordeaux. Graves possesses its own AOC appellation and a
ranking system similar to that of the red Médoc wines.

The only possibility of labeling confusion that you really need
worry about stems from the fact that some American bottlings of
Sauvignon Blanc call themselves Fumé Blanc. This is a practice that
began some years ago with Robert Mondavi, who wanted to distinguish his then-novel dry vinification of Sauvignon Blanc from the, at
that time, dominant sweet style. Nowadays few sweet versions ever
find their way to the market, and the two names, Sauvignon Blanc

and Fumé Blanc, are used almost interchangeably to designate a dry dinner wine.

One last piece of prologue: California Sauvignon Blanc is always composed minimally of 75 percent Sauvignon Blanc grapes, and usually much more than that. One-hundred-percent Sauvignon Blanc is not uncommon. The French wine, faithful to the traditions of the Bordeaux area, mixes Sauvignon Blanc grapes with Sémillon, in proportions that will vary significantly from maker to maker.

Okay, now you're ready to work, so go to it and check back here after you've made all your comments and/or talked yourselves out about these two wines.

## Appearance.

The appearances of these two wines should be very similar, with the Graves a slightly darker shade of straw than the Sauvignon. In any given flight, either one might look slightly paler than the other because of bottle variation, but the difference shouldn't be significant. And as you probably are tired of hearing by now, any darker colors—deep gold or especially brown tints—are sure to mean that that particular bottle is finished, either over the hill with age or destroyed by bad shipping or storage.

## Aroma.

Aroma may present some tasters with problems in the case of these two wines, because neither has what you could call a very pronounced or a very big bouquet. That's not a serious flaw in either wine, but it does qualify as a disappointment. Even though Sauvignon Blanc is not an intensely aromatic grape, some vinifications of it develop a very lively and very pronounced grassy aroma that is a real plus for the wine when present.

With these two wines we have aromas that most tasters describe as subtle or subdued, with the scent of the varietal Sauvignon Blanc being slightly more intense or powerful or marked than that of the Graves. Most people also call the two aromas faint, clean, refreshing, and pleasant. Those tasters who don't mesh with these wines tend to call the French wine slightly musty and the California a little acrid.

More specifically, the Graves is usually described as dry and soft-smelling, lightly fruity or spicy or floral, with herbaceous or apple-like overtones. You may even detect a faint, lightly ammoniac smell, not unpleasant, that reminds some people of young, fresh cheese.

On the other hand, the Sauvignon Blanc smells sweeter and more flowery to most tasters, with an often-remarked-on leafy or grassy component fairly prominent. The latter element is an identifying characteristic of the grape variety. Some people may also pick it up as the scent of straw, or, at the other end of the spectrum, as a citrus odor.

Taste.

In taste, even though once again neither wine has a big, overpowering flavor, they are usually easily differentiated. Almost everyone tastes the Graves as the softer, the Sauvignon Blanc as the more acid—though as usual you can get sharp differences of preference about those tastes. The French wine is most often described as soft, mildly fruity, with a dry finish, straightforward and uncomplex.

The California wine, on the other hand, is usually felt as slightly fruitier, drier, and more lively on the tongue. Because of its greater acidity, many tasters experience a slight tingling sensation, almost as if the wine were *pétillant*, even though it is not. Some may report discerning a distinct grapefruit flavor in it. Most agree that it has a good, dry finish, but like the first wine is rather simple and uncomplicated.

Speaking as objectively as is ever possible about wine, I'd say that both wines are good, sound examples of their breeds.

The Schyler is to my mind the essence of what used to be (it seems centuries ago now) classic French carafe wine, designed not to call too much attention to itself but to partner quietly and well with almost anything on a menu. The worst you should be able to say of such a wine is that it is bland and inoffensive, the best that it is pleasant, with enough body to take food well and enough flavor to satisfy without requiring analysis. As an introduction to the dry white wines of the Graves, it shows well the kind of balance and body they strive for, though it gives you only a rudimentary idea of the complexity of flavor they can achieve.

Similarly, I find the Gallo Sauvignon a good, middle-range representative of the grape's character as Californians handle it. It seems to me to have decent if not strongly accented varietal character, especially noticeable in those grassy/citrus/herbal scents and flavors. More important to me, it is not overly grassy, as some straight varietal Sauvignon Blancs can be. Some intense Sauvignon Blancs can make you feel you've been sent out to pasture. On the other side of the coin, it is not as rich in flavor and nuance as some other California Sauvignons either, though its fruit gives you some hint of what a more intense specimen might be capable of.

All in all, I would describe both as sound, well-made wines that are true to their materials and—what is most important for our present purposes—true to the style of their regions. The Graves is made by the firm of Schroder & Schyler, Bordeaux wine merchants since 1739 and the owners of Château Kirwan, a highly regarded classified growth Margaux. Gallo is Gallo, the largest single maker of wine in the United States, and producer of all levels of California wine, from sugary pop wines up to those of international-competition caliber. At most of those levels, Gallo offers very good value for dollar.

## Substitutes:

Younger vintages are always the first fallback. After that, Martini Napa Valley Sauvignon Blanc would serve well as a stand-in for the California wine; it's a bit crisper and more intense, but the main outlines are intact. Also good is Geyser Peak Sonoma County Sauvignon Blanc: very lemony, but otherwise similar to the wine described here. For the Schyler Graves, try the same wine—AOC white Graves—from B & G or another, equally reputable shipper, or an Entre-Deux-Mers from Schyler or B & G, or even Château Loudenne—only AOC Bordeaux Blanc but estate-bottled and usually of a quality beyond its appellation.

This is the conclusion of the Ninth Flight. There are several ways for you to proceed from here.

*Following the lead of your own preferences:*
    If you liked the first wine better, the Graves, go on to the Tenth Flight.
    If you liked the second wine better, the Sauvignon Blanc, go on to the Twelfth Flight.

*Following the kind of grapes:*
    Go on to the Tenth Flight.

*Following the wines of the country:*
    Wine One: Go on to the Tenth Flight.
    Wine Two: Go on to the Thirteenth Flight.

# THE TENTH FLIGHT

∾⨀∾

## *Château Carbonnieux 1989*
## *(Graves)*
## *and*
## *De Ladoucette Pouilly-Fumé 1989*

∾⨀∾

I N THIS FLIGHT you're still slugging it out with the Sauvignon Blanc grape. Once again, you will be tasting the Bordelaise style, a blending of Sauvignon and Sémillon (in this particular château, 65 percent and 35 percent), against a straight varietal vinification, in this case a Pouilly-Fumé, a wine from the northern reaches of the Loire, the region that provided the generally acknowledged model for California's current mode of handling Sauvignon Blanc.

Sancerre and Pouilly-Fumé (not to be confused with Pouilly-Fuissé, which is in another region entirely) lie far up the Loire in central France. This is almost exclusively white-wine country, and the Sauvignon Blanc is the dominant grape. Farther down the Loire, westward in the château country of Anjou and Touraine, the Chenin Blanc holds sway, and farthest west of all, at the mouth of the Loire, lies the domain of the Muscadet grape. While the Rhône and the Gironde systems fight it out for the title of France's red-wine river, the Loire is its uncontested white-wine stream (unless, of course, you consider the Rhine a French river).

Once again, as so often in this book, you should be concentrating on tasting differences and similarities, or differences within similarities, subtle as that may be. Just pay attention as you smell and taste; that and practice are the only secrets of wine tasting.

It occurs to me it's been a while since I reminded you that your *analysis* of a wine—your description of the things you smell and taste in it—is not the point of this book, nor is it the point of the tasting you are about to perform. What matters most is your preference, your decision about which sort of wine gives you more pleasure. The analysis only helps you see what causes you to like or dislike a particular kind of wine, so you can either seek out others like it or avoid it and its kin like the plague. So even if you find yourself smelling and tasting a particular wine very differently from the way it's described here, you're still attaining the object of your tasting.

Analysis and description are only the tools, never the goal. Taste fearlessly then and trust your own olfactory and palatal impressions. Above all, don't be cowed by what anyone else (and this definitely includes me) says about the wine; nobody else can taste with your mouth any more than you can drink with theirs.

Are you ready then? Okay, proceed with your full ritual of gauging appearance, aroma, and flavor—and don't forget to spit: you should certainly be doing that routinely by this point, without any lingering self-consciousness. The little bit you discard is negligible, and you can fully enjoy the wine better later for the small amount of it you "waste" now.

Appearance.

Both these wines are a deep, clear straw shade, with the Château Carbonnieux perhaps a slight bit darker or sometimes showing traces of greenish gold highlights. Both should be pleasing, clear, and live looking.

Aroma.

A few people might find these wines either elusive or overpowering, but most tasters are likely to describe both as fragrant but not intensely aromatic, meaning that they both have reasonably distinctive but not powerful scents. The majority of tasters, by a very substantial margin, like the aromas of both.

The range of descriptions people provide for the Château Carbonnieux is pretty wide. It includes mineral terms like "flinty," "chalky," or "limestone-smelling," as well as a more direct damp-stones or earth aroma. It also includes fresh grass and straw, herbaceous scents (sometimes mint is specifically mentioned), as well as fruit and spices (sometimes specifically cinnamon). Another sort of response emphasizes the fruit component of the aroma, describing it as a sort of peach with lemon-juice scent, very clean and lingering. Generally speaking, tasters find the aroma of this white Graves not big but complex and very composed.

The range for the Pouilly-Fumé is at least as great, but the emphasis is, for most tasters, quite different. The flinty tone some tasters observe in the Bordeaux wine tends to be more often and more prominently observed here (connoisseurs rightly or wrongly regard it as almost the defining characteristic of the Sauvignon Blanc wines from this part of France). Additionally, many people find the grassy, herbaceous, and fruity portion of the aroma spectrum more noticeable in this Pouilly-Fumé. Citrus especially (orange and grapefruit are possible as well as lemon) and wood (oak often) and spice tones (cinnamon most commonly) are among the most frequently cited specific components.

Generally speaking, most tasters perceive the aroma of the Pouilly-Fumé as slightly less powerful but just as complex as the scent of the Graves wine. This usually causes some surprise, since tasters have a quasi-logical expectation that wine made from a single grape should be more intense but also more monochromatic than wine made from a blend of grapes. In this case, however, the Sauvignon Blanc grape brings to the blending a lot more aroma than the Sémillon, which tends to subdue some of the Sauvignon's more pronounced fragrance elements.

Taste.

Most tasters react very favorably to this Château Carbonnieux. They tend to comment first on its balance: the first impression it makes on the palate is one of fullness, roundness, and elegance, all in one package. More specifically, they mention its nice bright acidity and what seems to be a small but firm tannic bite, coupled with its good, soft, and dry fruit. A few people may find its acidity a bit too high and talk about a tingly sensation or a sort of "hot lips" feeling, but the majority find it pleasing and lively.

Pushed for more specifics, tasters generally seem to describe the fruit of Château Carbonnieux as tasting predominantly of peaches, but subdued (by which they invariably intend a compliment: subdued as in well-bred or softspoken, not overblown). Mixed with that they also report a fairly distinct citrus component in the flavor. Most call it lemon, but some may call it lime, or grapefruit, or even pineapple. Some palates also detect a slight nuttiness and some wood-derived vanilla flavors. The wine is clean and extremely polished, with a good dry finish. Food rounds and softens it a bit.

Almost everyone comments first on the fruitiness of the de Ladoucette Pouilly-Fumé, which most find very attractive. For only a few is it either cloying or, at the other extreme (and because of the wine's acidity), too sharp. Perhaps only a few tasters will explicitly notice or mention the Pouilly-Fumé's acid, but that is what really makes the liveliness of its fruit flavors possible.

The flavors that will almost certainly be commented on can include grass (meant as a compliment: a fresh, vegetal flavor), generalized fruit, exotic fruit (some say kiwi), and citrus (some may taste orange or grapefruit). This Pouilly-Fumé strikes most people as dry, clean, and refreshing, with a dry finish. It feels a bit lighter on the tongue than the Graves and seems a bit higher—a tenor rather than a baritone. Like the Graves, it rounds somewhat with food but doesn't soften as much—its acid stays more forceful.

Preferences tend understandably to be pretty evenly divided between these two wines. This is, after all, a classic matter of taste. Both are very well made, sound, and flavorful wines, and the key differences between them are differences of style.

Most tasters will give the Graves the edge in complexity of flavor and nuance, the Pouilly-Fumé the lead in forcefulness and fruit. If I were choosing for myself, I'd want the straight varietal wine for drinking right now, because I think its present brightness and freshness and vivacity are the acme of what this grape and this region have to offer and because I think the wine is at or near its peak at this age.

On the other hand, I'd be very happy to put away some bottles of the Graves to drink in a few years, because I think additional bottle-age will bring out yet more flavors and subtleties in a wine of that type. At a guess, I'd say it would be at its best at about four or five years old and could probably hold well (properly stored, of course) for another five. That's a guess, mind you; I am not the oracle of Delphi. Part of the fun of estimates like that is putting away enough of the wine to check on your accuracy every now and then. It's the wine lover's equivalent of looking in to see what the kids are doing.

Château Carbonnieux is a classified-growth Graves estate of great age and repute. It produces both red and white wines under the

same name. It is distributed in the United States by Château and
Estates Wine Company, which also imports a good many other
excellent Bordeaux châteaux.

De Ladoucette Pouilly-Fumé is produced by Château de Nozet, a
family firm headed by Baron Patrick de Ladoucette, and imported
into the United States by Heublein's Palace Brands. In addition to
this wine, the house also markets a Sancerre Comte Lafond and its
top-of-the-line Pouilly-Fumé Baron de L., made exclusively from
very low-yielding old vines on one of the best vineyard sites in the
region.

### Substitutes:

A younger vintage of either wine would serve best. Failing that, try
Château Olivier for the Graves; for the Pouilly-Fumé, look for other
reputable producers, such as Château de Tracy, Joliver, Masson-
Blondelet, Redde & Fils, or Saget.

This concludes the tenth tasting session. There are several ways for
you to proceed from here.

*Following the lead of your own preferences:*
   If you liked the first wine better, the Château Carbonnieux, go
   on to the Eleventh Flight.
   If you liked the second wine better, the Pouilly-Fumé, go on to
   the Twelfth Flight.

*Following the kind of grapes:*
   This is the last tasting of wines based on Sauvignon Blanc.
   Have you tasted the earlier Sauvignon flights (the Third and
   Ninth)?

*Following the wines of the country:*
   Go on to the Eleventh flight.

# THE ELEVENTH FLIGHT

## *Mastroberardino*
## *Greco di Tufo 1990*
## *and*
## *Chapoutier La Bernardine*
## *Châteauneuf du Pape 1986*

THIS IS A UNIQUE FLIGHT. Here you are confronting what is by rational wine terms an oddball pairing, one French white wine and one Italian, neither from an area famed for its white wines. In fact, the Italian wine comes from an area not famed for fine wines, period. I think that by the end of your tasting, however, you will understand the idea behind the pairing and I hope you will find both wines enjoyable. I'm pretty sure that at least you'll have seen a graphic demonstration of the fact that no one really interested in fine wine should ever write off any region without doing at least a minimal amount of fact-checking and actual tasting. Good wine is being made all over the world, and snap judgments and prejudices will only cheat you of pleasure in the long run.

End of sermon. Taste on: see, swirl, smell, sip, savor, and spit. See you back here in a few minutes.

### Appearance.

Not a great deal of problem here. Both wines are light gold, the Châteauneuf du Pape slightly stronger in color than the Greco di Tufo. These colors may deepen a bit more with more bottle-age, but in all probability they will stay within the light-to-medium-gold color range. However, these two wines could develop deeper coloration without being oxidized, so even if your two bottles (or either one of them) are considerably darker than I'm describing, don't *in this case* automatically assume they're bad; taste first. If the wine is inert, lifeless, flat, then return it to your dealer and get another bottle.

## Aroma.

I think it's pretty safe to say that most of you were surprised by these two. Their aromas are very different from what you've been smelling in white wines up to this point; in fact, they differ pretty markedly from the aromas of the great bulk of white wines. For many people, this divergence from what they may have been coming to think of and expect as normal can be a shock, and all shocks have a way of being unpleasant, so there may very well be a lot of *initial* negative responses or indecision about both these wines. I say initial because the majority of tasters find that these are aromas they can warm up to after a few minutes; a little adjustment is all it takes to start appreciating what Greco di Tufo and white Châteauneuf have to offer.

Greco di Tufo: Almost everybody remarks on the strength or intensity of this wine's aroma. Not its bigness, mind you; it isn't one of those almost mythical wines with an aroma so huge it fills the room as soon as you pull the cork. Strength is the right word; there's a kind of muscularity here (possibly owing to alcohol) that demands respect.

The next quality most people mention directly or indirectly is complexity—what they sense here is not just one thing but a medley of aromas, some of them very unusual in white wines. Here are some of the more commonly mentioned possibilities: flowers, especially strongly scented varieties; ripe or fermented fruit, especially apples and strawberries; herbs and spices, especially licorice or anise; cheese, especially Parmesan cheese; and nuts, especially walnuts or hazelnuts. Any one or any combination of those may dominate a taster's impressions, and naturally like and dislike will vary tremendously. The majority of people, however find Greco di Tufo's scent intriguing; "pungent but pleasing" was the way one particularly concise taster described it.

Châteauneuf du Pape: The remarks about strength and complexity that I made about Greco di Tufo apply every bit as accurately to this wine. The biggest difference between the aromas of this Châteauneuf and the Italian wine is not in their attack but in their components, the different elements you can discern in each. Three separate classes of scents seem to have almost equal shares in the Châteauneuf's bouquet: spices, grass, and mushrooms. More specifically, people mention a whole shelf of spices they smell in it: cardamom, cumin, mace, mint, sesame (toasted seeds or oil). The grass smell comes across for some individuals as very intense—one taster reported it as smelling like arugola, which brings the grass scent right to the border of herbs and spices. So too with mushrooms: some tasters describe the clean earth smell of fresh mushrooms, others an intense fungous scent that borders on a slight odor of truffles. For some tasters, the combination of elements is strong and complex enough for them to compare this aroma to that of some red wines; for others, it's strong enough to be unpleasant.

### Taste.

People tend to respond to Greco's flavor just as they responded to its aroma. Either by directly remarking on it or indirectly by the number of elements they will list, they show that the Greco's complexity has grabbed their attention once again. However, the range of flavor components people mention seems to be a bit narrower than those of the aroma. Most common are alcohol, noticed as a fiery or winey characteristic; fruit, again most usually apples or strawberries; and nuts, most often hazelnuts or almonds—almonds especially in the finish, which many tasters remark on. The great majority of tasters enjoy the flavor of Greco, which they describe overall as pleasing, complex, balanced, dry, and round, with good body. Some people describe that last characteristic as a pleasing sense of weight on the tongue combined with a mouth-soothing oiliness. Tasters who have come to this flight directly from the wines based on Sauvignon Blanc seem to be particularly aware of this quality—Greco's rich "fatness"—as a dramatic contrast to the bright acidity of Sauvignon-based wines.

La Bernardine Châteauneuf du Pape: That fatness is one quality the Châteauneuf has in common with the Greco. It, too, is a rich, full-bodied wine, very round, with some of the same pleasing oiliness on the tongue. With both these wines, you know you've got something in your mouth; there is nothing frail or insubstantial about either of them. Of the two, this Châteauneuf seems somewhat more robust to most people, but that doesn't seem to imply any loss of subtlety. Tasters still remark on its balancing of fruit and alcohol, crispness and fruitiness. The elements they discerned in its aroma they tend to mention again in its flavor, particularly the spices, grass, and fruits. And many tasters are particularly pleased with the marked astringent finish of this wine.

Obviously these are very different wines, but they share some likenesses that for me make this pairing very revealing. These are both warm-region white wines; the Châteauneuf from the southern Rhône, Greco di Tufo from Campania, not far from Naples. Both are big wines, full-bodied, sturdy, completely dry, with reasonably high alcohol for white wines, and yet fruity, flavorful, and above all rich and complex. Both can take several years of bottle-age with improvement. Nevertheless they taste quite different from each other, operating in totally different segments of the flavor spectrum. Preferences will go as individual palates dictate, though I could be happy with either most of the time.

As you may have gathered by now, I'm a fan of both, and not just because after all those moderately light and fruity wines I really appreciate a wine with guts—though that's true, too. But the reason for my enthusiasm is more fundamental than that. For me these two wines exemplify something that I call the southern style in wine-making. It's not very fashionable right now—in fact, when people talk about southern wine style they usually mean it as a put-down, implying the kind of sunbaked, high-alcohol, coarse wines that used to be the norm from Sicily or from California's Central Valley.

What I mean by it I think you can figure out from these two wines: complexity of flavor coupled with fullness of body, a richness both of fruit and of nuance, all of which can be achieved only with fully ripened grapes and the most careful vinification. It makes for wines that, in these days of fashionable superslimness and light-mindedness, are unmodishly robust, wines that almost rudely demand you pay attention to what you're drinking. In a world where everything seems to be in the process of being microminiaturized, Greco di Tufo and Châteauneuf du Pape and wines like them are uncompromisingly, untrendily big. I wish there were a lot more like them.

Needless to say (but I'll say it anyway), these wines are not at their best as aperitifs or cocktails, though they may perfectly well be enjoyed alone. They are wonderful dinner wines, not only with any of the dishes you would normally choose a white wine for but also with some you wouldn't. I would happily drink a white Châteauneuf with a steak or a Greco di Tufo with a bistecca pizzaiola or with a dish of bresaola or a Piedmontese veal tartare. These are substantial wines, and they will stand up to a wide variety of foods.

Mastroberardino is the name of a family-owned winery based in Avellino, high in the hills east of Naples. Its winemaker, Antonio Mastroberardino, is widely regarded as the best winemaker in the Italian south and one of the handful of premier winemakers in Italy. The winery turns out a complete line of Neapolitan wines at the highest quality level. Most of these are imported to the United States by Heublein's Palace Brands.

Chapoutier is a 175-year-old firm based in the northern Rhône but owning properties throughout the whole valley. It produces almost the whole range of Rhône wines, all of them made to the highest standards in a very traditional style. They are imported into the United States by Paterno Imports.

## Substitutes:

The only real substitute for this Greco di Tufo is a younger vintage. That would also be the best alternative for La Bernardine. If that is not available, you could try a white Châteauneuf from such estates as Château de Beaucastel, Château Rayas, Château de Vaudieu, or Domaine de Mont Redon.

This ends the Eleventh Flight of white wines. There are several ways for you to proceed from here.

*Following the lead of your own preferences:*
  If you liked either the first wine, the Greco di Tufo, or the
  second wine, the Châteauneuf du Pape, go on to the Fourteenth
  Flight.

*Following the kind of grapes:*
  There are no other flights tasting these grapes.

*Following the wines of the country:*
  Go on to the Twelfth Flight.

# THE TWELFTH FLIGHT

◦~◦◦◦~◦

## *Bollini Trentino Chardonnay 1990*
## *and*
## *Mâcon-Lugny Les Charmes 1988*

◦~◦◦◦~◦

YOU ARE NOW STARTING a series of tastings of wine vinified
from what is widely considered the premier white-wine grape
of the world, Chardonnay.

Whether it is the best is, like so much else in wine, definitely a
matter of taste, but there is no doubt that Chardonnay is currently
the hottest, the most glamorous, of the noble white grapes. It is
enjoying a vogue among wine lovers and winemakers all over the
world, and is being planted in climates and soils very different from
its native Burgundy, where it has been for centuries the heart of
what are pretty universally thought of as the greatest white wines in
the world. Again, whether white Burgundies are or aren't the
world's greatest white wines is very much a judgment call—but in
the world of wine connoisseurship, they serve as benchmarks for
quality white wine in general and any Chardonnay-based wine in
particular.

That, however, should not mean a hill of beans to you, especially
not with Chardonnay learning every day to "speak in accents yet
unknown" when the Burgundian style was first formulated.

Chardonnay usually makes a full-bodied wine, but the grape is
versatile and can be vinified in several different styles. The idea of
the next few flights is to let you learn the basic taste of the Chardonnay variety and to show you its different styles and let you choose
the one that suits you best. To be honest, if money is an object, you

had better hope you don't prefer the classic Burgundian style. Burgundian whites are right up there with red Burgundies in the retail-price stratosphere, and a real fondness for them could mean the start of your personal economic recession. I've been as kind to your pocketbook as I can in making the selections for this book, but the flavor of white Burgundy never comes really cheap. Be brave about it.

Your first Chardonnay flight comprises two of the most popular reasonably priced examples available in the United States, both imports: an Italian, Bollini, and a French, Mâcon-Lugny Les Charmes. In your tasting, try to pay attention both to similarities of the basic grape's flavor and to differences in style resulting from either the region in which the grapes are grown or the methods of vinification. In other words, sameness and difference once again.

All set? Then work through your infamous s's and check back here when you're finished.

## Appearance.

Both wines should show a characteristic young Chardonnay color, a clear, clean straw with some gold or green highlights. Older Chardonnay wines, particularly those that have received some wood-aging, will show deeper and more golden than these.

## Aroma.

Most people perceive the aroma of the Bollini as a bit on the delicate side—subdued but complex. It is in many respects a typical Chardonnay aroma, distinctive yet hard to describe. Tasters seem to be about evenly divided between describing it as fruity or as leafy. The fruit backers usually name pears and apricots, sometimes more exotic fruits. The leaf people usually just stick with that, though some will say freshly mown grass, some nominate mint, and some add fresh-turned earth as well. The great majority of tasters agree that this aroma is, overall, fresh, clean, and pleasing.

Les Charmes has an aroma of about the same magnitude as the Bollini, though different sniffers will rate it slightly bigger or slightly smaller. Almost all tasters describe it as predominantly fruity, though less defined than the Bollini's fruit: they will probably mention pears, perhaps also leaves or grass. Some tasters describe this Mâcon-Lugny's scent, in comparison with the Bollini's, as softer, damper, and weightier—more earthy, mushroomy-smelling. All of that, for those of you who may not be mycophiles, is definitely intended as a compliment.

Taste.

Most tasters find that the flavors of these two wines match quite closely with their aromas, the Bollini fruity and lively, the Mâcon-Lugny fuller and rounder.

More specifically, the kinds of responses the Bollini elicits are usually in the nature of fresh, bright, very fruity. People claim to taste in it things like apples, pears, and bananas. Traces of citrus fruits are rarely ever discerned in this wine (remember how frequent they were in Sauvignon Blanc, for instance?). There is a small trace of bitterness—some people love it, others are unmoved—that could be due either to the wine's fairly high acidity or to the Chardonnay grape itself. Most tasters pick out the bitterness particularly in the wine's finish; those who like it describe it as a good bitter-almond flavor; those who don't make small disparaging noises. Most tasters, however, find this wine very enjoyable, if not particularly big or muscular.

By contrast, Les Charmes is fuller and weightier on the tongue; almost everybody can feel the real impression of heaviness it makes. Objectively speaking, this wine is not a true heavyweight: medium-bodied would be about the most accurate description. But just as its fruit seems subdued, minimized, after tasting the Bollini Chardonnay, so, too, its body seems exaggerated and magnified. The fruit is still there, however, even if it is not so forward as the Italian wine's. As with Les Charmes's aroma, most tasters describe the fruit in its taste as soft and somewhat undefined. They may suggest pears, and perhaps in this wine a slight touch of citrus—lemon or orange most likely—and maybe grass. Most people find an excellent long, dry finish in the Les Charmes.

Both wines seem to respond very well to food, though the French wine's lower acidity and greater body may make it a bit more adaptable with rich or creamy dishes.

I think you have here a textbook illustration of the differences of national styles in handling the Chardonnay grape.

The Bollini Chardonnay is a very representative example of the dominant (but not exclusive) method of vinifying white wines in Italy today. Most Italian winemakers, with most white grapes, are striving for and attaining fresh, clean fruit, with a good but not overpowering taste of the variety and a lot of acid to keep the wine all bright and lively. Italy is making oceans of sound, pleasing white wines like this from any number of grape varieties in several provinces. They are above all wines meant to be drunk young and enjoyed as aperitifs and with non-solemn meals. The best examples of them, should you wish to pursue this branch of wine, seem to come from the two northern regions of Trentino–Alto Adige and Friuli–Venezia Giulia. They would include international varieties such as Chardonnay, Sauvignon Blanc, Pinot Blanc, Pinot Grigio, Gewürztraminer, and Riesling, as well as purely local varieties such as Verduzzo and Tocai.

This Mâcon-Lugny furnishes an equally fair representation of the French approach to white wine in general and the Chardonnay grape specifically. There is evidently less desire for fruitiness and a greater striving after body and balance. The wine has more roundness, more muscle, and probably a greater ability to survive in the bottle. I don't mean this is a particularly long-lived wine, but it does show every sign that it will last essentially unchanged for about three or four years from bottling. On the other hand, I wouldn't plan to keep most Italian white wines around that long; their bright acid style doesn't seem to have that much staying power. The French seem to desire greater maturity from a wine and a more sophisticated, balanced attack, rather than all that youthful *esprit* and *élan*. That, at any rate, is the style that is cultivated throughout the whole domain of the Chardonnay, from Dijon to Lyon, including Mâcon-Lugny's more famous sibling, Pouilly-Fuissé (not to be confused with Pouilly-Fumé, which is a Sauvignon Blanc wine), Chablis, and all the famous villages of the Côte d'Or.

You could argue—and you might well be right—that these essential differences in style stem from the differences between the two national cuisines the wines normally accompany. But what do you make then of French red wines, like Beaujolais, that are meant for quick drinking, or Italian white wines, such as Greco di Tufo or Torre di Giano, that are meant for laying down? There comes a point with wine where logic breaks down. That is the right point to think less about it and drink more of it. Onward.

Bollini Chardonnay is imported into the United States by the Kobrand Corporation. Les Charmes is produced in the Mâcon by a cooperative of small growers called Cave de Lugny and it is imported to the United States by Château and Estate Wines.

## Chardonnay's Kingdom

The realm of the Chardonnay grape actually encompasses a good deal more than what the wine lover thinks of as Burgundy, which tends to be largely the Côte d'Or, the thirty-or-so-mile-long strip that runs south from Dijon through Beaune to Chagny. Northwest of Dijon, near Auxerre and almost halfway to Paris, lies the Chablis district, one of Chardonnay's major fiefdoms. South of the Côte d'Or, lying beside the river Saône and along the direct route to Lyon, the Côte Chalonnaise produces important white wines as well as reds. The major townships for whites are Rully, Mercurey and Montagny. And directly south of the Côte Chalonnaise lies the Mâconnais, where once again Chardonnay dominates the wine production. Mâcon wines appear on the market as simply Mâcon, Mâcon Villages, Mâcon with a specific village name attached (as our wine, a Mâcon-Lugny), or single village name alone, such as St-Veran, Pouilly-Fuissé (which for reasons known only to fashion often commands the same prices as the white wines of the Côte d'Or), or Pouilly-Vinzelles. South of the Mâconnais, red grapes take over again: the Beaujolais district runs almost to the Lyon city limits.

Just for the record (you never know when you're going to need the odd fact to break the ice), the town of Chardonnay, which gave its name to the grape, is located in the Mâconnais.

**Substitutes:**

First choice, younger vintages of these wines. Alternatives for the Mâcon-Lugny Les Charmes would be Maufoux's Château de Viré Mâcon-Viré or Drouhin's St-Veran. Labouré-Roi Mâcon Villages is fine, though a bit more elegant than the average Mâcon. Similarly usable but more elegant than average is Collavini's Dei Sassi Cavi Chardonnay (Atesino) and Puiatti's Collio Chardonnay.

This concludes the twelfth tasting session. The paths begin to converge here.

*Following the lead of your own preferences:*
   If you enjoyed either the first wine, the Bollini Chardonnay, or
   the second wine, the Mâcon-Lugny Les Charmes, go on to the
   Thirteenth Flight.

*Following the kind of grapes:*
   Go on to the Thirteenth Flight.

*Following the wines of the country:*
   Wine One: This is the last flight that includes an Italian wine.
   Check to see if you have tasted all the relevant earlier flights
   (the Third, Fourth, Fifth, and Eleventh).
   Wine Two: Go on to the Thirteenth Flight.

# THE THIRTEENTH FLIGHT

~~∾ᔐᔐ∾~~

## *Moreau Chablis*
## *Premier Cru Vaillons 1989*
## *and*
## *Louis M. Martini Napa Valley*
## *Reserve Chardonnay 1989*

~~∾ᔐᔐ∾~~

I N THIS FLIGHT you will start to move away from the simpler, fruity style of Chardonnay and toward its more complex, elegant, and fuller incarnation. Once again the comparison will consist of juxtaposing a French example with a different region's handling of Chardonnay—in this case, California. French vintners set the original standards for wines based on Chardonnay, and California winemakers really began to achieve international acclaim when, in the 1970s, some of their Chardonnays showed better than some French vintages in international exhibitions.

Despite the reciprocal emulation, imitation, and competition between French and American winemakers, it would be a great mistake for you to taste these two wines only to see which is better. Forget that idea entirely. Not only is "better" in an objective sense frequently indeterminable in wine tasting, but "better for you" is really all you should be interested in. Chardonnay grows differently in California than it does in France. The California way of vinifying Chardonnay has evolved in its own special direction. And American taste in wine is not necessarily, even at the level of connoisseurship, identical with French taste. What you should be thinking as

224

you approach this flight is that you are about to taste two completely different wines that happen to share the same grape variety, and what you should be looking for, once again, are the kinds of same-nesses and differences that enable you to say (to yourself or any-body else who cares), "The thing I like about this wine is . . ."

Got that? Okay, go for it: do the infamous s's and then check back at headquarters.

## Appearance.

Little or no problem: both wines should be showing a bright golden straw color, very attractive and definitely live. In any particular pair of bottles one or the other wine could appear a slight bit more golden, but it should only be a very slight shading, not a marked difference.

If either is deeply golden, there is a fifty-fifty chance the wine has not gone wrong, so taste very carefully. Well-made Chardonnays can take a surprising amount of bottle-age without harm and often with real improvement. When mature, such wines often show a deep golden tinge that can resemble the color of a maderized wine. ("Maderization" is the five-dollar word for spoilage of a particular kind, the sort of oxidation in the bottle that causes wines, partic-ularly whites, to lose their flavor and turn brown. The color of a wine so spoiled sufficiently resembles the perfectly proper shade of the fortified wine Madeira for its name to be pressed into service— more accurately, disservice, at least to Madeira.) Chardonnays like the two you are tasting here can sometimes undergo an accelerated development, going through what would normally be, say, a ten-year cycle of maturation in just a few years. So you might have a chance here to taste a more developed flavor than would ordinarily be available.

## Aroma.

Just about all tasters report small to middling aromas of some complexity in both these wines, with the balance tilting toward the Chablis as more complex and the Martini Chardonnay as slightly stronger.

The great majority of tasters perceive a fresh, clean scent in the Chablis, though they may describe it in any number of ways: as lightly floral; as spicy or herbal (some people find thyme in there); as grassy or lemony or leafy; as delicately fruity; or as smelling like cool earth and stones or freshly shucked oysters. A lot of how that is expressed obviously depends on the individual taster's experience and associations. Many people pick up as well a vivid acid sharpness, which may or may not link for them with other elements to give the odor of flint that is traditionally associated with the aroma and taste of Chablis.

The Martini Chardonnay smells stronger to most people, riper and deeper. It is still not what anyone calls a huge aroma, nor do people think it particularly complex. Most tasters pick up a compound of vinous, citrus, and alcohol scents that they may or may not separate from the kind of Chardonnay fruit aromas they described in the twelfth white-wine flight. The fruit aroma tends to be mixed up with a fresh wood scent that is definitely oak: this wine has been given some barrel-age. Some tasters will describe a faint odor of toast or buttered toast: that too is Chardonnay fruit and oak in combination.

## Taste.

There are a lot of variables here, because the flavors of both wines contain enough diverse elements for different palates to respond to different stimuli. On the broadest level, most tasters react favorably to both wines, finding them pleasing and reasonably complex, the Chablis more vivid and the Chardonnay more composed.

Specific reactions cover a wide range. People remark on the Chablis's lively acidity (most discernible as a gentle prickle on the tongue) and its good fruit (grapefruit and not fully ripe pears). Despite its acidity, some detect a buttery quality and a bit of softness more usually found in white Burgundies from farther south. For many tasters, it hints at sweetness without actually being sweet, an effect both intriguing and enjoyable. Above all, for almost everyone this Chablis tastes fresh and clean, dry and fruity, in what seems almost a perfect combination for a versatile dinner wine.

Tasters describe the Martini Chardonnay first in terms of broad similarities to the Chablis: good fruit, good acid, a little bit tart, a little soft. The numerous differences follow. The Chardonnay is fuller, rounder, more tannic (from its wood aging). It has a buttery, toasty flavor most people pick up quite clearly, and its fruit is more subdued than the Chablis's, more restrained or balanced by the amount of tannin present. It seems very complete and balanced, though on a relatively small scale.

Most people tasting these two wines side by side find it fairly easy to distinguish in the Martini the basic varietal flavor of Chardonnay from the overlay of flavors that derive from the wood. Nevertheless, they may still find it hard to verbalize the differences they taste, a problem to which—at this point in this book—I am deeply sympathetic.

Loosely speaking, in this wine the range of sensations and tastes that includes tannin and the pucker it causes (try very hard not to confuse it here with acid prickle), as well as the flavors in the tea-and-toast range, are all traceable to oak. Their interplay with the already rich flavors of top-quality Chardonnay grapes gives the best Chardonnay wines the complexity and layering of flavors that make them the nonpareils of the white-wine world.

Needless to say there are lots of possible variations on the wood and fruit theme. You can probably by now guess all those due to the grapes—climate, soil, degree of ripeness, vinification method, etc.—but wood-aging introduces a whole new range: what kind of oak and from where, whether the cask is new or has been used and for what, how it has been treated (charring, for instance, can bring up that toasty flavor), and so on.

But the relation of wood flavors to grape flavors in this Martini Chardonnay can pretty well stand as a decent example of how (in California at any rate) those components are going to mesh. Move up and down from this Chardonnay on your imaginative intensity scale, shift the balance back and forth from fruit to wood: if you can taste for a while with your mind's tongue, you can find in this Chardonnay a very useful yardstick with which to measure your expectations and other wines' accomplishments.

It is not belittling this wine in any way to describe it as a scale model of a topflight Chardonnay: at its price, that is an accomplishment to put most other vintners to shame.

This Chablis too furnishes a good example of a whole class of wines, in this case the new style in Chablis. Old-fashioned Chablis used to be characterized as flint-and-steel, bone-dry wines with intense but austere fruit and plenty of structure. That may all sound a bit forbidding, but they were wonderful wines, among the most satisfying white dinner wines in the world, and quite capable of prolonged life in the bottle, too. Although a good number of Chablis makers continue to work in this old-fashioned style, you are more likely to encounter it among the *grands crus* than among the *premiers crus.*

The recognized AOC designations of Chablis are Petit Chablis, Chablis, Chablis Premier Cru, and Chablis Grand Cru. Among the last two designations you may find single-vineyard wines as well as shippers' blends. Generally speaking, Chablis Premier Cru most often turns up in the United States as dealer's wine from a single named township (such as Vaillons), while most Chablis Grand Cru appears as single-vineyard, estate bottlings. The *grands crus* appellations are very limited in number: Blanchots, Bougros, Grenouilles, La Moutonne, Les Clos, Les Preuses, Valmur, and Vaudesir.

Thanks once again to modern technology, Chablis is now a much more consistent wine than before—if its highs were stratospheric, its depths used to be abysmal—and most of it is fresher tasting and fruitier. The new Chablis are made as is this Vaillons: softer, with gentler and lusher fruit, more forward in development and more accessible to the taste. They are very charming and enjoyable wines, of very high quality and—especially in comparison to other Burgundy whites—*very* reasonable price. And they are not in any sense a falsification of Chablis: the best of them have, as this Vaillons does, a sturdy spine and a good healthy acid bite that identify them quite readily as Chablis.

I hope this flight pleased you. These are both enjoyable wines and instructive ones: for my purposes (which I sincerely hope are your purposes as well), quite a perfect combination.

Vaillons is a highly regarded Chablis Premier Cru designation. The maker, Moreau, is a large and well-reputed grower and shipper in the area. This particular Chablis is imported to the United States by Frederick Wildman.

This Chardonnay is one of the Martini family's reserve selections, which means it received a little extra aging (whether bottle- or barrel- is not clear) before release. It is typical of the high-quality, moderate-price wines the Martinis, a Napa Valley institution, have been producing for many decades now.

### Substitutes:

First try for younger vintages of these same wines. Failing that, look for Chablis Vaillons from other shippers—Louis Michel, for instance, or Drouhin, or Long-Depaquit—or medium-priced Napa or

Sonoma Chardonnays from a range of reputable makers, including
Buena Vista, La Crema, Simi, Sonoma-Cutrer, and Sterling—and
don't forget Gallo's Limited Releases.

This is the conclusion of the thirteenth tasting session. There is only
one way to go from here: all roads lead to the final flight.

*Following the lead of your own preferences:*
   If you enjoyed either the first wine, the Chablis Vaillons, or the
   second wine, the Martini Chardonnay, go on to the Fourteenth
   Flight.

*Following the kind of grapes:*
   Go on to the Fourteenth Flight.

*Following the wines of the country:*
   Go on to the Fourteenth Flight.

# THE FOURTEENTH FLIGHT

## *Drouhin Chassagne-Montrachet 1989 and Château Montelena Alexander Valley Chardonnay 1989*

IN THIS LAST FLIGHT—yes, this is the last pair of white wines— you put your toe in the door of what is, in terms of price certainly and of prestige probably, white wine's biggest league. Once more, what you should be tasting for here is to discern, at this high level of quality, the sameness provided by the basic flavor of the Chardonnay varietal and the differences caused by soil, climate, and wine-making techniques.

By this stage of the game, a task like that should be child's play for you. Go to it.

**Appearance.**

Both wines should be showing distinctly yellow or golden straw, very clean, bright, and attractive. Slightly darker coloration is possible without necessarily indicating defect. In any given pair of bottles, one or the other may seem a bit lighter or darker. Such variation means almost nothing as long as both wines are within the same general color range; you only have to start worrying when there is a really marked difference between them.

Aroma.

With these two wines you have a chance to experience those scents that professionals regard as characteristic of Chardonnay. Actually, that is a complete misnomer, because the sorts of aroma that professionals and connoisseurs have in mind when they talk about "a Chardonnay nose" are typical only of the very highest levels of Chardonnay vinification. You've been smelling far more typical Chardonnay aromas in the two flights that have preceded this one. Unfortunately, a lot of people new to wine read about these ideal (and that is really what they are) aromas and then, because they can't perceive them in the less expensive Chardonnay they're drinking, wrongly conclude that they are insensitive or can't appreciate wine or that it's all a bunch of hokum anyhow.

I hope that you who have been working through these wines with me have by now gotten enough confidence in your own taste buds and your own judgment not to be buffaloed by that sort of thing, but it probably doesn't hurt to remind you once again that most wine writing describes the best that a grape or wine attains, not the average, while what most of us—and this includes wine writers, most definitely—drink most of the time is average wine. Great wine is almost by definition a special occasion thing for all save the wealthiest of us.

And just to eliminate the last possible confusion: the phrase "average wine" is emphatically not a put-down. We are lucky enough to be living in a time when the average level of winemaking skill turns out wines that run from pleasantly drinkable up to very fine, so "average wine" includes an awful lot of very enjoyable bottles, a lot of wines that I personally would not want to be without.

I guess that was all preparatory to giving you your diploma. You are getting pretty near graduation, you know—but first we've got to finish up these Chardonnays. Another tough assignment.

Reactions to the aroma of the Chassagne-Montrachet tend to be very uniform. The few differing reactions almost always come from tasters who simply do not like the Chardonnay grape, and their tendency is to find the aroma of this and many other Chardonnay-based wines synthetic-smelling and displeasing—a bit like acetone, in fact.

Most people, however, respond very favorably to the aroma of Chardonnay, and the majority will describe the scent of this

Chassagne-Montrachet, at least in part, as recalling buttered toast. It's remarkable how many people spot butter in that aroma: some will say burnt toast and butter, some butter and earth, some butterscotch, but the butter usually gets in there. Other elements that are frequently mentioned include alcohol, grass, fruit (especially pears), spices (especially cinnamon), and fresh sawdust or related woody odors.

Reaction to the Château Montelena Chardonnay seems to be less monolithic but nevertheless pretty regular also. Again, with the exception of people who just don't like Chardonnay, the great majority of tasters respond very favorably to this wine. They will usually describe its aroma as similar to the Chassagne-Montrachet's, but with important differences. Some will say the Château Montelena smells more woody and tannic. Others perceive it as smelling more intensely fruity, even slightly sweet, as if the fruit were very, very ripe. Peaches, nectarines, and apricots—sometimes even bananas—are what most tasters specifically mention. Others find grassy or herbal—especially minty—elements in it. And still others may pick up the scent of fresh mushrooms and wet woods, a clean earth-and-forest scent.

Just for your information, the trio of butter, fruit, and wood (especially oak) is pretty much the connoisseur's stereotype for Chardonnay's aroma.

Taste.

The distinctions between California style and Burgundy style began to manifest themselves in the aromas of these two wines. Their flavors complete the lesson. Most tasters perceive these wines as markedly different not only in style but in flavor as well. Usually, the minority of people who dislike Chardonnay entirely tend to perceive these two wines as similarly artificial-tasting and unpleasant.

Most tasters describe the Chassagne-Montrachet first of all as big: full-bodied, weighty, dry. They often remark on its perceptible alcohol or report a warmth or pleasant sting that could result from alcohol or acid or even tannin (most good Burgundies and California Chardonnays receive some wood-aging). For the most part, however, they find the wine very balanced and harmonious, even elegant. Specific flavors, for most people, follow very closely what they discerned in the aroma: butter, toast, butterscotch, fruit (pears can become very prominent), and spice (sometimes a new introduction here, such as clove). For most people the wine partners beautifully with food and finishes well, long and dry and slightly almondy.

The majority of tasters find that the Château Montelena also delivers on its aroma. Most of the specific elements that people will discern in its flavor are the same or related to those they found first in its bouquet—butter and toast again, fruit especially, and sometimes sweet fruit (peaches and apricots most often), alcohol, and often a strong tannic sensation (for some, reminiscent of over-steeped tea). The wine usually creates an overall impression of great fruit, big but soft body, and tannic dryness with an intriguing and almost paradoxical underlay of sweetness, as if the fruit were either incredibly ripe and deeply flavored or there was the smallest trace of residual sugar. Many tasters discern cedar in the finish.

Both wines seem to respond equally well—imperturbably—to food.

Most people find themselves pretty hard put to express a preference, and for good reason. You're dealing here with excellent wine-making working with first-rate materials. The quality level is equal in both wines, so the only real point of preference is your reaction to their differing styles—the French wine big, authoritative, polished, and somewhat reined in, the California wine also big but more brash, spirited, with its fruit all up front. Your own palate should dictate your choice—and you certainly apologize to nobody for your preference, not this close to graduation.

The Chassagne-Montrachet is made by Drouhin and imported by Dreyfus, Ashby & Company. The firm of Joseph Drouhin is an old and respected Burgundian house, dealing for many decades in almost all of the wines of the Côte d'Or, and at every level, from a simple white Burgundy to wines from prized villages like this one to estate-bottled, single-vineyard wines.

Château Montelena is a Napa Valley winery noted particularly for the quality of its Chardonnay and for its exuberant Cabernet Sauvignon and Zinfandel.

Substitutes:

Younger vintages of either wine would be the best. Otherwise, try a Chassagne-Montrachet from another excellent *négociant* (Leflaive, for instance, or Maufoux, or Jadot) or a Chardonnay from such fine makers as Chalone, Robert Mondavi, Simi, Sonoma-Cutrer (especially the Reserve of all these). Trefethen is also excellent, but be aware that its "Library Releases"—older Chardonnays that have been reserved for longer aging—are so Burgundian in style that they would almost make a better substitute for the Chassagne than for the California wine.

This finishes the white-wine tastings, but there are still several ways for you to proceed from here.

*Exploring other wines related to whites:*
   Go on to the rosé wines and the sparkling wines.

*Following the kind of grapes:*
   Go on to the Second Flight of the sparkling wines if you have already completed the Twelfth and Thirteenth flights of the white wines.

*Following the wines of the country:*
   Wine One: Go on to the Second and Third flights of the rosé wines, the Second Flight of the sparkling wines.
   Wine Two: Go on to the First and Second flights of the rosé wines, the First, Second, and Third flights of the sparkling wines.

# ROSÉ WINES

# THE FIRST FLIGHT

❧❧

## *Lancer's Rosé*
## *and*
## *Seghesio Northern Sonoma*
## *White Zinfandel 1990*

❧❧

ROSÉ BY ANY OTHER NAME is a white wine. Surprised? Well, you're probably not alone. Most people assume—or have been led to assume—that rosé is a very distinctive kind of wine, made by some mysterious process that renders it a) pleasing to everybody and b) perfect with any food. Both are outrageous falsehoods.

In the interest of total honesty, I've got to tell you from the outset that I am a curmudgeon about rosé. I've rarely met one I've liked, and I think the public by and large has been sold a real bill of goods about them. Generally speaking, most rosé falls for me into the category of imitation wine, and I would much rather get on to the real thing. Nevertheless, I realize that there are good rosés in the world and that for many people they offer an attractive and engaging entry into wine, so we (that is to say, you) will taste a brief survey of rosé wines, starting with some of the most popular varieties.

Before you begin, however (you didn't really think I'd let you off the hook that easily, did you?), you ought to know a bit about what rosé really is: how it gets that color, what grapes it's made from, what dishes it does go well with, etc.

Let's start with the grapes it's made from. Popular wisdom takes it

237

for granted that rosé can be made only from a limited number of varieties. If you in your wine wisdom assume that popular opinion has once again committed a vulgar error, you're absolutely right. Pink wine can be made from any red grapes or mixture of red and white grapes. Any. Anywhere. And it is: almost every spot on the globe that makes wine at all can and does make a rosé wine. If you look around any decent-sized wineshop, you'll find rosé from California and New York, Chile and Argentina, Spain and Portugal, France and Italy. You'll find rosé of Grenache, rosé of Cabernet, rosé of Merlot, a white Zinfandel that's actually rosé. You'll find rosé that is in fact rose-colored, rosé that is cherry, rosé that is orange, rosé that is very close to colorless. You'll find rosé vinified still, crackling, and sparkling, sweet and dry.

Get the idea? Whatever rosé is, it is certainly not one thing. Rosé is every bit as varied and variable as any other kind of wine.

Another popular mistake about rosé is to think of it as a blending of red and white wines: add a little red and little white and keep juggling until you get the color you want—voilà! rosé. Very definitely not true. The core of rosé—the thing that makes it rosé and not white or red—is a technique of vinification.

You start with red grapes or a blend of white and red grapes. You press them in the normal manner. At this point, if you were making a white wine, you would separate the musts and the solids immediately and proceed to ferment the musts by themselves. In wine jargon, this is known as vinification *au blanc*. If you were making a red wine, you would allow the must and solids to ferment together for anywhere from four days to four weeks. But if you are making a rosé, you will let the musts and solids ferment together for a very carefully controlled and very brief amount of time—often only a few hours, rarely more than a day.

This is because grape juices are mostly colorless when pressed: a red wine becomes red during fermentation, when color leaches from the grape skins into the musts. So early removal of the skins yields a lightly colored wine by shortening the dyeing process. That interruption curtails other processes as well, since the grape solids contribute many other things to red wine besides color—particularly tannin and other extracts that affect the wine's body and longevity.

After the skins have been removed, the musts are then fermented *au blanc*; that is, they are treated exactly as if they were going to make a white wine. These days this usually entails controlled, low-temperature fermentation to preserve fruit and freshness, and the use of stainless steel or Fiberglas tanks rather than wood to prevent the introduction of any other flavors than those the grapes themselves possess. So from the point of view of the finished rosé, therefore, the chief result of this whole process is to make a wine that, despite its reddish tinge, is structurally and palatally closer to white wine than to red. That is the most important single thing you should know about rosé.

You've probably already figured out what follows from that. If rosé is actually more similar to white wine than to red and not, as the color suggests, something that stands midway between them, then it is probably going to taste better with the same sorts of food that white wines accompany. That is in fact the way it is: you can only drink rosé with everything, as folklore has it, in the sense that you can drink any wine you like with everything. Like any other wine, rosé goes better with some foods than others, and the better the rosé itself is, the more important the wine-food combinations become—as with any other wine.

Okay, I think that's really enough preliminary. Sorry if I sounded a bit preachy, but as I warned you, I'm not a real fan of these wines. Anyhow, now it's your chance to find out whether you are or not, so off you go to your first rosé tasting.

I'm making things relatively easy for you to start—two very popular rosés, one Portuguese and one Californian. Nothing too complex here, so taste away—not forgetting the infamous s's, all six of them.

## Appearance.

With rosé wines, there is somewhat more to say here than you're used to, isn't there? These wines will sharpen your eye, if nothing else.

The Lancer's normally shows a medium-pink color with highlights of other tones throughout, gold or copper or peach depending on your bottle and, to some extent, your lighting. It is also slightly carbonated (a degree of sparkle that is usually called "crackling"), and those little bubbles give it a very lively, somewhat festive appearance. The Seghesio's usual color is a pale, peachy pink, a relatively pretty hue. As a class, white Zinfandels are both misnamed and widely variable in color. While they are almost never clear, they may be any shade from the faintest onionskin through to vivid cherry.

Aroma.

Reactions here tend to be pretty uniform. Almost all tasters find the Lancer's aroma quite faint. They chiefly discern an acidic, tart element linked with fruit, which they may describe as citrus or apple or coppery or even as a fresh cucumber smell, all nevertheless faint. There is slightly more division of opinion about the Zinfandel. Some people find its aroma initially faint though growing stronger as it opens. Others find it restrained throughout. Almost all describe it as smelling sweet and slightly fruity, but the range of fruits they discern is wide: cherries, mangoes, nectarines, peaches. For most people this fruit aroma has a definite sweet quality, and for some it is also accompanied by a clear presence of alcohol or a small, yeasty smell.

Taste.

The greatest variable here is the individual taster's sensitivity to sugar and tolerance for it. The greater the appetite for sugar, the drier these wines will appear.

Responses to the Portuguese wine, for instance, can run the whole gamut from pleasing dry/tart freshness to sweet and acid. Whatever the degree of sweetness perceived, most tasters describe a pleasant, generalized light fruit flavor (prunes or apples are sometimes mentioned) and a sweet finish, all enlivened by the slight sparkle of the wine.

The vast majority of tasters find the Seghesio drier than the Lancer's and drier than its own aroma led them to expect, with a kind of vague sweet-and-sour fruitiness—the sour usually predominating. If a specific fruit comes to the fore, it's almost always identified as berry. Some people report small herbaceous or grassy flavors as well as a salty, not unpleasant, seawater taste. Almost everybody agrees that the Zinfandel is rounder, softer, and slightly fuller than the Lancer's, with a distinctly tart finish.

Just about everybody also agrees that these are not complicated wines. There isn't a whole lot more to say about them, other than that they are both surprisingly pleasant quaffing wines, especially when served as well chilled as their producers intend them to be. They do illustrate very nicely, however, the two basic schools of rosé: the light-bodied, often acidic, frequently sweet (even if only slightly so) style and the usually drier, fuller, more austere style. The choice between them is purely a matter of taste. Right now in America white Zinfandel seems to suit an awful lot of people's palates, even though I regard it as a waste of good red grapes. *Chacun à son goût*: just be aware that the range of sweetness in white Zinfandel is almost as great as the range of color—what we've been tasting here is one of the drier specimens.

### Everything's Coming Up Rosés

Of course, Zinfandel isn't the only grape that makes rosé in North America, and a good many winemakers all over the United States have for years been producing all sorts of rosé, usually from blends. In California, Grenache was for years a staple of inexpensive rosés, though now it is beginning to get more respect. Because of the ever-increasing popularity of white wines and a temporary glut of red wines, more and more California vineyards have been turning out *blancs des noirs* and *rosés des noirs*—white and rosé wines from essentially red-wine grapes. So you'll now find Rosé of Cabernet Sauvignon and Rosé of Pinot Noir right alongside White Zinfandel on the shelves, just as they're likely to be side by side in the color spectrum too.

Lots of these wines are coming out with highly imaginative and poetic names attached, and some of the wines even manage to live up to their names. But it is impossible to offer any useful generalizations about them to arm you for shopping. Makers go their own way with these wines, and you have to read each label carefully for clues even to such basic facts as sweetness or dryness. Let the buyer be wary is the best rule.

By the way, lest it be thought that all this sliding around the color scale was not well considered, you should know that a new name has been conferred on this new generation of rosé-type wines. They are now officially known as "blush wines." Whatever marketing genius invented that beauty deserves not one but two raises.

Lancer's is a fair representative of a popular group of Portuguese wines, all vinified from mixed grapes and slightly sweet, and all with a touch of sparkle, whether from trapped gasses or from added ones. This isn't all there is to Portuguese wines, not by a long shot: if you can find them, try some full-bodied, dry Dao reds.

Seghesio is a family-owned firm in Sonoma; it makes—and makes well—the whole range of California wines.

Substitutes:

A younger vintage of the Seghesio White Zinfandel should be your first choice; failing that, try a White Zinfandel from Sutter Home. If Lancer's Rosé isn't available, try Mateus Rosé, also from Portugal and also nv, though not crackling.

This is the conclusion of the First Flight of rosé wines. There are several ways for you to proceed from here.

*Following the lead of your own preferences:*
   If you liked either the first wine, the Lancer's Rosé, or the
   second wine, the Seghesio White Zinfandel, go on to the
   Second Flight.

*Following the kind of grapes:*
   Wine One: There are no other tastings of these grapes.
   Wine Two: There are no further tastings of these grapes; have
   you tasted through the red Zinfandel flights?

*Following the wines of the country:*
   Wine One: There are no other Portuguese wines in these
   tastings.
   Wine Two: Go on to the next flight.

# THE SECOND FLIGHT

## Joseph Phelps
## Vin du Mistral 1990
## and
## Moc-Baril Cabernet d'Anjou
## Rosé 1989

AGAIN, a California rosé and a European. The Anjou rosé represents an ancient and honorable breed, while the propri-etorally named California wine exemplifies the newfound respect the Grenache grape and its other Rhône Valley relations are now receiving from American winemakers.

These two wines are vinified from very different grapes (Grenache and Cabernet Franc, respectively), so there should be a lot of obvious differences for you to spot. The similarities ought to be subtler and more difficult, since they stem largely from the fact that these two wines have been vinified in a similar manner. They are distant cousins rather than kissin' kin, and that may or may not make your task tougher. In any event, I know that you are hardened to this arduous duty from the rigorous training you've been through, so get in there and taste!

Full drill: see, swirl, smell, sip, savor, and spit. Ask no quarter and give none.

### Appearance.

In talking about the exact shadings of different rosés, you will probably use more adjectives and get a wider spread of descriptions

243

than you encountered in speaking of the appearance of all the red
and white wines combined. Even in the context of the same wine,
the color variation from vintage to vintage can be enormous. This
Phelps Vin du Mistral, for instance, has been described as everything from watery claret to pale pink to pink with marked or-
angey/coppery overtones. The Anjou rosé has been called simply a
pretty pale pink, pink with a lavender tinge, and salmon. There is
near unanimity that both wines are brilliant—that is, very clear and
bright—and very attractive.

## Aroma.

About the aromas of these two wines there is an unusual level of
agreement. Just about everyone credits the Vin du Mistral with a
nice, light, fresh aroma, with marked but difficult to pinpoint fruit
tones. Light fruits, like greengage plums or some citrus fruits, are
among the popular candidates, with mint and strawberries also in
the running.

   And just about everyone finds the scent of the Anjou wine also
fresh, but fuller and more savory. They name fruits less often,
though a sweet, peachy scent is frequently remarked on, and more
generalized smells frequently—fresh cheese especially, and vegetal
odors and fresh wood. The aromas of both wines rate as pleasing
and/or intriguing with the majority of tasters.

## Taste.

More marked differences of opinion emerge in the actual tasting of
these wines. Those who respond favorably to the Vin du Mistral
usually find it light, slightly acid, and refreshing. They describe its
flavor as simultaneously sweet and sour or as good fruit on the
borderline of sweet. In either case, what they are responding to is a
small amount of residual sugar balanced nicely by acidity and soft
tannin. Berries, apples, plums, and even some citrus fruits loom
large among the specific flavors named. Those who don't like this
wine are usually reacting to its acidity and/or tannin, and they
consequently describe it as sharp, tart, or bitter, with a finish in the
same vein. Tasters pleased by this wine tend to praise its soft, dry
finish.

   Most tasters find the Rosé d'Anjou lightly but definitely sweet,
and rounder, fatter, and less acid than the Vin du Mistral. They

usually describe it as having more fruit: berries, peaches, and nectarines seem to be the most popular candidates. Like the Vin du Mistral, this Anjou rosé finishes dry and pleasing. Those who don't react favorably to it usually fault its sweetness: they tend to find it too simple—sugar and water—and sometimes flabby. Tasters pleased with it invariably say that it has ample acid to balance its small sweetness.

In the wine world, both these wines are usually typified as charming, which is really meant both as a compliment to them (they *are* charming) and a condescension (that's all they are).

Both of them ought to be drunk as young as possible: bottle-age does not improve them. Both are meant to be served chilled, though not iced to numbness, and both are thought of essentially as warm-weather drinks or light aperitifs, roles in which it would be difficult indeed to fault them. To my mind (though perhaps not to yours), they are less satisfactory as dinner wines, but I'd probably change my mind if I were having that dinner in the open air on a warm summer night somewhere on the banks of the Loire or the shores of the Pacific, where these wines hail from and where they seem not only appropriate but practically inevitable in every situation.

Vin du Mistral is the name invented by prestigious winemaker Joseph Phelps to distinguish his new, "Rhône Ranger"–style Grenache rosé from the old-fashioned, sickly-sweet pink treacle that used to be the common grave of all the Grenache grapes of California. Other winemakers equally serious about the potential of Rhône varieties in California have devised their own names for their own versions of this wine.

Anjou is a province on the middle Loire, famous alike for beautiful châteaux and gentle wines. Rosé d'Anjou is perhaps the gentlest of them all. It is usually made from a blend of red grapes, but the better examples, like this bottle, are vinified from the Cabernet Franc, which is the vinous aristocrat of the region. Moc-Baril is the trade name of the family firm of Albert Besombes, a long-established Loire *négociant*. It is imported into the United States by Kobrand.

## Substitutes:

As always, younger vintages of these two wines should be your first choice. Otherwise, look for examples of quality Grenache rosé from other California producers such as Bonny Doon (Vin Gris de Cigare)

or McDowell Valley Vineyard (Les Vieux Cepages): they will not be
identical to Vin du Mistral, but they will still provide a good introduction to the breed. For the French wine, if Moc-Baril is not available, try a Rosé d'Anjou from another maker (odds are it will be
sweeter) or go a completely different route with a bone-dry
Provence Rosé such as L'Estandon (J. Bagnis & Fils).

This concludes the second rosé flight. There are several ways for you
to proceed from here.

*Following the lead of your own preferences:*
  If you enjoyed either the first wine, Phelps Vin du Mistral, or
  the second wine, Moc-Baril d'Anjou Rosé, go on to the Third
  Flight.

*Following the kind of grapes:*
  Wine One: The grapes closest to this can be found in the red-
  wine Nineteenth Flight. Surprised?
  Wine Two: There is no other tasting involving a significant
  amount of Cabernet Franc.

*Following the wines of the country:*
  Wine One: This is the last California rosé.
  Wine Two: Go on to the Third Flight.

# THE THIRD FLIGHT

～～～

## *Mastroberardino*
## *Lacrimarosa d'Irpinia 1990*
## *and*
## *Château d'Aqueria Tavel 1989*

～～～

THIS TIME YOU FACE an Italian and a French rosé, both big wines by rosé standards. In connoisseur circles, the two wines you are about to taste are thought of as being just about the highest that rosé reaches. So get ready to concentrate: taste carefully and—as always—be prepared to run into a surprise or two. Forward!

Do not, under pain of having your taste buds confiscated, omit the full ritual of tasting procedures.

### Appearance.

Marked differences leap to the eye (a grotesque phrase, don't you think?). The Lacrimarosa is very pale, barely rosé. It usually shows the color that some California vintners call "eye of the partridge" (another grotesque image). A better way to state it is to call it an onionskin shade, pale, coppery, bright, and pretty. The Tavel, on the other hand, shows a definite pink coloration, really a light cherry tone or a fleshy peach-and-pink combination—a good hue, quite clear and brilliant.

### Aroma.

Here is where the surprises begin for most people.

The scent of the Lacrimarosa is pronouncedly different from

247

those of the other rosés you've dealt with, so much so that many tasters are a bit put off by it at first. Don't be thrown off by shock: let it sit and come back to it a few times until you acclimate.

Everybody agrees this is an authoritative aroma, not necessarily huge, but insistent. Most tasters discern at least two main bodies of scent in it: cheese and herbaceous odors. By cheese most tasters do not mean fresh cheese, as we've had in some other wines, but the nutty, dry smell of mature cheeses like aged Parmesan or aged Gouda. And by herbaceous elements they tend to mean rooty, stemmy, leafy underbrush scents—what one taster called "sawdust and soil"—as distinguished from more usual floral or herbal scents. On a more general level, many people notice an absence of acid components in this aroma and a presence of aromatic oils in their stead. Almost everyone agrees too (whether it pleases them or not) that this wine has a quite complex aroma.

Almost all tasters also find the aroma of the Tavel big and complex, though in a manner very different from the Lacrimarosa's. Most also find in this wine two main aromatic components: a kind of woody or oaky scent mixed up with leaves and grass on one hand and a body of distinctly fruity odors on the other. The woody/grassy elements are usually described as very fresh and clean-smelling, the fruit as only hinting at sweetness and more marked by an attractive acid sharpness, even a little sourness. There is little unanimity about the specific fruit scents contained here: you might get peaches or melons or sour cherries or something as unusual as kumquats. Most people find this aroma more immediately appealing than the Lacrimarosa's and no less complex.

**Taste.**

The surprises continue.

The first thing almost everybody reacts to on tasting the Lacrimarosa is its surprisingly big body, and the second is the presence of plenty of acid in the taste despite its absence from the aroma. Most find that acid very adequately balanced by something that they are prepared to call fruit but which doesn't seem to be fruit in the way they've become used to encountering it in white and rosé wines. Most say it *is* fruit (cherries, lemons, and even unsweet mangoes get mentioned), but fully dry and present more in the manner of a red wine than a white. Some tasters describe the sensation by saying that with your eyes closed you wouldn't know whether you were drinking a red or a white wine. Many also mention a lingering, astringent finish that adds to the mixed impression of austerity, complexity, and elegance the wine makes on them. Almost everybody finds this wine very balanced and very impressive. For a small percentage of tasters, it's just too big and powerful. Generally, all agree that this is by no stretch of the imagination a delicate aperitif wine but rather a first-class dinner wine.

The Tavel has some surprises for most tasters as well. Few expect it to be as fully dry as they find it, and many discover a little tannic pucker in there that catches them off guard. Most describe the wine as fruity and acidic—sour cherries and citrus fruits, especially grapefruit, are often mentioned—with its balance just beginning to take hold: it gives the impression that it has further evolution in front of it. Most tasters call it medium-bodied, a bit lighter than the first wine and softer in the finish, though every bit as intriguing and perhaps a bit more attractive. As with the Lacrimarosa, most also agree that this is a more substantial wine than any in the first two flights of rosé and that it should definitely be used as a dinner wine rather than as an aperitif.

Tavel and Lacrimarosa are very close to, if not at, the ceiling for rosé wines: they just don't make them much better than these, and only in a few places do they make them this good. Rosé is a limited option in wine. It reaches its apotheosis (for my palate at any rate) in rosé champagne, where the additional body extracted by fermenting Pinot Noir on its skins raises an already superb wine up a notch higher on the pleasure scale. Interestingly enough, that's also one of the very few cases in which a rosé wine is made by blending fermented red wine with separately fermented white.

Lacrimarosa d'Irpinia is an extremely localized and unusual wine. It is made primarily by one house, Mastroberardino, in a small growing area not far from Naples, and vinified from the Aglianico grape, which otherwise yields a full-bodied red wine (Taurasi) of great breed and longevity. Mastroberardino's wines are imported by Heublein's Palace Brands.

Tavel is the much more famous name of the two wines in this flight. Indeed, Tavel is the most respected rosé appellation in France. Produced on the west bank of the Rhône near Châteauneuf du Pape, Tavel uses almost the same grapes as that big red wine, but particularly Grenache. Château d'Aqueria is a family-owned property that produces textbook Tavel.

## Substitutes:

Younger vintages of either wine are the first fallback position. For the Lacrimarosa d'Irpinia, there really is no other option. You could try other makers (Château de Trinquevedel, Domaine Lafond, or Domaine Maby) or *négociants* (Maufoux makes quite a decent Tavel) as alternatives for the Château d'Aqueria.

This finishes the rosé section. You may either move directly on to the sparkling wines, or

*Following the lead of your own preferences:*
    If you liked the Lacrimarosa d'Irpinia better, go back to its
    cousin in the white-wine Eleventh Flight.
    If you liked the Château d'Aqueria Tavel better, try its burlier
    kin in the red-wine Nineteenth Flight.

*Following the kind of grapes:*
    Wine One: There is no other tasting of the Aglianico grape.
    Wine Two: See the rosé Second Flight.

*Following the wines of the country:*
    Wine One: Go on to the sparkling-wine Third Flight.
    Wine Two: Go on to the sparkling-wine Second Flight.

# SPARKLING
# WINES
# AND
# CHAMPAGNES

# THE FIRST FLIGHT

~~oOo~~

## *Korbel Brut California Champagne and Freixenet Cordon Negro Brut*

~~oOo~~

IF IT IS POSSIBLE for one kind of wine to be the victim of more disinformation and confusion than all the others combined, sparkling wine is my candidate for the dubious distinction. With regard to the difference between sparkling wine and champagne, more fuss has been made and more words written by more people (myself among them) about these mere words than about most others in my long memory. *C'est la vie.*

Champagne is a sparkling wine made in the Champagne region of France: thus "champagne" is a geographical name, like "port" or "sherry," so it stands to reason that "real" champagne comes only from Champagne.

Any sparkling wine anywhere in the world can be made by the champagne method, if the winemaker is willing to go to the trouble and expense of doing so, but that shouldn't—and within the European Common Market doesn't—allow that wine to be called "champagne," any more than a blend of Cabernet Sauvignon and Merlot made in the Napa Valley should be called Bordeaux.

The problem arises simply because words like "champagne" and "chablis" and even "burgundy" have been used outside of France as wine names rather than as geographical identifiers. To speak of the wines of Burgundy is one thing, but to talk of California burgundy is quite another. But if you are willing to risk exactness—an increasingly bold undertaking in the waning years of the twentieth century—the case is simple. Here is all you need to know about it: All champagne is sparkling wine, but sparkling wine is a category that includes much more than champagne. Or, if you prefer the snobbier formulation: champagne comes only from Champagne— all the rest is only sparkling wine.

The difference between the champagne method—*méthode champenoise* is the technical phrase you will usually see on labels (though as the French move to legally protect even that phrase, you will also see *méthode traditionelle* and *méthode classique*, in various languages, to designate the same thing)—and other ways of making sparkling wines, however, amounts to considerably more than a matter of words. The champagne method is painstaking, costly, slow, and laborious, and to this point in history it results in sparkling wines that are almost always perceptibly better than those made by other methods.

Time was that the champagne method was practically a monopoly of the Champagne region. Now, however, winemakers in a good many other parts of the globe have learned and are utilizing its techniques, with the result that Spain, Italy, and the United States at least are presenting increasingly impressive challenges to champagne's hitherto unquestionable supremacy among the world's sparkling wines. Needless to say, none of these sparkling wines exactly reproduces champagne. That's not even the goal of the winemakers: what they're after, and what some of them are achieving, are wines of champagne quality with the peculiar characteristics of their districts, their grapes, their style.

The tastings that follow in this section are designed to give you a chance to explore the range of styles that are possible within the broad category of champagne-method sparkling wines. As a preliminary, it would be just as well to unfreight yourself of either or both of the two most widespread—and, interestingly enough, contradictory—prejudices about sparklers, should you happen to believe them.

The first prejudice says that all sparkling wines are just too la-di-da, too snooty or pretentious or serious. The second prejudice has it that they aren't serious at all, that they are pure fun wines, to be tossed down without thought or appreciation. The first prejudice misses all the pleasure of these wines completely; the second gets only half of what they have to offer, like smelling a rose but never looking at it, or sniffing freshly baked bread but never eating any.

### Turn on the Bubble Machine

The steps of the *méthode champenoise* are as follows. First the grapes are carefully selected. Each village in the Champagne growing area is rated, and champagne makers compete strenuously for the best grapes. Further selection and elimination of unsound or unripe berries occurs just before pressing. After pressing, the juices are fermented in the ordinary white-wine manner, and in the following spring they are bottled off. At the same time, each bottle of still wine receives a small amount of sugar and yeast solution. It is then tightly corked.

The yeast and sugar cause a second fermentation in each bottle, which, because it occurs in a completely closed environment, generates gasses that are forced into suspension within the wine. This is both the origin of champagne's characteristic sparkle and the reason champagne is always packaged in heavy bottles with mushroom-shaped, wired-down corks: the pressure inside a champagne bottle is five times greater than that in the normal atmosphere.

Champagne is then aged for whatever period the maker's policy determines. Before shipment, however, the sediments thrown by the second fermentation must be removed. This is accomplished by a process called riddling. The bottles are placed neck downward in specially perforated boards called *pupitres*. These are gradually raised to steeper and steeper angles, until the bottles are almost standing on their heads. In addition, the bottles are regularly rotated so as to move the sediments down the neck and against the cork. Finally, the necks are plunged into a freezing brine solution and the corks quickly extracted (in some firms, still by hand). This, if all is going well, extrudes the wad of sediment, leaving the wine clear for topping up and recorking.

Along with topping up, each bottle receives a final *dosage*, an addition of a sugar solution which will determine the final dryness or sweetness of the champagne.

Sure, sparkling wines are fun. All wines are fun. Why else bother to drink them? The world is filled with lots of other things that are good for you. The factor that puts all wines miles ahead of cod-liver oil is the pleasure they give, and that pleasure is definitely heightened in sparkling wines. There is something indefinably and undeniably festive in their simple appearance, and that quality is amply reinforced by the power of custom and tradition, which have made sparkling wines the irreplaceable centerpieces of all major celebrations. Weddings, births, anniversaries, graduations: all lose their sparkle when they lack a sparkling wine.

But that isn't all there is to these wines. In fact, that's mostly the power of our own associations and our own attitudes. The most basic fact to remember about sparkling wines is that they start out life as still wines like any others, and each one of them is just as good—or as bad—as the wine it's based on. Good grapes make good wine make good sparkling wine, and you can and should taste sparkling wines for the very same things you would look for in still wines—*plus* the added lift that a well-orchestrated sparkle should give them.

Though the Korbel is not a true champagne in the sense that the wine comes from Champagne, the firm, like others from other parts of the United States, freely uses the champagne name, to the outrage of French growers. Both the Korbel and the Freixenet are made completely according to the champagne method, but neither uses exactly the same grape varieties from which traditional champagne is made. In fact, it's more than likely that these two sparkling wines use such a diversity of grapes that they don't even have one variety in common. So your mission is to go boldly where your palate has gone many times before, but this time with a little twist. Try to discern here, while you are tasting the big differences due to grape varieties and climates and soils, what similarities of flavor or style you can trace to the similarities of the wines' treatment. That should keep you occupied for a bit.

By the way: The best glasses for serving champagne or any sparkling wine are not those broad, shallow, fruit-dishy looking things that tradition in the United States seems to hallow. Anything that wide and shallow simply dissipates the bubbles, so why bother with a sparkling wine at all? Rather, choose a tall, narrow glass, flute- or tulip-shaped, with enough of a stem so your hand won't warm the wine, and pour your sparkling wine deep enough in it so you can appreciate fully its special charm.

Purists never use any kind of soap or detergent to clean glasses intended for champagne (or any other wine, for that matter), and they use only the finest quality, lint-free towels to dry them. Other equally knowledgeable wine drinkers regard all that as preposterous affectation. It all depends on just how sensitive your nose and eye really are.

Okay, wine trekker, taste away: see, swirl, sniff, sip, savor, and spit.


## Appearance.

Right away, being the wily bird that you are, you noticed that sparkling wines have introduced a new element into what used to be the most routine part of your tasting procedure, checking the appearance of the wine. Bubbles. Bubbles change everything, don't they?

The color of these two wines is not radically different from anything you've been looking at up till now: the Korbel is a pale shade of straw, the Freixenet perhaps a little darker or yellower. But the bubbles completely alter the appearance of the wine and make what would be a perfectly ordinary-looking wine seem very gay and lively.

Since that appearance and impression of liveliness in a sparkling wine is highly desirable, whatever contributes to it is good and whatever detracts from it is bad. So if one of your glasses is making a steady, rapidly ascending stream of fine bubbles while the other is making only a few sluggish, large, and vulgar-looking bubbles, it doesn't take an advanced degree in esthetics to tell which is more pleasing and attractive to the eye and which, therefore, is the better-made sparkler.

Among connoisseurs, that stream of bubbles is usually referred to by one of the nicer pieces of jargon in the wine trade: it is called *perlage*, which is a French term denoting, loosely, the quality of the beading or the pearling of the wine.

Under ideal circumstances, both these wines should generate a persistent, lively stream of what are, in the range of wine sparkles, just about medium-gauge bubbles. Remember, however, that there can be great variation not only from bottle to bottle but even from glass to glass, depending on the glass's shape and how it was cleaned.

Okay, now that you have picked some new pieces of technical language and data and increased your sophistication enormously thereby, let's get on with the tasting.

### Aroma.

Most tasters find a readily identifiable broad distinction between the aromas of these two wines. The Korbel strikes most people as smelling somewhat sharp, with a wheaty overlay and fainter fruity—apple is the one most often mentioned—and grassy scents coming after. Some tasters discern leafy or minty overtones, all relatively light and subdued. The great majority of tasters describe the Freixenet, on the other hand, as smelling strongly wheaty, even as smelling like fresh or toasted bread, with fruity tones—peach is the candidate here—following after. Very few people detect even the slightest trace of sweetness in either aroma.

A small note of caution: It is possible with almost all white wines, but especially with sparklers, occasionally to smell a trace of sulfur when the bottle is first opened. Almost always this passes off within a few moments. Obviously, if it persists it is a serious flaw in the wine.

### Taste.

For most tasters, the broad differences indicated by the aromas continue into the actual flavors of these two wines.

People are likely to describe the Korbel as some combination of light, dry, lively, and/or fruity, with a slight touch of sweetness, and they may taste in it apples or apricots or peaches or white grapes. They may term it acidic (many people find it strongly so, and taste a nearly unpleasant sourness because of it) or aggressively carbonated. Overall, the most common responses depict a light, bright, active wine, which most people tend to like.

On the other hand, most tasters find the Freixenet markedly dry by comparison, perhaps even austere. At the same time, it is slightly fuller and weightier, with high acid and elegantly subdued fruit. The most frequently discerned flavor seems to be toast or a nonspecific, pleasing fruit that suggests sweetness without being sweet. The overall impression is of a somewhat austere, restrained, and balanced wine, more elegant than zestful.

Some people may summarize the differences between the two by seeing the Korbel as starting from a more interesting and fruitier base wine and the Freixenet as being the better-constructed sparkling wine, a distinction which goes to the heart of a great deal about these wines.

That is because the Korbel wine is vinified from California grapes, which almost always possess plenty of fruit and flavor, which, when well handled, make interesting wine. Freixenet makes its sparkling wine from native grapes, Spanish *vinifera* varieties, which seem to possess some of the delicacy that American grapes often lack but only a shadow of their fruit.

Both Korbel and Freixenet make what are among the least expensive champagne-method sparkling wines on the American market, and both offer sparkling wines at several levels of quality. Korbel, founded as a sparkling-wine house in 1882, is unquestionably the largest such firm in California. Freixenet is probably the largest maker of champagne-method sparkling wine in the world and has been producing such wines since 1915.

## Substitutes:

None should be necessary, since these wines are among the most widely distributed in the United States, but just in case—for the California sparkler, try Wente Brothers Brut or Hans Kornell Brut; for the Spanish sparkler, Codorniu Brut Clasico.

This concludes the first flight of sparkling wines. There are several ways for you to proceed from here.

*Following the lead of your own preferences:*
  If you enjoyed either the Korbel or the Freixenet, go on to the
  Second Flight.

*Following the kind of grapes:*
  There is nothing else like these grapes in these tastings.

*Following the wines of the country:*
  Wine One: Go on to the Second Flight.
  Wine Two: The only other Spanish wine in these tastings can be
  found in the red-wine Fifth Flight.

# THE SECOND FLIGHT

❦

## *Codorniu Napa Brut*
## *and*
## *Veuve Clicquot Brut*

❦

I N THIS FLIGHT your challenge, once again, is to taste for regional and stylistic differences in two wines made from the same
sorts of grapes and in exactly the same manner. Both of these wines
are nv, nonvintage, a category that constitutes the major portion of
the production of any champagne or sparkling-wine house. Because of that, all winemakers take special pains to preserve a conti-
nuity of flavor and body and attack in their nonvintage bottlings and
to create in them a readily recognizable house style.

That makes this class of sparkling wines ideal for the sort of
sophisticated comparison at which you've become so expert; so go
to it.

Don't forget to perform the whole ritual: see, swirl, sniff, sip,
savor, and spit. Meet you back here in a few minutes.


**Appearance.**

The Codorniu Napa Brut should show a clear straw color, rather
delicate looking, with a persistent stream of middling-sized bubbles. The Veuve Clicquot Brut ought to be a slightly paler straw than
that, with a fine, steady perlage. Both are good-looking wines.

## Aroma.

Both wines fall into the category of light or delicate aromas: no blockbusters here, nor are they very common anywhere in the world of sparkling wines.

Tasters seem to divide pretty evenly about what they smell in the California sparkler: one group picks up mostly yeast and alcohol and wheat; the other group largely discerns delicate green-leaf and fruit scents—sometimes as specific as mint, but usually more generalized than that. Almost all find the aroma of the Codorniu Napa clean and fresh, and most—at least after sniffing the Veuve Clicquot—recognize these aromas as belonging to the packet of classic champagne smells.

There tends to be more unanimity about the champagne: almost everybody discerns yeast, or freshly baked bread, or buttered toast, or some other variant on that class of aromas, once again delicate rather than powerful. The only major departure from that—and it is not really very big—is the occasional mention of something like a warm, earth smell. As with Codorniu Napa, most tasters find the aroma of this Veuve Clicquot fresh and clean. Many tasters, in fact, describe it as in some important respects a development of the scents of the California wine, as if—as one taster put it—the same ingredients had been cooked rather than served raw.

## Taste.

Here of course is where the real differences in style between these two wines are going to show themselves most strongly. The Codorniu Napa strikes most tasters as lively and bright, with a medium body and a whole truckload of fruit that somehow or other doesn't make it fleshy. Most people taste it as fully dry, with modest acidity and a pretty, peach finish. Some people describe it as a lean wine, but no one would ever call it steely or austere.

By contrast, most people feel the Veuve Clicquot as heavier: they may call it anything from medium- to full-bodied, but what they mean is a greater sense of weight on the tongue and a genuine sensation of fullness, almost roundness, in the mouth. They tend to describe it as softer, smoother, and more giving than the Codorniu Napa, with a definite wheaty element in the flavor, as well as a definite fruit flavor—dried apricots, or perhaps peaches. Many tasters also report a lovely long finish, dry and distinctly nutty.

### Champagne Vintages

In champagne, vintages do not simply occur: they are declared. The norm in champagne is nv, a blend of wines from different grapes (Pinot Noir, Pinot Meunier—both red—and Chardonnay), from different vineyards and areas (for example, Montagne de Reims or Côte des Blancs), and from different years. Each house maintains reserves of wine for blending, in order to be able to preserve a continuous and recognizable flavor and style from year to year. The wine so produced constitutes the bulk of each house's line. Vintages are exceptional, and are declared only in those years when the house decides it has access to enough superior grapes to make a wine sufficiently distinct from its nv to warrant separate labeling. This is an individual decision, and not all champagne makers choose to bottle a vintage wine for the same harvest. In 1982, almost all the houses declared a vintage. In 1983, some, but by no means all, made a vintage wine.

Fine as both wines are—and they are practically paradigms of top-quality sparkling wines from their respective regions—not everybody likes them. For some, all sparkling wines are just a dead issue and they taste nothing but acid or a little prickle on the tongue. Others find the Codorniu Napa too hard or too one-dimensional. And yet others find the Veuve Clicquot too heavy and insufficiently zestful—a little too old-and-tired-tasting for their palates. But most people, by and large, respond very favorably to both wines, though perceiving large differences between them. Overall, consensus gives the Codorniu Napa an edge in muscularity, the Veuve Clicquot a lead in complexity.

Speaking as objectively as one ever can about wines (which of course is still very subjectively), I would say that the Codorniu Napa Brut has been vinified in a style I would call full Blanc de Blancs.

What on earth do I mean by that? I'm so glad you asked.

Let's start with some champagne basics that usually surprise people. Three grapes go into champagne, and two of them are red: Pinot Noir, Pinot Meunier, and Chardonnay. What happens to the color? Well, except for pink champagne (about which more later), the musts from the grapes for champagne are fermented off the skins—that is, the liquids are separated from the solids immediately after pressing. Most grape juice is clear: the color in red wine leaches from the skins into the musts over a period of time. This is not allowed to happen with champagne.

Fascinating, no doubt, but what has it got to do with anything we're talking about? Well, it is the red grapes that give body and flesh to champagne, and the blending of the different kinds that provides champagne with its complexity. Nevertheless, some houses make—and it is very popular right now—a Blanc de Blancs champagne, a white wine made exclusively from white grapes, in this case Chardonnay. Such a champagne is almost always paler in color, lighter in body, more delicate and less complex than conventional champagne. If you'll forgive a pun, Blanc de Blancs is monochromatic.

Nevertheless, within the limitations of Blanc de Blancs there is still room for house style to express itself. The wine can be soft or hard, very fruity or very restrained, delicate or assertive. This Codorniu Napa, which is made with a very high percentage of Chardonnay (half, to be exact), reminds me of a Blanc de Blancs champagne in the full style: its bright, stylish muscularity is to my palate characteristic of that particular kind of champagne. Taken as a whole, this wine offers a fine example of how very sophisticated California winemaking has become.

Nevertheless, the differences between these two wines still show the differences that persist between the California style and the French style, which can be summed up in the California sparkler's emphasis on fruit and the French wine's elegant restraint, its gloved power. The Veuve Clicquot shows just exactly the kind of complexity and balance that I would expect from a very well-made champagne containing the usual three grape varieties, with Chardonnay making up its more customary one third of the blend. In fact, just because this particular wine is rather full-bodied and weighty, I would expect, even if I had not known, that it contains a substantially higher percentage of red grapes than white. They—especially Pinot Noir—provide the grounding for champagne: they give it its bass notes.

That is why, by the way, a genuine pink champagne is no airy-fairy, effete drink. Pink champagnes, which derive their color from allowing some Pinot to ferment for a while on its skins, are usually among the most full-bodied and robust of sparkling wines. A Brut Rosé from a good champagne house usually ranks as one of its special cuvées ("cuvée" is the term used in Champagne for any blend). Such a sparkler can teach you a lot of respect for pink wines.

That's an awful lot of champagne lore for you to digest at one sitting, so pour yourself a glass of bubbly and read through it again to make sure you've got it straight. Then go on out and swank the neighbors.

Codorniu Napa is a new California winery specializing in sparkling wines, a scion of the giant Codorniu firm of Spain, and an indication of the intense interest the success of California wines has aroused among the great winemakers of Europe.

Veuve Clicquot is one of the *grandes marques*, the great champagne houses upon whom so much of the prestige of champagne rests. It produces wines that are highly regarded examples of the big, full-bodied style in champagne. In addition to this nonvintage wine, Veuve Clicquot markets in the United States both vintage champagnes (blanc and rosé), a charming dessert champagne (demi-sec), and its great *tête de cuvées* (the champagne term for the top-of-the-line, no-expense-spared blend), La Grande Dame.

Needless to say, both France and California, not to mention Spain and Italy, are rich in producers of fine *méthode champenoise* wines, so if this sort of sparkling wine appeals to you there is a whole world for you to explore. Here are some names to work with.

California: Domaine Chandon, Hanns Kornell Cellars (interesting wines reminiscent of the best German *Sekt*), Mumm Cuvée Napa, Schramsberg Vineyards

Spain: Codorniu, Freixenet

Italy: Ca' del Bosco, Cinzano, Equipe 5, Ferrari, Fontanafredda, Gancia, Martini & Rossi, Riccadonna

France: Bollinger, Charbaut, Deutz, Charles Heidsieck, Heidsieck Monopole, Krug, Lanson, Laurent-Perrier, Moët & Chandon, Mumm, Perrier-Jouet, Piper Heidsieck, Pol Roger, Ruinart, Taittinger

Most, if not all, of the French houses (and some of the others) in addition to their regular nv bottlings produce vintage champagnes, pink champagnes, Blancs des Blancs, and special cuvées of various styles and ages.

## Substitutes:

If either the Cordorniu Napa or the Veuve Clicquot is unobtainable, try the following: for the California wine, Mumm Cuvée Napa brut; for the French, Bollinger Special Cuvée brut, Pol Roger brut, or Moët & Chandon Brut Imperial (the latter will not be as full-bodied as either Veuve Clicquot or Bollinger).

This is the conclusion of the second tasting session. There are several ways for you to proceed from here.

*Following the lead of your own preferences:*
  If you liked either the Codorniu Napa Brut or the Veuve Clicquot Brut, go on to the Third Flight.

*Following the kind of grapes:*
  See the Chardonnay flights among the white wines and the Pinot Noir flights among the red wines.

*Following the wines of the country:*
  Wine One: Go on to the Third Flight.
  Wine Two: This is the last flight of French wines.

# THE THIRD FLIGHT

❧ ❧

*Schramsberg Napa Valley*
*Crémant Demi-Sec 1986*
*and*
*Granduca Asti Spumante*

❧ ❧

THE TWO FLIGHTS before this have been your hors d'oeuvre
and entrée. This, now, is the dessert course: two sparkling
wines that are less than bone-dry. With white wines, no matter how
you duck and dodge, the sugar always comes back at the end.

Before you start your tasting ritual, let me take a minute to explain
why a wine labeled demi-sec (half dry), as is the Schramsberg, is
likely to be anywhere from slightly to distinctly sweet. It isn't just
part of the International Wine Conspiracy to keep you confused and
feeling dumb and inadequate.

It came about because in the nineteenth century, in France especially, champagne was made very sweet. Public taste (English taste
in particular) began to demand drier and drier champagnes, and as
the makers gradually reduced the sugar in their wines they evolved
a series of names indicating increasing degrees of dryness. They
obviously thought they had gone about as far as common sense
would take them when they created *sec* (dry), but they were quickly
pushed beyond that to *extra sec* and finally to *brut*. To give you some
idea of what some more conservative champagne makers thought of
all this, *brut*, which we now use unthinkingly to mean dry champagne, literally translates as "rough" or "raw."

Almost all of these grades of champagne are on the market today.

266

Just remember that if it says dry or sec at all, it's got some sugar in it, and if it admits to *douce*, or sweet, it's got a lot. The sweeter champagnes are usually served with dessert (though some people, especially in France, also take them as an aperitif), the dry with a dinner's earlier courses. And just for your information, some champagne and sparkling-wine houses also make a wine drier than brut: it is usually called *nature* or *dosage zéro* to indicate that it has no sugar whatever.

"Crémant," by the way, is a champagne term denoting a wine having about half of champagne's normal internal pressure and therefore producing a rather gentle creamy foam when poured, rather than champagne's more explosive fizzing. The word implies nothing about a wine's sweetness or dryness. In some sparkling wine–producing areas outside of Champagne, the term "crémant" is beginning to be used to distinguish top-of-the-line bottles from more ordinary sparkling wines.

Appearance.

Both wines are very pretty—limpid, straw colors, with fine, persistent perlage. The Schramsberg Crémant is visibly a bit more golden than the Asti Spumante, and its perlage is a trifle more irregular.

Aroma.

Everybody describes the aroma of the Schramsberg as light in comparison with the Asti's. Almost everybody calls the Schramsberg fresh and fruity as well: some smell apples, many smell oranges. A few tasters may even find it reminiscent of Riesling, with a delicate floral aroma and hints of spice. Many also pick up in the aroma a distinct scent of yeast, sometimes even of toast—somewhat like the brut champagne of the last flight. Practically all tasters, except those who abominate even the slightest trace of sweetness, agree that this wine's nose is complex, clean, and refreshing.

The Asti Spumante's aroma is, it almost goes without saying, very different from the California wine's, absolutely unmistakable for any other wine scent and nevertheless very difficult to describe. It is first of all a strong aroma, about as deeply fragrant as you will ever find in a sparkling wine. And it is a deep, heavy aroma, a baritone to the Schramsberg's tenor. And it is markedly fruity, even sweet-smelling. About 99 percent of the people who try Asti will agree to all of that without any trouble—but how do you describe what that scent is like to someone who's never encountered it? What you are smelling in the Asti is the characteristic scent of its single grape, the Moscato or Muscat grape. The best that most tasters can come up with to define it is to compare it to the aroma of concentrated fruit essences, like pear or apricot leather or prunes or other dried fruits. Most people love it and find it almost intoxicating, but for some it is overpowering and cloying.

**Taste.**

Tasters may encounter a few surprises here.

The California sparkler strikes the majority of people as lively and fresh, very bright and acidic—an essentially and surprisingly dry wine with an accompanying, almost peripheral, sensation of light sweetness. Its fruit is unexpectedly big and vivid, much more pronounced in flavor than the aroma seemed to most people to predict. That fruit hits different tasters different ways. Some will taste ripe peaches in it, some apricot. Almost everybody discerns orange or other citrus flavors. Some even claim to pick out ginger and green, growing things—herbs and grasses and suchlike. But whatever they taste, most will describe the total flavor as rich, hardly sweet at all, and finishing like an organ blast, with everything evident and echoing long afterward.

With regard to the Asti, all but unanimity reigns. Practically everyone gets an enormous burst of fruit on the palate, strongly flavored but very clean: some describe it as golden raisins, others as intense berry flavors. The wine strikes most tasters as soft and—choose your word—fat, big, round, full-bodied, rich. For all its opulence and all its sweetness, however, most people don't find this sparkler at all cloying or sugary. Its sweetness seems in balance with the intensity of its fruit, and there is a lot of acid in there to keep the whole mass animated, even though it is not acidic in the same way the California wine is. Many tasters remark on its excellent finish, which they describe as surprisingly dry and giving a final burst of pure Muscat flavor. Most tasters, even if they don't care for this sort of wine, find this example very well made and very interesting. Many get enthusiastic about Asti, but some just find it all too much—too rich, too aggressive, too sweet.

There can be little argument that these are both very well-made wines in totally different styles, the Schramsberg fruity and muscular in a half-Californian, half-French style, the Asti Spumante lush with fruit yet balanced in a very typically Italian fashion. Most sparkling wines labeled demi-sec will show their sweetness a lot more readily than this particular crémant does, but for my money this kind of wine or one the merest touch sweeter makes the best accompaniment to dessert. A really sweet wine on top of a sweet dessert is not only simply too much of a good thing, but the two sweets in effect cancel each other out, and you lose the effect of at least one and maybe both of them. In my opinion, you don't serve a wine like this Asti Spumante with dessert: you serve it *as* dessert, and you bless the day you dried out your palate sufficiently to really appreciate the wonder of a well-made sweet wine.

The Granduca firm, under the direction of its highly regarded president and winemaker, Michele Chiarlo, produces the whole range of traditional—and mostly red—Piedmontese wines, from fine Barbera up to noble Barolo. Its wines are imported to the United States by Kobrand.

Schramsberg Vineyards makes only *méthode champenoise* wines and probably has the highest reputation for them among California vineyards. Most use the traditional champagne grapes, but this lovely crémant is vinified from a grape called Flora, a cross between Gewürztraminer and Sémillon.

## Substitutes:

There's really nothing else quite like Schramsberg's Crémant, but if the Granduca Asti Spumante isn't available, you could substitute the same wine from several other reliable makers: Martini & Rossi, Cinzano, Contratto, or Santo Stefano.

# CODA

Well, boys and girls, men and women, you've made it. Here you are at the end of the book, with all those wines under your belt, all those notes in your files, and all that knowledge in your head. I can't give you a degree or anything like that, not even a certificate, much as I would like to and much as I think you deserve it for your perseverance. (You did persevere, didn't you? You're not just skipping over a lot of wines and sneaking a look at the end, are you?)

But if you've really been working with me through all these pages, you can give yourself something that will show just how much you've profited from all this effort: you can go out and buy yourself a special bottle of wine that you'll really enjoy. If this book has done its job well, you'll now know exactly which one that is.

Happy days!

# APPENDIXES

APPENDICES

```
      ⌒୨୧⌒
```

# How to Read a Wine Label

```
      ⌒୨୧⌒
```

NOW THAT YOU'VE cut through all the mumbo-jumbo and mystic rites of wine lore and found that wine is really pleasurable, there is still one last obstacle in the way of your simply enjoying it. That is penetrating the arcana of the wine label to find the wine you're looking for, or a reasonable facsimile thereof. And it ain't easy. Wine labels seem to be the last refuge of untrammeled self-expression. No two are alike: facts are put in different places, sometimes prominent, sometimes hidden. Different type faces and type sizes emphasize or disguise different things. The same sort of wine can go under several aliases: varietal name, type name, regional name, brand name. The purchaser confronts forests of print, spiky legions of gothic letters, an octopus-wriggle of copperplate script, not to mention illustrations ranging from antiquarian to avant-garde, classic to commercial. In all that, figuring out what is the essential information looks more like a task for a CIA-trained cryptographer and codebreaker than for a hapless wine lover.

Take heart, however. Things aren't as bad as they seem: those labels only *look* like pure anarchy. Legally, certain minimal and fairly precise kinds of information must be there on the label, and once you know what you're looking for it can usually be found lurking somewhere. The thing to be aware of is that the requirements of truth in labeling and the requirements about the kind of information to be conveyed vary from country to country, just as much as winemaking practices and wine tastes do. So on a French wine label you will look for different data than you would seek on an Italian label, which in turn will be different from a German or Californian label.

Already, from your many wine tastings throughout this book,

you know a lot of the items to look for in the different nations' wines. For your convenience, what I'm going to do here is pull that information together in one place and fill in any gaps that may be left. To make this really useful, I'll risk a certain amount of repetition and talk about typical wine labels from the four areas that have absorbed the greatest part of our attention in the tastings: California, France, Italy, and Germany.

## CALIFORNIA

We'll start at home. Most of what there is to say about California wine labels will be true for other U.S. winegrowing regions as well.

First, take a look at a classic California label.

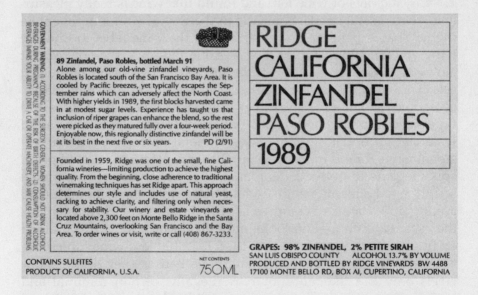

Ridge's labels have always been models of clarity and mines of information. All American wine labels won't be this easy to read, but this one is practically a schematic diagram of what an American wine label can and can't tell you.

Here are the relevant data, from top to bottom.

**Ridge.**

Usually the first and most prominently displayed item on the label is the brand name or winery name or vineyard name. With the

proliferation of would-be quality wineries in California, this information is not always as useful as it might be to the consumer,
especially to the new wine drinker. Nevertheless, many California
wineries have already achieved a level of recognizability and reliability, and more—in California and all over the United States—
are doing so every year. So this piece of information will matter
more and more to you as you learn more and more about American
wine.

## California.

Every wine has to indicate its place of origin somewhere on the
label. The general rule of thumb is, simply, the more precise the
designation of origin, the greater the wine's potential for excellence.
That is a theory to which, alas, there are often exceptions, but do
hold it as a working principle nevertheless. U.S. labeling law requires that 100 percent of the grapes from which the wine was
vinified must have come from the area named: no alien infusions
are allowed. In California there are many possible geographical
designations:

- California, simply indicating that all the grapes are from within
  the state;
- North Coast counties, or some similar indication that the grapes
  originate in a single but broad growing area;
- Sonoma or Napa or Monterey or similar county name, indicating
  that all the grapes were produced within that one county;
- Alexander Valley or Carneros or (as further down this label) Paso
  Robles or similar, indicating a very restricted growing zone, usually a township or a smaller geographical feature.

The Bureau of Alcohol, Tobacco, and Firearms (believe it or not, that
is the agency with jurisdiction over wine) is in the process of approv-
ing areas as specialized wine zones, so you can expect to see many
more precise growing-area designations appearing on labels.
Names like Carneros, for instance, or Stags Leap District will be
strictly controlled and applied only to wines grown and produced
within very tightly defined limits. In effect, this marks the serious
beginnings of an American system to parallel the European AOC
and DOC: legally controlled names of the regions of origin.

## Zinfandel.

After the name of the winery, the second most prominently displayed piece of information on the label is the name of the wine. In this case, following (up-until-now) normal practice for California's quality wines, it is the name of the grape variety. By law, any varietally labeled wine must contain at least 75 percent of the named variety. Almost all makers in California far exceed that minimum, and many would not consider making anything other than a 100 percent varietal wine. Some go so far as to report on the back label when they have mixed batches of the same varietal from different fields, giving percentages of each in the crush. Ridge has from its earliest bottlings provided exact information about the components of its wines (look at the small print at the bottom of this label) and the conditions of the harvest (see the "back flap"—the left-hand portion—of this wraparound label). For the average consumer, this much information may constitute overkill, but if you reach the point of connoisseurship where you are tasting and enjoying such slight differences, you will no doubt surprise yourself by just how interesting you find data of this sort.

One final word about straight varietal wines and blended wines. There is, of course, nothing intrinsically wrong with blended wines; many of the world's most sought-after wines are blends. It is simply a matter of fact that Californians first succeeded with varietal wines, while—until quite recently—their blended wines generally got a comparatively bad press because of the prevalence in the market of inexpensive blends bearing the names of European wine regions or wine kinds to which they had no relation at all. Chablis and burgundy are good examples of this type, which are known in the trade as generics. To distinguish their wines from these generics, back when California wines of quality were struggling for their proper recognition, many winemakers reacted by going to the opposite pole and refusing to blend their grapes at all. Now that the potential quality of California wine is universally believed, more and more serious U.S. winemakers are experimenting with quality blends—mellowing the asperities of Cabernet Sauvignon with small percentages of Merlot and Cabernet Franc, for instance, or modifying Zinfandel with Petite Sirah, or in white wines blending varying percentages of Sauvignon Blanc and Sémillon as is done in Bordeaux. The Mondavi-Rothschild Opus One sets the pace for most of these "Meritage" wines, as they are collectively called.

## Paso Robles.

A more precise designation of origin than the broad California appellation, this and the back-label information indicate the area from which this wine's grapes originated. Like many California wineries, Ridge produces wines not only from its own estate vineyards but also from other vineyards with which it has (usually) long-standing arrangements. So Ridge bottles several California Zinfandels, each differentiated on the label by this line naming the place of origin. Not all wine labels will give this information, of course, since not all wines, even at the very highest levels of quality, will of necessity come from a single grower or farm. But where the vineyard is a prized one and where its grapes have been vinified and bottled separately, as is the case here, those facts will be clearly presented. Of course, such wines will cost more than simpler, less restricted bottlings.

## 1989.

The vintage year, not the bottling year or the year of release. Many wines rest in barrel and in bottle for several years before becoming commercially available. Vintage information can be of crucial importance in determining not only the quality and value but also the readiness or unreadiness of a wine for drinking. Paul Draper, the winemaker at Ridge and one of the masters of California wine, has traditionally added his ideas about that to the wine's back label, a practice that many other wineries now emulate.

## Grapes: 98% Zinfandel, 2% Petite Sirah.

Precise data about the wine's components, as explained above.

## San Luis Obispo County.

This is where Ridge's Paso Robles vines are located. Each Ridge wine will bear this information in this same place, right after the breakdown of the blend.

## Alcohol 13.7% by volume.

American law requires a statement of alcoholic content on the bottle. This is usually done by volume, a measure that includes both the actual and the potential amount of alcohol in a wine. Potential alcohol means the amount of unfermented grape sugars remaining in the wine. The sugar measure most commonly used in the United States is Brix: a rough formula of conversion holds that 2 degrees of Brix yield 1 percent of alcohol. In a dry wine like this, the alcohol by volume measurement is going to be very close to, if not identical with, the actual alcohol in the wine. In a sweet dessert wine, where a good deal of unfermented grape sugar still survives in the finished wine, the difference between alcohol by volume and the amount of alcohol actually present in the wine can be quite substantial.

## FRANCE

Here you have a visual layout not entirely different from the preceding California label. The emphases, however, are widely divergent, and what is given the place of honor typifies the difference in focus and attention between France and California. Nevertheless, this fairly typical French label presents on the whole much the same information; only its arrangement is truly different.

For example, "Volnay 1$^{er}$ Cru" dominates the top of the label. This is not the name of the winery or firm or brand, but a place name, one of the esteemed red-wine communes of Burgundy's prestigious Côte d'Or. Already-hooked wine lovers don't need to glance a few lines farther down to find out that this is a Burgundy: they know simply from the name Volnay—which is why it comes first on the label. In French wines, place almost always takes precedence over people and over grapes; it is the *terroir* that over the centuries has shaped the characteristics of the wines. Consequently, almost all of France's great wines bear the names of places (the wines of Alsace are the single important exception), and almost all the places have received ratings according to the excellence of the wines they produce (to this, Alsace is no exception).

Consequently, right along with the place name, and sharing pride of place with it in prominence and print size, is the wine's rating, "Premier Cru." (See p. 115 for a fuller discussion of Burgundy's rating system.) By itself, this designation would mean that this wine was probably blended from several *premiers crus* vineyards, which is not at all bad, but neither is it as prestigious or as good (in theory at least) as a wine made from a single *premier cru* vineyard. That, of course, is what this bottle contains, as the next two lines

"Le Clos des Angles"
Appellation Volnay 1<sup>er</sup> Cru Controllée

specifically inform us. That AOC confirms all three key elements of the wine's identity: commune, ranking, and individual vineyard. After that heady stuff, the wine's broader regional affiliation— "Burgundy Table Wine"—appears almost as an afterthought.

Definitely not an afterthought, however, is the next piece of information, set carefully apart from what precedes it and in a typeface only slightly smaller than the vineyard name: "Domaine Boillereault de Chauvigny." In the patchwork of vineyards and plots within vineyards that make up the Côte d'Or, the name of the proprietor of the vines is the next most vital bit of data after their location. So, in the typical Burgundian scenario implied by this line and the next two ("Mis en bouteilles par Maison Prosper Maufoux / Négociant à Santenay (Côte d'Or) - France"), we can deduce that the reputable *négociant* Prosper Maufoux purchased, while it was still in barrels, the single-vineyard Volnay wine of the equally reputable grower Boillereault, and that Maufoux bought enough of it—perhaps Boillereault's whole production—and that it was of a vintage good enough for the *négociant* to bottle it separately and sell it on the strength of the vineyard's name rather than his own, which he relegates to relatively small print (the importer's name looms larger, for instance) near the bottom of the label.

Two common items are missing from this label: the vintage, which would appear elsewhere (on a neck label most probably), and the words "estate-bottled" ("Mis en Bouteille au Château"). The latter are absent because, of course, this wine was not estate-bottled. Only the Domaine Boillereault could have done that for this particular wine, and like many small proprietors in Burgundy it chose rather to sell its new-made wine in bulk.

The estate-bottled distinction used to mean more than it does now, when almost every small farm throughout France—and California—seems to be dubbing itself a château and bottling its own wine. In the days when many wines were shipped in the barrel and bottled on arrival at their market, estate-bottling served as a preventative against adulteration. The owner's name was on the bottle and his reputation rested on its contents, so—if he wanted to continue to get the best possible price for his wine—he was unlikely to stretch his harvest by the additions of lesser wines. Today the estate-bottled designation serves mainly as a reassurance that the entire production of the wine has been watched over by the proprietor, who still has a vested interest in preserving the quality and integrity of his product. In areas such as Burgundy where the *négociant* has traditionally been involved in the sales and distribution of wine, the *négociant*'s name is as important a guarantee of quality as the grower's.

## ITALY

Italy's wine legislation, like that of the United States, is young and yet evolving, despite the fact that Italy is one of the oldest wine-producing regions in the world. Italian winemaking, too, is going through a period of intense change and modernization, and the consequences can be, from the consumer's point of view, very confusing. Add to that the fact that Italian wine labels may bear the traditional names the wines carry in their region (for example, Lacryma Christi) or commercial names (for example, Rubesco), or place names (Chianti), or varietal names (Pinot Grigio), and many people conclude that no sense can be made of the chaos.

There's no need to despair, however. The labels still tell the truth about the wine, and they are no harder to read than any others. Here, for instance, is an Italian wine label that is as typical and attractive as it is clear.

The center of the label is taken up by a simple logo and the two

IMBOTTIGLIATO NELLA CANTINA VIETTI CASTIGLIONE FALLETTO ITALIA
ANNATA 1980

**Vietti**
BAROLO

DENOMINAZIONE DI ORIGINE CONTROLLATA E GARANTITA
DELLA LOCALITA' ROCCHE
DELLE 10.500 BOTTIGLIE QUESTA E' LA N. 00000
13,00% BY VOL. - BOTTLED BY VIETTI - RED WINE - 750 ML
incisore gianni gallo    PRODUCT OF ITALY    stampatore gianni cozzo

key items of information: the wine's name and its maker's name. We haven't seen much in the way of a logo on the labels we've been looking at, but—as any wine drinker knows—they are common and often gaudy: medals, crests, scrolls, realistic or stylized portraits of the winery or vineyards or château or castle—everything up to originally commissioned works by major artists (Château Lafite Rothschild). This more modest print (the artist and printer are identified in the bottom corners of the label) of almonds and hazelnuts and grapes is more pleasing to my eye and more appropriate to my way of thinking, but it serves the same essentially decorative purpose as more ornate specimens. The hard information is contained in the two words "Barolo" and "Vietti."

Barolo is both the wine name and a place name, that of a small town near Alba in the Italian Piedmont. If you didn't know that Barolo was one of Italy's great wines, you might reasonably infer it from the fact that the wine is not simply DOC but DOCG (*Denominazione di Origine Controllata e Garantita*), a classification so far reserved (with the single embarrassing exception of the white wine Albana di Romagna) for the finest red wines. In regard to whether the stress falls on place or on people, Italian labels stand about midway between French and Californian. The places and zones *are* important. Frequently they determine the wine's right to a particular appellation, as in the case of Barolo: a 100 percent Nebbiolo wine made elsewhere than in the delimited zone around Alba just wouldn't be Barolo and couldn't call itself so. But there are Barolos and Barolos, so the maker's name and stamp on the wine are just as important: hence the large Vietti at the center, and the proprietary-bottling information at the top ("Imbottigliato nella Cantina Vietti Castiglione Falletto Italia"), just above the vintage. In the same sort of balancing act—for every mention of the winemaker there is a corresponding mention of place—right after the DOCG the label specifies the prestigious site within the Barolo zone from which this wine originated: "Della Localita' Rocche." Rocche, Brunate, Cannubi and a few other sites are the Piedmontese equivalents of *grands crus* communes in the Côte d'Or, so this bit of information is far from insignificant; though (because the Barolo sites and Italian crus in general are much less well known than the French or even the Californian equivalents) it is not markedly emphasized on the label.

For the most part, Italian wine labels are no more confusing than this, once you become familiar with their layout. Italian varietal wines invariably bear a regional DOC as well as the grape's name, so you will find Cabernets that are DOC Friuli or DOC Trento, Trebbiano from Tuscany or Lazio, Chardonnay from several provinces. Even wines with purely fantasy names will give you at least geographical information about their origin and often about their grapes.

The great number of wines Italy produces is both its blessing and its curse, just as it is for the consumer. For people just beginning to learn Italian wine, the maker's name is often the most useful and most reliable piece of information. A good rule of thumb is to stick with a maker whose wines please you, try all his varieties, and use them to measure others. Reputable winemakers, in Italy as anywhere else in the world, work hard to keep their quality up and their product consistent. Where there are so many other variables and such a great profusion of wines to choose from, that is a very helpful constant.

# GERMANY

Wine drinkers probably have more difficulty with German wine labels than any other. Even seasoned wine shoppers have been known to lose their way among the swirls and curlicues of German labels. But the information contained on those labels is quite precise if you know what you're looking at. Here's a typical example.

Pay no attention to that wonderfully florid crest: the pertinent information lies alongside and beneath it. The top and bottom lines of this label provide us with the broad frame within which to understand the kind of wine we're looking at. "Rheingau" tells us the large region from which it comes, in this case one of the prestigious Rhine Valley growing areas. The bottom line of the label describes the wine's grade—"Qualitätswein mit Prädikat." The simple designation "Qualitätswein" would place it at the doorstep of Germany's ascending ladder of sweetness grades; the words "mit Prädikat"—"Qualitätswein" with a descriptive word attached— mean that this wine has started climbing that ladder. The descriptive words in question designate differing levels of sweetness: Kabinett, the driest, followed by Spätlese (late harvest, in effect), Auslese (selected picking—of very ripe bunches is understood), Beerenauslese (picking of very ripe grapes), and Trocken- beerenauslese (picking of ripe, partially raisined grapes). In terms of establishing a German wine's price range, these grades are the single most important factor. To see how high on that ladder this wine rises, we must look elsewhere on the label.

This particular label is arranged rather symmetrically and clearly. The second line down from the top and the second line up from the bottom identify the producer of the wine, Schloss Schönborn, a.k.a.

Domänenweingut Schloss Schönborn, an ancient, family-owned winery headquartered in Hattenheim, an important wine village in the Rheingau. That lower line also informs us that this particular wine is estate-bottled ("Erzeugerabfüllung"), implying that it merits more than ordinary attention.

You've probably noticed that all the ornate Gothic script is reserved for the winery's name. The key facts about the wine itself are all set forth very clearly in bold, san serif print and very prominently clustered dead center on the label. First the vintage—"1989"—is announced. Then the label indicates the wine's township of origin, Erbach (*Erbacher* translates as "from Erbach") and the vineyard from which it comes, Marcobrunn, the most famous site in the appellation. That is the usual pattern for revealing these facts on German wine labels: the village or township name almost always ending in "er" to make it into an adjective modifying the following vineyard name. By the way, Erbach is the next village east of Hattenheim, and the Marcobrunn vineyards abut the Hattenheim line, so this vineyard lies very close to home for Schloss Schönborn.

The final data—grape variety from which the wine is made and its exact *Prädikat*—are given in the next line: "Riesling," which as Germany's noblest grape is almost predictable in these circumstances, and "Auslese," a late harvesting of selected, very ripe bunches of grapes to yield a wine of marked sweetness.

Essentially that same sort of information must be present somewhere on the label of every German wine, and the absence of various pieces of it moves you regressively down the line of prestige. If there is no *Prädikat*, that is one step; if no vineyard name but only a village, another. If there is not a village name but a *Bereich* designation—a *Bereich* is a much larger region—that is yet another step. And finally, if there is only the broadest regional designation—Rheingau or Mosel for instance—that is yet another step. As with all the other labels we've looked at, the greater the degree of particularity about origin, the greater the potential quality of the wine.

There are other niceties about German wine labels that can illuminate or confuse the buyer, but I've given you the basics here. They ought to see you safely through your first few forays into German wine. After that, if you're hooked on Hock or Mosel you'd better invest in a German pocket dictionary.

That just about covers what I can tell you about label lore in anything shorter than an encyclopedia. No doubt you'll come across some exceptions to the general explanations I've given you, but don't let that throw you. One of the real charms of wine, you discover after a while, is that it is more or less all exceptions, and the "rules" are the first thing you throw away after you've found out what you like.

Happy hunting!

# Wineshops, Wine Merchants, and Wine Drinkers: A Comedy of Errors

**M**Y INTENTION IN WRITING this little note is simply to try to give you a little information that will, as you get more involved with wine, help you recognize a good wineshop or wine merchant and avoid bad ones. That should be straightforward enough, but the buying and selling of any alcoholic beverage in the United States is so surrounded by federal, state, and local regulations (not to mention taxes) that most citizens can acquire marijuana with greater ease than they can a specific bottle of wine.

If you are so miserably unfortunate as to live in a state where all wine sales are handled through state stores, nothing I have to say here is going to help you. I can only say I grieve for you. Most states impose merely primitive and incommoding conditions on the wine drinker: state stores and their concomitants are not even up to the level of Neanderthal. I have had the dubious pleasure of watching a selection committee for one state's alcohol control board tasting wines. Is anyone going to be the least bit surprised when I say that they knew nothing about wine and were moreover the only individuals at the tasting who got rip-roaring drunk? So much for alcohol control.

On the other hand, if you are lucky enough to live in a state where the stores are free to let you taste the wine you may buy, a lot of the troubles that plague the rest of us are lifted from your shoulders. All you have to do is find a dealer you respect and stick with him—which is exactly what I want to talk to you about.

286

How do you know a good wineshop? How can you tell a really knowledgeable wine merchant from a glib salesperson? There are ways. They are not infallible, but there are things to look for, both good and bad, that can save you time and trouble and shorten your quest. The really great wineshop, with terrific selection and reasonable prices, and the really fine wine merchant, knowledgeable and helpful but not hard-sell, are the Holy Grail of every wine enthusiast, and unless you are stupendously lucky or very well friended, you are not going to stumble on them right away. But they do exist, so be patient.

Keep your expectations realistic. Don't enter a small neighborhood shop that does most of its business in vodka and Scotch to search for a specific vintage of a specific vineyard, and don't go into a rage when the shop doesn't have it. Remember you're dealing with business people who have to move their stock in order to pay the rent.

If the shop is really conveniently located for you and you honestly believe you might do a lot of business there, talk to the owner or manager. Tell him what you mean by a lot of business. See how cooperative he is. Some shopkeepers are interested in increasing their wine sales, others don't want to be bothered. If this one falls into the latter camp, just move on: don't waste your energy trying to make a convert. If he is interested, try to set up something on a trial basis so you can both see how it works out.

Remember, in a small shop every new wine the merchant brings in means something else he or she no longer has room for, and it means cash out of his or her pocket, so don't be surprised if a shop owner doesn't clap hands with delight every time you suggest a wine you think you'd like to try. In any event, you have to reconcile yourself to the fact that there are real limitations to what a small, neighborhood shop can provide for an increasingly serious wine enthusiast.

There are exceptions to this, of course. Sometimes, especially in smaller towns where cellar space comes cheap and competition may not be so intense, you find a merchant who is a wine enthusiast, too, and who has been able to turn a neighborhood shop into a specialty store. That sort of place can be a treasure trove if you recognize it and treat it properly.

First, some obvious things to warn you off.

If the window display is filled with flavored wines and pop wines, the odds are not strong that you'll find what you want inside. The window display pitches to the customer the shop caters to, or wants to cater to. If the window holds a display of what you consider good wines but the bottles are all standing upright in full sun, be dubious. If they look as if they have been that way for a long while, be very distrustful. If you enter the shop and all the wine is standing upright on all the shelves, with not a single horizontal display or storage shelf to be seen, run, do not walk, to the nearest exit. Wine drinkers patronizing such a place deserve the spoiled wines they will almost certainly get.

Other warning signs come from the personnel. Don't even bother to attempt to explain to the clerk or merchant who wants to sell you a five-year-old Beaujolais or Pinot Grigio. The odds are that he or she already knows that those wines are supposed to be drunk young but just doesn't care. Be suspicious also of the dealer who always tries to move you up the price ladder from your initial interest. That dealer may be trying to steer you to a better wine, but if it happens all the time he or she is probably only trying for a better mark-up, whether the wine is actually better than what you requested or not.

Above all, avoid like the plague the shop where the owner or manager is constantly marking up the prices with each new edition of *Beverage Media*. Very few places move stock that fast, and what you're witnessing, in many cases, is simply gouging a bigger margin out of old stock, a practice that is immoral at best and in some places downright illegal—but it happens, so watch for it.

So what are you looking for then? Let's talk about the ideal, and you can scale down from that to a realistic model for your region and your needs.

First, personnel. The staff—whether it consists of the owner or owners alone or of a whole group of clerks, stock people, and delivery people—is absolutely crucial to the success of a wineshop. The people in the store have to know about wine beyond the rudimentary level of responding to queries for a light white wine or a dry red one. This doesn't mean that every single individual has to know everything there is to know about wine (it isn't possible, anyway) but that somebody on the floor should be able to respond accurately to questions like "Were the Rhône reds any good in the '81 vintage?" or "Isn't this '86 Chianti over the hill already?"

And certainly the floor people should know their own stock. You should get very suspicious of a store with a lot of wine that nobody on the premises has ever tasted: that often means that it was stocked only because the price was advantageous. That, in turn, does not mean that you won't be able to get good buys in such circumstances—but you'll have to rely on your own knowledge and luck entirely, because no help will be forthcoming from the staff.

Attitude is a good indicator, too. Serious wine merchants realize that a wine drinker has to start somewhere, that even a great connoisseur once didn't know the difference between Bordeaux and Burgundy. Knowing that, they are usually patient with beginners and thoughtful in answering questions, insofar as time and the pressure of business will allow. Naturally if you walk into a shop on a busy Saturday afternoon or right before a major holiday and present the dealer with a list of questions the length of *War and Peace*, you are not going to receive all the deference and courteous respect that is, no doubt, your birthright. But at slower times— which is when you should appear if you really have a lot of questions—you will be able to recognize a good wineshop by the thoughtfulness with which your queries are answered.

Finally, the staff should show a certain amount of pride as well as knowledge, a bit of enthusiasm as well as information. They should be able to show you wines you won't get just anywhere, and they needn't be the costliest rarities, either. A good wine staff should be just as happy to be able to offer a good, sound everyday wine as a noble vintage.

That brings us to stock, which probably is what you're most interested in.

The first criterion is completeness. No single shop could stock even one bottle of each of the world's wines, so exhaustiveness is out of the question. Who would want all of them anyway? Completeness in this context means that our ideal wineshop would stock the major kinds of wines of the major producing areas of the world and at a good mix of price ranges. I would say also that it wouldn't hurt a bit if in addition to that sort of completeness the shop or its owner or its staff also possessed a specialty, an area of wine in which its stock and their expertise were exceptionally strong.

The second criterion is accessibility. That marvelous selection of wines should be so displayed that you can actually see what's there to choose from, pick up the bottles, read the fine print and the back labels. I find very unsatisfying, not to say uncomfortable, the system of some European shops, where you sit in antiseptic splendor and choose your purchase from a catalog. I want literal hands-on experience with the wines I'm going to buy. I'm not even happy with (though because of space limitations I can sometimes see the necessity for) the practice of keeping only one vintage of a particular wine on the floor and holding the others in storage.

Especially for people just starting out in wine, I think it is important that they familiarize themselves with the different bottles, the labels, the vintages, the different data given on each. Not that they're going to memorize it for some giant wine quiz—they say the right vintage and a foie gras comes down—but simply to get comfortable with such things, to build up a level of easy recognition. Besides, there is also a bit of romance, which no catalog can supply, involved in actually handling a rare old bottle, and romance is one of the attractions of wine for the enthusiast and one of its selling points for the dealer.

The third criterion is pricing. A shop can meet those first two criteria and still be a nightmare rather than a dream if its prices are always pegged at maximum markup. You as a customer must feel you're getting good value for your money. Your enjoyment of wine and your satisfaction in it are diminished if you think you've overpaid. You want to feel you've made a good buy, not ransomed a hostage from terrorists.

That doesn't mean every wine has to be steeply discounted either: good merchants are entitled to their profits. A reasonable balance between all-that-the-market-will-allow and no-frills-no-services-plain-pipe-racks is the ideal. The quickest way to assure yourself that a particular shop is actually dealing fairly with you in this regard is to watch its sale offerings. Are the items quoted really on sale or merely lightly discounted from prices inflated to begin with? Are there any genuine bargains in the sale or do these prices merely bring the merchandise into a range regularly or frequently available elsewhere in your region? Are there only one or two spectacularly discounted items—loss leaders—and the rest not a sale at all?

Those are the questions to ask, and if the answers you get start turning up in the wrong column then you are probably dealing with a robber baron rather than a real wine merchant. And don't be intimidated at this stage by prestige or reputation either: some wine dealers count on both to justify preposterous prices—but you can't drink pretension, so neither should you pay for it.

Once you have found a wineshop to your liking, introduce yourself to at least one of the regular staff. Let someone in the shop get to recognize you, and fill him or her in on your circumstances and your taste insofar as you can. Pick your times right—not in the middle of a busy spate—and genuinely confer with this person about the wines in the shop. Exchange opinions and information and enthusiasms. This will enable your regular clerk to help you better and give you a basis for judging how likely it is for a wine that he or she enjoyed to please you. And don't just go back to the shop with complaints. Stop by occasionally and let them know how much you enjoyed that petit château they recommended, or how well the Barolo went with the leg of lamb, just as they said it would. You're building a relationship that could go on for years, to both your benefits, so try to think about it not just in a business context but in a human one. That's where wine belongs anyway.

Good buy, and good luck.

# Index

Page numbers in **boldface** refer to principal explanations of terms.

293

# *About the Author*

A contributing editor of *Wine and Spirits*, Tom Maresca writes regularly for major travel and food magazines. He is a professor of English at the State University of New York, Stony Brook, and lives in New York City with his wife, Diane Darrow.